C0-AYJ-595

COLS
WRIGHT STATE UNIVERSITY
UNIVERSITY LIBRARY
0 00 13 01 52866 5

EDUCATION AND SOCIAL CHANGE IN EGYPT AND TURKEY

Also by Bill Williamson

THE POVERTY OF EDUCATION: A Study in the Politics of Opportunity (with D. S. Byrne and B. G. Fletcher)

EDUCATION, SOCIAL STRUCTURE AND DEVELOPMENT

CLASS CULTURE AND COMMUNITY: A Study of Social Change in Mining through Biography

Education and Social Change in Egypt and Turkey

A Study in Historical Sociology

Bill Williamson

Senior Lecturer in Sociology
University of Durham

MACMILLAN
PRESS

First published 1987

Published by
THE MACMILLAN PRESS LTD
Houndmills, Basingstoke, Hampshire RG21 2XS
and London
Companies and representatives
throughout the world

Phototypeset in 10/12pt Times Roman by
Styleset Limited, Warminster, Wiltshire

Printed in Hong Kong

British Library Cataloguing in Publication Data
Williamson, Bill. *1944-*
Education and social change in Egypt and Turkey:
a study in historical sociology.
1. Education—Social aspects—Turkey—
History 2. Educational sociology—Turkey
3. Education—Social aspects—Egypt—
History 4. Educational sociology—Egypt
I. Title
370.19′09561 LC191.8.T9
ISBN 0–333–40709–1

Contents

Preface

The research upon which this book is based was made possible by a grant from the Centre for Middle Eastern and Islamic Studies of the University of Durham. I wish to record formally my thanks for this. In some ways more important was the help given to me by the staff of the centre and staff of the Oriental Studies Library of the university. Their careful professionalism has ensured over the years that Durham is an excellent place in which to carry out research on the Middle East.

Colleagues in the American University of Cairo, Ain-Shams University, the Middle East Technical University, Ankara and the Bosphorous University in Istanbul will recognise my debt to the conversations I had with them. So, too, will many Turkish and Egyptian friends who, both in their own country and in Durham, have shared with me their thoughts about education.

The weaknesses of the study are entirely my own. There would have been many more than there are, however, if it was not for the careful way in which Mrs Lynda Nurse of the Department of Sociology and Social Policy of Durham University typed the manuscript, corrected its errors and discussed the whole project with me in such helpful ways. I am deeply grateful to her for this.

My family, once again, have suffered the writing of a book with me, and without the help of my wife, Diane, in checking sources, tables and text I am not sure it would have ever been finished.

BILL WILLIAMSON

Introduction

This is a study of the educational systems of Egypt and Turkey, two of the largest states of the Middle East. Each in its own way is critical to the geopolitical stability of the whole area and what role they play there depends on how and whether either state achieves economic development. They are states with a common Ottoman past in which determined attempts have been made both in the nineteenth and twentieth centuries to modernise traditional social structures along lines modelled on those of Europe. Change in education has been at the forefront of those efforts. The relative failure of both societies to realise these goals fully provides us with an interesting context in which to examine once more the subtle and ever-changing relationship between education and socioeconomic development.

The fact that Egypt and Turkey are in the Middle East adds two special features to discussions about education and development. The first is religious and concerns the role of Islam in the modern world. The second is about the relative autonomy of nation states and the degree of their control of education. Both Egypt and Turkey are part of the world of Islam and for almost four hundred years Ottoman rulers claimed religious leadership of the Muslim world. Secularising trends in the nineteenth and twentieth centuries reflected particularly in the growth of a secular nationalism, have not altered the fact that both societies have predominantly Muslim populations.

In recent years, in both societies, religious divisions have assumed political connotations. President Anwar Sadat of Egypt was murdered by an army officer and devout Muslim who went to his own death believing his place in Paradise was assured as one who had destroyed someone who was destroying the faith. In Turkey, prior to the military *coup d'état* in 1980, religious divisions were exploited by both right-wing and left-wing groups for their different political ends and the situation degenerated into a virtual civil war.

Religion is important, however, not just because it is part of the politics of the Middle East but also because of what it implies for the way societies of the area should develop. The question is whether what Hegel once called 'the majestic ruin of Islam' is in any way consistent with socioeconomic development in the modern world and with exploiting science and technology and the social forms which have accompanied them in the West or in the Soviet Union.

The second feature which the Middle East adds to the education and development debate is the importance of assessing the ways in which the external relations of a society give shape to its internal structure. This problem has two aspects, one concerned with the role of the state in development, the other with how the effective boundaries of a social formation (society, nation state), can be drawn.

Prior to the end of the First World War almost the whole area of the Middle East was, at least nominally, under Ottoman control. That control had once been strong and had resulted in a social and political formation – the Ottoman Empire – with a social structure essentially different to that of Europe, which developed from the medieval period onwards. The growth of the nation state and of modern industry in Europe took place under and created very different conditions to those which prevailed in the Ottoman Empire in the nineteenth century.

This had decisive implications for the form of Ottoman modernisation and the social groups which inspired it. Modernisation was necessarily of a defensive sort to prevent further encroachment into Ottoman lands and sovereignty by expansionist European powers including Russia. It had to be centrally engineered and had to overcome resistance within the Ottoman state itself. This resistance had both a cultural and political form and features of that resistance still remain even today in attitudes and values and social structures which oppose modernisation along Western lines. In the nineteenth century, however, modernisation had to be mobilised to attempt to save a social order which seemed to many incapable of preventing its own further decline.

That decline and that mobilisation cannot be understood, however, unless the changing relationship of the Ottoman Empire to the rise of modern Europe is grasped for the growth of one catalysed the demise of the other. It is against this backcloth that the educational reformers of the nineteenth century must be seen for they attempted to import into the empire the science and technology of modern Europe and thereby opened their societies to values and ideas potentially threatening to the Islamic and Ottoman ones which were politically dominant. In this sense the uniqueness of the Ottoman state provides us with a sharp contrast to the experience of several societies of Europe and, indeed, of several societies including Japan, Russia, France and Germany, which experienced the 'late industrialisation effect' (Gerschenkron, 1962) and 'defensive modernisation'.

In the Ottoman case the state was an obstacle to the development of modern industry; in Germany, France and Britain it was a major force in mobilising economic development. Any generalisations which social scientists seek to make about states and economic development must be sufficiently qualified to embrace this contrast.

The second feature referred to earlier is that of how the boundaries of the social structures of different societies are actually to be drawn for the purpose of assessing the role of education in development. It is the issue of the nation state and the international division of labour and the ways in which these influence the structure of education in the Middle East. Much of the literature in the field of studies of education and development presupposes the framework of the nation state capable of taking decisions to influence policies towards particular ends. In the case of underdeveloped societies this implicit model of government was always somewhat naive. For those societies which experienced colonisation directly the issue is clear enough. Metropolitan colonising powers like Britain and France and later Germany, took the important decisions in the colonies. Societies like Turkey have never been colonised and the word itself may have too many other connotations to describe properly the Egyptian case from the British occupation in 1882 onwards, and under Ottoman rule it is not possible to talk of nation states although, indeed, there were nationalist movements gnawing away at its roots. The nation state itself was something which reformers in Egypt and later in modern Turkey had to construct; it was not something which was already there and which could be used to engineer reforms. It had to be constructed almost three hundred years after European states had been formed.

Furthermore, the two nation states discussed here had to be formed in conditions which threatened to undermine any autonomy they could gain for themselves. A permanent military presence in Egypt to defend British Imperial interests, the Suez Canal route to India and a balance of power in Europe, and a government careful not to develop the country beyond manageable limits – all set the parameters within which Egyptian nationalism developed in the late nineteenth century just as Ottoman rule had been decisive earlier. The economic backwardness of the Anatolian heartlands of the Ottoman Empire set the constraints within which Mustafa Kemal (Atatürk) had to fashion Turkish independence in the 1920s. In both cases, economic backwardness maintained the vulnerability of the two economies to a world market dominated by the more powerful economies of Europe and, later, the United States and Japan. What it amounts to is this: the changes in social and economic organisation to which Ottoman reformers had to respond and which the modern governments of Egypt and Turkey must control, developed under external stimuli. These changes cannot be explained except *relationally*, i.e. in terms of the way both societies are and have been constrained by the wider international order of which they are a part.

Modernisation in Egypt and Turkey necessarily implied and implies measures to develop industry, science and technology which alone guarantee national independence. But in seeking to achieve this both societies have suffered from their role as dependent states in an international division of labour. Their search for distinctive models of develoment for their people and their attempts to plan carefully their resources have been frustrated continually by dependency and the attitudes it nurtures.

The themes in their economic history, describing how each society has sought to overcome these problems, are set out in subsequent chapters of this book together with detailed accounts of their educational policies at different stages in their history. For the moment it need only be noted that both societies still display features of what might be called dependent peripheral economies. This is exemplified in the contemporary period in the case of labour migration, a phenomenon of crucial importance to the future development of the two states.

In relation to Western Europe Turkey was until the early 1970s a labour-reserve economy. The migration stream which developed in the 1960s from Anatolian village to Turkish town and city and then onwards to Western Europe to Germany, Switzerland and the Netherlands was the result. Turkey supplied the booming economies of continental Europe with a labour force without which their economies would not have grown the way they did. Turkey itself was thus able to export a good part of its own unemployment and strengthen its foreign exchange balance with migrant remittances. But like bank credit this only gave the country breathing space in which it could confront the structural weaknesses of its own economy. The breathing space was not well used and the consequences, at least in part, were seen in the violence which prompted a third post-war military take-over of power.

Egypt, too, plays the role of labour exporting peripheral economy. For reasons which will be set out later, Egypt has come to be a labour reserve economy for the whole of the Middle East and for the Gulf

States in particular. Egypt too relies heavily on the earnings of migrants for foreign exchange and because her economy, like that of Turkey, is open to the international economy Egyptians, like Turks (or at least some of them), can calculate their life chances not only on what they might be able to achieve in their own societies but also on what they might earn working abroad. This has major implications for the way labour markets function in the two societies and for education. If investment in education is justified on the grounds that it generates a good personal rate of return then in the case of both Egyptians and Turks the calculations involved take into account likely earnings from work abroad and not just what they could command at home. This has a major distorting effect on the nature of the demand for education in the two societies as well as on other features of economic planning. It amounts to this; the demand for education in Egypt and Turkey, varied though it is and has been along the well-known parameters of class, sex and urban or rural backgrounds, must be assessed against the background of how these societies relate to a changing international division of labour.

The role of the state in providing education of a particular type must be seen in the same light. The provision of education in any society rarely follows a calculation of the human resources needs of an economy; it reflects political considerations too. In the two societies discussed in this book there are educational systems which articulate ineffectively with the ways in which successive governments have perceived their political and economic priorities. The relative autonomy and backwardness which educational systems have displayed can only be explained in terms of the values attached to learning which have been inherited from the past. Important, too, are shifting alignments of an international division of labour which define the real opportunities of the labour markets which operate in the two societies. Neither society can be understood therefore in purely national terms.

In subsequent chapters this argument is developed and illustrated, the purpose of which is to show how many of the concepts employed in studying the education-development relationship and the role of education in reproducing social structures in societies of the Western capitalist type and former colonial societies are not so helpful in the context of the Middle East. This is not a claim that the societies of the Middle East are in some ways set apart from the world of modern capitalism. Quite the opposite: they are part of that world; they play a particular role as peripheral and dependent societies in the changing structures of that world. But to make sense of their experience we have to consider carefully how education systems function and reflect the past in societies of this type. It is a past fused with the history of a major world religion and a powerful empire. The features of both relevant to the study of modern Turkey and Egypt are discussed in the next chapters. In this respect this book is intended as a contribution to what is now a growing field in comparative and historical studies in the sociology of education.

COMPARISON, DEPENDENCE AND HISTORICAL CHANGE

The rationale for comparative studies is that, by varying the circumstances under which ostensibly similar social relationships or social processes take place, it is in principle possible to arrive at generalisations which will hold true in all societies. Comparison, then, like an experiment in the natural sciences, is a controlled process of theorising and hypothesis testing leading to verifiable statements about societies.

The problems of doing comparative studies in the social sciences are, however, enormous. The absence of comparable data on different societies is only part of the problem and perhaps the least difficult to overcome. Of much greater significance is the fact that comparison involves theorising and there is little agreement among sociologists about the theories they should use. Moreover, societies are not static structures; they exist in time and their structures change. In any case, all societies are unique; they have distinctive histories and cultural patterns so that entities which are essentially alike can never actually be identified.

Two features of the approach developed in this book to overcome such difficulties are first, to characterise particular societies in relationship to a more generally identified ideal type, in this case dependent societies; and secondly, to discuss their structure in terms of the same analytical categories. The categories chosen reflect a more general idea of how educational systems function in relation to processes of cultural transmission, social reproduction and social change (Williamson, 1979).

The overall purpose of comparison conceived in this way is to establish the value of general theoretical propositions about how education systems function and to set the limits of their applicability. The propositions themselves must allow us to *explain* different aspects of education functions and not just describe them.

Throughout this book Egypt and Turkey will be discussed as underdeveloped, dependent societies playing a particular role in an international division of labour. Dependency is discussed however, not just as a relationship which changes through time. It is an asymmetrical relationship between underdeveloped societies and the developed societies of the world but it also involves distinctive kinds of relationships within the underdeveloped societies themselves. In a state dependency is experienced as a set of *constraints* and *opportunities* which permeate throughout the whole of society. In general the constraints are of a kind which limit the autonomy of governments to pursue policies independently. Autonomy is curtailed with respect to resources – the dependent society, in general is a poor one – but also by political factors reflecting the distribution of power in society.

There are, too, cultural aspects to dependency reflected in the kinds of expectations different social groups have about life styles, life chances and living standards. A sharp ostensible contrast between a modern urban sector in an economy and a rural traditional sector is a recurrent feature of dependency. And it is one with a powerful cultural overlay in which marked contrasts of attitude and outlook and aspirations within a society can be found.

In the two societies examined in this book clear contrasts will be noted in attitudes and expectations of peasant producers and educated urban dwellers working in the modern sectors of the economy or state bureaucracies. Both groups are politically mobilised in different ways and place very different values on education. At the same time they face different constraints and opportunities with respect to education (and, of course, other services). Nevertheless, their fates are linked and it is misleading to characterise the urban-rural divide as one of the co-existence of two different social forms. Internal migration in response to poverty, changes in agriculture and population growth has linked the two worlds. Rural areas have been opened to the full blast of the market economy and cities have been 'peasantised'. Changes in attitude and outlook which in Europe took over one hundred years to mature have, in the case of many underdeveloped societies including Egypt and Turkey, been telescoped over one or two generations.

Against such a background the acquisition of an education can imply profound changes in personality and outlook and severe disjunctions between generations. It implies a volatile juxtaposition of attitudes, some of which are modern and secular while others remain traditional, part of an older religious framework. Cultural discontinuity, conflict and misunderstanding are such outcomes of rapid change and obvious features of educational expansion.

Dependency is not a static condition but changes through time. The constraints and opportunities which different groups face and the terms in which they understand them are also historically variable. It is necessary, therefore, to understand the changing forms of dependency historically. The societies over which Atatürk and Nasser presided are very different from those controlled by Presidents Evren and Mubarak.

None the less, there are historical continuities. In the first two chapters the ways in which both Egypt and Turkey had to cope with an Ottoman and Islamic past is examined. The themes of these chapters are the ways in which educational change in the two societies came to be seen as a contribution to the modernisation of social structures and the construction of nation states.

At this point, however, a further comparison enters inexorably into the account: that between the long-term decline of the Ottoman Empire and the world-changing development of Europe from the sixteenth century onwards. The two are inextricably connected but how they might be explained remains one of the more complex conundrums of historical scholarship.

Ottoman successes in the sixteenth century commanding the great trade routes to the East and threatening European states from the south-east was one factor in a vortex of changes which transformed the medieval economy of Europe. Other factors included the great journeys of discovery, the import of silver from the new world, the growth of trade, the development of science and improvements in technology, profound changes in the religious outlook; together they prompted, in Tawney's words, 'the enormous tilt of economic power from the south and east to the north and west' (Tawney, 1972, p. 77). 'Art and scientific curiosity', wrote Tawney, 'and technical skill, learning and statesmanship, the scholarship which explored the past and the prophetic visions which pierced the future, had all poured their treasures into the sumptuous shrine of the new civilisation' (Tawney, 1972, p. 76). But that was in Europe. In contrast, in the Islamic world the story is one of the intellectual decline and stagnation and of the persistence of state forms and economic structures both incapable of and prohibited from offering any serious challenge to the expansion of capitalism in Europe (see Tibawi, 1972; Gibb and Bowen, 1969).

The consequences of this difference have been profound. For the

Ottoman Empire they spelled out a future of political and economic decline, military defeat and growing dependency on Europe. By the close of the eighteenth century the need to modernise the empire was glaringly apparent. The history of the next hundred years is one of further decline and of increasingly desperate attempts to arrest it, a history defining the debris out of which Atatürk had to construct both a state and a modern economy.

In Europe, the story is one of growth, of expansion overseas, of the application of science and technology to the economy and of the birth of a new kind of society, secular in outlook, bourgeois in disposition and freed of economic traditionalism. Karl Marx grasped the difference in the distinction between modern capitalism and the asiatic mode of production (see Anderson, 1974). Others have grasped it differently. Some of these issues will be examined in the chapters which follow. It is important for the moment to note that while the forces which effected these transformations were political and economic there was a cultural dimension, too, which relates to the differences in the development of education in the two cultures and in their attitudes to learning and to science and to technology. The Ottomans neglected to their cost what European states embraced with conviction. By the middle of the nineteenth century the gap was so great that Ottoman reformers were forced into modernisation defensively and in a way which left them dependent on and vulnerable to European technical and economic and military superiority. In the following two chapters the historical dimension of educational dependency will be discussed.

Since dependency is a feature also of the political structure of a society the account of education which is given is developed in terms of the changing distribution of power in the two societies. This, of course, turns out to be a task in which the different perceptions and political orientations of distinctive social groups have to be described. The social structure of the Ottoman Empire was essentially different to that of Europe. For instance, Perry Anderson (1974) has noted that 'The economic bedrock of the Osmanli despotism was the virtually complete absence of private property in land' (Anderson, 1974, p. 365). Among other things this defined political structures very different to those of the absolutist states of Europe and effectively prevented the growth of a Turkish mercantile bourgeoisie reviving Roman law, engaged in trade, and diplomacy which could give precise meaning to the idea of private property.

My point for the moment, however, is that such differences in social structure gave rise to very different patterns of social differentiation and political domination. The most obvious difference is what Şerif Mardin once called the absence of 'civil society', i.e. urban bourgeois society, in the Ottoman Empire and hence the political domination of the Sultan and his slave bureaucracies in a state dependent on tax farming and control of trade rather than a growing economy (Mardin, 1969).

The educational relevance of this is that the expectations of different social groups from the past about education have to be described for they give shape to their political demands and influence what kinds of educational institutions actually developed. In Europe the conditions were ripe for a renaissance in learning and a diffusion of scholarship, something which cumulatively reinforced economic expansions. Ottoman lands, in contrast, remained in the grip of economic backwardness and a body of religious experts, the *ulema*, corrupt and incapable of responding creatively to the challenges of modernisation and new knowledge. The institutional contrast involves the expanding universities of Europe and the learned societies - Gresham College, the Royal Society, the French Academy of Sciences - which encouraged research and discovery and the declining *madrasa* system of the Ottoman Empire, which propped up an increasingly incompetent class of religious officials and denied the Sultan access to expertise of a practical kind. The present day educational systems of Egypt and Turkey, or anywhere else, can only be understood in terms of their past. In the first two chapters the historical residues of these contrasts are outlined to clarify the context of Ottoman and later nationalist modernisation.

But it is not just a matter of sketching in the historical background. Philip Abrams (1982) put this succinctly when he stressed that historical sociology of the sort attempted here is not 'merely a matter of recognising the historical background to the present. It is the attempt to understand the relationship of personal activity and experience on the one hand and social organisation on the other as something that is constructed in time' (Abrams, 1982, p. 16). What will be sought is a description of the changing patterns of Turkish and Egyptian education in the context of the educational action of different social and political groups of these societies at different periods in time to show how, to use Max Weber's striking phrase, an 'ideal of cultivation' became institutionalised in educational practice. The gist of the case presented here on the development issue is that the ideal of cultivation which has developed in the two societies is not one which promises a break, at least in the education field, with dependency despite the progressive rhetoric in which educational policies have been liberally wrapped.

EGYPT AND TURKEY

Productive comparison presupposes both similarities and contrasts. The comparison of Turkey and Egypt can be justified, partly, at least, on the grounds that there are many points of similarity between them. It has been stressed already that they share a common past through the political, cultural and religious configurations of Islam and the Ottoman Empire. Both societies have a modern history of determined attempts at modernisation both in the nineteenth century through the *Tanzimat* reforms in Turkey and Muhammad Ali's industrialisation projects in Egypt, and in the twentieth century through the policies of Atatürk and Colonel Nasser. Both societies, in this way, have experienced 'revolutions from above' (see Trimberger, 1978). Education has been regarded in both cases as a vehicle for national integration, economic regeneration and modernisation. In both cases their revolutions have faltered through the absence of mass-based political parties sufficiently rooted among the people themselves to effect fundamental change in social structures. Neither the secular nationalism of Atatürk or the socialism and pan-Arabism of Nasser penetrated fully to the periphery of the two societies.

In terms of their broad socioeconomic profiles and developmental potentialities there are further points of similarity. Both societies have large populations The Table I.1 indicates some of the more obvious and measurable aspects of their social structures. Both have a serious demographic problem in that about one-third of their total populations is made up of young people. Both societies are modern in the sense that they have nation-wide networks of schools and extensive public bureaucracies. In terms of potentialities for development both societies are very richly endowed. The opportunities they have for agricultural development, solar energy, mineral exploitation, tourism and industry are enviable. They are culturally integrated societies and unlike many states of the region suffer from no shortages of labour. Both societies are strategically placed, as they have always been to engage readily in extensive international trading networks and unlike many other societies of the area both Egypt and Turkey have long-standing national systems of education and a

Table I.1 Population and education in Egypt and Turkey

	Turkey		Egypt	
	1970	1977	1970	1978
Total population (000s)	35 321	42 010	32 820	39 870
% population 6–17	29.5	28.9	31.2	28.6
Enrolment × level (%)				
1st	77	66	69	60
2nd	20	30	26	33
3rd	3	4	4	7
Public expenditure as % GNP	2.9	5.4	4.8	5.4

Source: International Yearbook of Education, vol. XXXIII (Paris: UNESCO, 1981).

capacity to produce their own supply of scientists and technologists and professional workers of all kinds. So great is their capacity relative to the ability of their economies to employ such people that both states have become exporters of scientific and technical human resources. Both societies share some rather serious problems of underdevelopment. Aspects of this are indicated in Table I.2. These data are crude; what matters, however, is not so much the precise statistics given but their pattern. In comparison with the industrialised countries of the world, Egypt and Turkey remain predominantly agricultural economies with large rural populations, a relatively small proportion of the labour force engaged in industry and still quite significant demographic profiles with high birth rates and lower life expectancy. The data for Egypt and Turkey more closely resemble the data for the middle-income and low-income economies of the world. In this sense at least the comparison attempted in this book is between societies which are economically and demographically similar.

In the field of education, as will be seen in detail later, there are yet more broad similarities. These include:

1. the overproduction of university graduates who cannot properly be employed;

Table I.2 Socio-economic indicators: Egypt, Turkey 1960–82

	Turkey			Egypt			Low income countries			Medium income countries			Industrialised countries		
	1960	1978	1982	1960	1978	1982	1960	1978	1982	1960	1978	1982	1960	1978	1982
Crude birth rate per 1000	44	32	31	45	37	35	48	39	30	40	35	35	20	14	14
Crude death rate per 1000	17	10	9	19	13	11	24	15	11	14	11	10	10	9	9
Life expectancy at birth (yrs)	51	66	M 61 F 66	46	54	M 56 F 59	42	50	M 58 F 60	54	61	M 58 F 62	69	74	M 71 F 78
% Labour force in agriculture	78	60	54	58	51	50	77	72	72	58	45	46	17	6	6
% Labour force in industry	11	14	13	12	26	30	9	11	13	17	23	21	38	39	38
% Labour force in services	11	26	33	30	23	20	14	7	15	25	32	34	45	55	56
Urban Population as % of total population	30	47	44	38	45	45	17	21	21	37	51	46	67	77	78

Key: M = Male; F = Female
Source: Adapted from *World Development Report* (World Bank, 1984).

2. great inequalities of educational opportunity as between social classes, regions of the country and between men and women;
3. a system of education which does not produce sufficient technically trained people;
4. labour forces of teachers which include a high proportion of untrained people and in which motivation is often low;
5. poor educational provision in rural areas where shortage of books, buildings and personnel are serious;
6. high drop-out rates from formal education and inadequate provision for adult and informal education and training;
7. intense political disagreement about the aims of education and suitable teaching materials;
8. educational diarchy – the co-existence of a state school system and a traditional religious system;
9. inadequate mechanism of educational planning;
10. a dependence on external scientific and technical expertise;
11. overcrowding at all levels in the system leading to highly formalised teaching methods;
12. low levels of remuneration among teachers at all levels leading to low morale and, in some cases, corruption with teachers charging fees to give students extra tuition;
13. a heavy reliance on formal examinations as a way of assessing people which leads to a kind of veneration of certification and highly stylised learning stressing memorisation of facts rather than the development of analytical skills;
14. the high value of education for the opportunities it affords for employment in the state bureaucracies;
15. the high cultural gap between the educated and the uneducated, which often produces both an exaggerated respect for the educated and a disdainful superiority on their part for their poorer countrymen.

Such cultural disjunctions have played a significant role in preventing the leaders of the two societies from relating politically and ideologically to those they lead.

These are interconnected issues and are fully discussed in subsequent chapters of this book. Spelled out in this way, however, these characteristics are much too generally identified; they could apply to many other societies in the developing world. It is intended that this book illustrates the ways in which they are uniquely exemplified in two specific cases and how they are actually an *almost* inevitable consequence of dependency. The qualification, *almost*, is, of course, needed; there is no way in which social structures can be shown to be necessarily as they are and not something else. The structure of education described will be shown to be the outcome, sometimes intended, most often unintended, of choices which have been made in the light of particular models of development by the leaders of the two states. But since, as Marx once pointed out, 'men make their own history, but not under conditions which they themselves choose' it is necessary to examine how the institutionalised choices of past governments have set the constraints on the choices of governments which have followed them.

Comparison should also involve contrast. Egypt and Turkey are, after all, very different societies. In language, political traditions and culture they differ considerably. They differ, too, in patterns of land-ownership and in agricultural methods and technology. Turkey is a much more secular society than Egypt, particularly in urban areas and Turkish villages are likely to be much more modern, e.g. in their use of agricultural machinery, than villages in Egypt. And the dominant ideals of cultivation which prevail in Turkey are much more involved with those of Europe than those in Egypt which are rooted much more firmly in the Middle East. This matters greatly for the way in which different groups of Turks and in particular the 'guardian elites' which, since Atatürk, have dominated Turkish state institutions, particularly the army, conceive of development and modernisation. In the education field, for example, the Turkish government insists on secularism and nationalism and science – the famous principles of Kemalism – whereas in Egypt, the values of Islam, socialism and pan-Arabism, at least until Sadat, have been heavily endorsed. This was so during the Nasser regime although there have since been some major ideological shifts. These will be discussed later but for the moment it is important to emphasise the differences in the values and models of development of the two states.

There are far more subtle differences, too, which travellers in the two countries would easily recognise. They span different patterns of social differentiation and modes of social recognition on the one hand all the way through to music, art and religious orientation on the other. Each society lays claim to a unique and glorious past each with its own myth and legend and the cultivated pride in the nation itself is symbolically elicited in very different ways in school texts, national ceremonies and political rhetoric. There comes a point, therefore, when comparison becomes impossible, though still necessary, and perhaps more than a little insulting. But differences pale once more into similarities if the perspective from which both are observed is that of modern Europe and other developed economies of the world.

It is the aim of this book to examine the structure and functioning of education in these two developing societies. In the first five chapters an historical analysis of education is set out in which the role of post-medieval developments in Western scholarship, education and economic life are examined in their implications for the societies of the Middle East. The purpose of these chapters is not to sketch in the historical background to the present. Rather it is to clarify the nature of the constraints which, at different points of time, have defined the structures of underdevelopment of the two societies. Underdevelopment in the two societies is presented as something active, a process which bears directly on how actions to combat its consequences today have come to be defined and legitimated.

Chapters 6, 7 and 8 provide an account of the modern systems of education of Egypt and Turkey with an emphasis on what takes place in the field of general and technical education. Throughout an effort is made to trace the ramification of the changing dependency relations of the two societies on their systems of education.

Chapters 9, 10 and 11 are concerned with higher education and the scientific and technological aspects of dependency relations. The book ends with a brief discussion of the practical possibilities for educational change of a kind which would aid independent development in the two societies. The thrust of the argument at this point is that change in the Middle East depends crucially on linked changes in the West; if underdevelopment is indeed a relationship then both parties to it must change at the same time.

1 Education and Society: The Medieval Period

> If one can imagine an impartial and omniscient observer surveying the prospects of the world's peoples in the fourteenth century, it is rather doubtful whether he would have predicted the triumphant future of Europe. (Holmes, 1975, p. 230)

The education systems of modern Egypt and Turkey both reflect and partly define the specific features of each country's state of underdevelopment. Underdevelopment is not as has been stressed in the introduction, however, a condition. It is rather a relationship in which the social structures and institutions of one society are rendered subordinate to those of another. Such subordination can be either direct, as in the case of military conquest or colonisation, or indirect through the control of economic life, as in the case of imperialism. Among those stark possibilities there are others, combining elements of both direct and indirect control. Neither Egypt or Turkey have in any sense been colonised but the economic weaknesses of both states are a consequence of some historically specific facets of the way their respective patterns of social and economic development have been constrained by the stronger capitalist economies of the West and, in the case of Egypt, in an earlier period by the Ottoman Empire.

The roots of that dependency in the two societies now must be traced back to the late medieval period because it was then that the constraints and opportunities which set the conditions for the development of both Europe and the Middle East were effectively defined. For my purposes two sets of constraints are critical. First, those arising from the nature of the relationship between the societies of the Middle East, and those of Europe. Secondly, those which are specific to each social formation itself and emerge in the patterns of their cultures, their religion and styles of life and forms of government. The two particular features of Middle Eastern society which have to be understood in this context and which must be seen in a particularly long historical light, are Islam and the patrimonial structure of the Ottoman state.

The purpose of this chapter is to discuss those aspects of both relevant to an account of the development of forms of education and learning in the Ottoman Empire and the modes of thinking and styles of life and motives for action to which they gave credence. For the particular religious thrust of Islam and the social and political forms of the Ottoman Empire defined a framework for economic action and ideology which contrasted radically with those of Europe.

Max Weber understood the difference as one of *ethos*. The ethos of feudalism as a structure of domination nurtured attitudes in marked contrast to those of patrimonialism (Weber, 1978). The feudal society placed a value on honour and personal fealty to a lord and was hostile to impersonal commercial relationships which it regarded as undignified and vulgar. The solidarity of feudal society, argued Weber, 'is based on a common education which inculcates knightly conventions, pride of status and sense of honour' (Weber, 1978, p. 1106). In contrast, a sense of distinct honour or dignity on the part of subjects is a serious potential threat to the patrimonial ruler where the whole emphasis of administration is on the preservation of tradition and public peace. The emphasis in education and training in patrimonial systems is administrative training for bureaucracy and for accounting and clerical systems unknown to feudalism. Both systems are hostile to bourgeois capitalist development. But capitalism can advance 'within the interstices of the feudal system' (Weber, 1978, p. 1102). While opportunities for individual acquisition were fewer in the medieval period in Europe than in the Ottoman Empire where officials could use their office to acquire wealth, they were, none the less, by that fact widened by channelling capital into essentially bourgeois activities of trade and manufacture. 'The more successfully the feudal stratum prevented the intrusion of *nouveaux riche*,' wrote Weber, 'excluded them from office and political power, socially "declassed" them and blocked their acquisition of aristocratic landed estates, the more it directed this wealth to purely bourgeois capitalist uses' (Weber, 1978, p. 1102).

Status and power both in the Near East and Occident in the medieval period were closely connected, though in different ways, with education. To understand why the institutional forms of the Occident were able to fuel the development of modern capitalist society and why those of the Near East hindered that development, some account of how learning and education was organised has to be given. It is though, only one element in a very complex equation and one during this period subsumed, in any case, by religion.

ISLAMIC TRADITION AND OTTOMAN EDUCATION

At a time when Europe was semi-barbaric Islamic scholarship flourished. Indeed, it was through the work of Muslim scholars that Greek learning was rediscovered and made available to the scholars of Europe. Islam established the world's first universities and it was from within Islam that major advances were made in the pre-medieval period in science, mathematics and philosophy.

Throughout the medieval period, however, and through the European Renaissance, this situation changed. Islamic learning ossified and the important itellectual developments of the age occurred in Europe. European development from the fifteenth century onwards towards domination of the world economy and to leadership in scientific and military affairs was the *force majeure* which eclipsed the Ottoman Empire, which by this time had become the political scaffold of Islam itself.

But there were, too, facets of the Ottoman social formation itself which prevented it from responding to changes taking place beyond its own borders. The historic irony is that these facets, which explain the success of the Ottomans from the twelfth century onwards in gaining political leadership of a vast empire, were the same as those which from the sixteenth century onwards explain its demise.

Two themes need elaboration to make the point fully: the religious organisation of the empire and its political organisation as a state. Islam gave the empire a coherence which transcended the divisions of tribe, race and culture and justified its expansion through the Balkans into Europe. The system of government Ottoman rulers evolved made it possible for the state to finance its military campaigns from revenues drawn from diverse minorities and accommodate their interests within the state itself. Mobile cavalry made the military adventures of the Ottomans successful. But what made the cavalry successful was a system of government elite recruitment and landholding which generated revenues and political allegiance for Ottoman rulers which they could exploit militarily in the interests of the state and of religion.

It is the purpose of this chapter to describe the social formation of the Ottoman Empire up to its high point in the late sixteenth century. A system which made it possible for Ottoman armies to threaten Vienna was unable subsequently to cope with the consequences of the expansion of Europe. This historic failure explains what the constraints were on Ottoman and Egyptian attempts to modernise their societies in the late eighteenth and throughout the nineteenth centuries. Since it was these nineteenth century attempts at modernisation which themselves gave shape to how development was conceived in the twentieth century it is vital to appreciate their intellectual and political roots.

The specifically educational aspects of this account concern the nature and form of traditional Islamic learning which the Ottoman state inherited and developed. What they developed was a system of education which was moulded specifically in the interests of the state itself but one which was none the less reliant on the traditional canons of the religion and the teaching of religious leaders. Parallel to the systems of religious education the state operated a system of recruitment and training - the *devshirme* system - which supplied it with appropriately trained functionaries of slave soldiers and officials. It was a system, however, which relied for its success on continued expansion of the Empire, a condition which could not be met from the seventeenth century onwards.

TRADITIONAL ISLAMIC EDUCATION

Pre-industrial societies range in complexity from small tribal units to world empires. They are rooted in economic structures as simple as subsistence agriculture and as complex as long-distance trade. Forms of property in such societies have been both individual and communal. Forms of political domination, to use Weber's term, range from traditional forms (including patrimonialism and feudalism) to legal-rational ones of a centralised state dominated either by economically powerful classes or coteries of experts or religious functionaries.

The societies of Islam in the pre-colonial period cannot be neatly described by any of these terms although reflections of each can be found. Within a hundred years after the death of Muhammad (AD 632) the Arabs had established a caliphate which encompassed the territories of the Persian Empire and the Byzantine Empire and which stretched along the Maghreb right through to European Spain. Within this vast territory there were many different cultures, forms of society and religious outlooks. What fashioned such diversity into political coherence was the faith itself and long-distance trade. Max Weber described Islam during its 'first period' as 'a religion of world conquering warriors, a knight order of disciplines crusaders' (Weber, 1970, p. 269). Maxime Rodinson (1980) has attempted to explain the economic basis of this religion in the extensive markets of long-distance trade which flourished during the early centuries of the Muslim state. It was a state embracing several different modes of production.

The 'decisive stratum' of the Muslim community (the *umma*) was not a feudal ruling class whose power rested on the control of land, but a military and bureaucratic elite whose power lay in the control of trade. Central to that control was the bureaucratic administration of towns drawing on the support of powerful local families, Arab tribal chieftains and, perhaps most important of all, Muslim religious leaders. As Lapidus puts it, 'Without the loyalty of village headman, elders, landowners and divines the system could not have been formed' (Lapidus, 1967, p. 5).

The ideological warp of this diverse society was, of course, Islam and the importance of education is that it draws the social perimeter of the *umma* and legitimates the only institution which spanned the myriad differences of culture, language and style of life, namely, Islamic law with its quite precise rules governing property, family life and religious duties (Gibb, 1978). It is this part of the Islamic tradition which persisted through to the climax of the early period till the tenth century and through subsequent invasions from the East to the ending of the historic caliphate with the sacking of Baghdad in 1258. Mamluk rule in Egypt and the Ottoman rule which followed it represented distinct political fractures and transformations in the historic empire but the central core of the faith itself remained intact and its mystical elements were strengthened by the Sufi orders in the towns.

In a society such as this the relationship between central political authority and the ruled populations is precarious. The diversity expressive of pre-Islamic differences of religion and culture was accentuated by division among tribes and in modes of production. And as several writers have emphasised the towns were not always able to contain the tribesmen within the strict frameworks of the faith (Gibb, 1978; Gellner, 1981). The faith itself is a universal one but ideas must be anchored in institutions. For a religion without a church or a priesthood the mechanism which fits best the task of disciplined proselytising is the school. Islam reserves a special place for the educator and seeker after truth.

Although the institutions of traditional Islamic education cannot be deduced from Islamic theology, at least not directly, since the meaning of traditional education varies according to context and through time, it is the religion itself which defines the pedagogical ends to which education is directed and the development of schools was part of the development and diffusion of Islam itself. Any account of education in Islam must begin, therefore, with the central tenets of the faith.

The holy book of Islam, the Koran, contains, for the believers, the divine words of God. The prophet, Muhammad, was only the man through whom God communicated his message to mankind. The central article of faith is captured in the expression 'there is no other God but Allah and Muhammad is his Prophet'. The words of the Koran are not those of men and Muslim teaching has this end: to instruct the believer in a knowledge of the Koran and what it enjoins upon the faithful. The message of the Koran can not be communicated indirectly; musical or dramatic representations of it are unthinkable. The word of God must be received in its pure form. The art of man can never embellish the absolute beauty of the words of God. God spoke to men directly, not through a church. There is no priestly class in Islam. All men are required to defend and represent the faith. There are no barriers between man and God. Islam is a faith for all men joined in brotherhood irrespective of race or nation. The barriers of ignorance which prevent men knowing God must be destroyed and the weapon is education in the form of direct instruction in the word of God.

Two problems had to be solved before this could happen. The first was to record with absolute exactitude the precise words of God and legitimate the authenticity of that one text. By the end of the reign of Othman, the third Orthodox caliph, this task had been accomplished and all previous versions of the Koran destroyed. The second problem was to devise ways to instruct the diverse people of an expanding Islamic Empire. It was required, therefore, of all Muslims that they should study and instruct others. The saying, 'The ink of the learner and the blood of the martyrs are of equal value in the sight of heaven' is one attributed to the Prophet (Williams, 1939, p. 36). Williams explains further:

> During the Jahitiya (Times of Ignorance) that preceeded Islam, it had been customary at literary fairs to recite long poems. These were not in writing but transmitted orally. The insitution of the Koran inspired a widespread desire to learn how to read and write and the first Kuttabs or elementary schools made their appearance. In the year 17 the Caliph Omar sent teachers in all directions, to instruct the Bedouins, and commended people to test their knowledge, and when a man was found who knew nothing of the Koran he was beaten, sometimes to death. (Williams, 1939, p. 35)

Williams quotes from the reports of a medieval traveller, Ibn Battuta that one feast day somewhere in West Africa, he found the children of the Kadi in chains. When asked if he would set them free the Kadi replied, 'I shall not do so until they learn the Koran by heart' (quoted Williams, 1939, p. 35).

The Prophet is believed to have said, 'A father can confer upon his child nothing more valuable than a good education.' The second problem, therefore, that of controlled proselytising was solved in Islam through the development of schools – *Kuttabs* – sometimes attached to mosques but also standing alone supported by the faithful themselves and without any central funding.

The philosophy of education which permeated through the teaching in such schools was strict. Children were required to learn by heart the words of the Koran. These must be recited openly and learned with absolute precision. There was no attempt to analyse and discuss the meaning of the text. Punishment was inflicted on the lazy and teachers expected obedience. The relationship between teacher and pupil was spiritual and not simply practical. In that sense the relationship between pupil and teacher was a personal one and not an institutional one (Tibawi, 1972, p. 39). It was a system which relied on rote learning, on memory and obedience. Practical training in skills related to trades or commerce or animal husbandry or military matters was not given.

Max Weber located Islamic education on a continuum which at one pole includes an education to awaken magical or heroic qualities and at the other to impart specialist training. What lies between these poles 'are all those types which aim at cultivating the pupil for a *conduct of life* whether it is of a mundane or of a religious character' (Weber, 1970, p. 426). Traditional Islamic education was of this type. Based on the Koran itself it sought not to develop specialist skills but to instruct the faithful in what God required of them.

There was, of course, a specialist training involved for those who would become specialists in Islamic Law and Theology, the *ulema*. Their 'pedagogy of cultivation', to use Weber's term, focused on the development and clarification of Islamic law and sciences and their status in Muslim cities as teachers, judges and their control of urban wealth through the administration of endowments (*waqf*) gave them a central position of authority in the faith and complete monopoly of the means of education (see Keddie, 1972).

In this sense, the fountainhead of Islamic learning was distinctly urban. The *ulema*, throughout the societies of the arid zone from Hindu Kush to the west coast of the Atlantic represented what one writer calls 'The Great Tradition' of Islam. (Gellner, 1981). Parallel to this tradition were the myriads of folk traditions of Islam and in contrast to the urban ascetism of the *Ulema* Islam produced Sufism and mysticism and many different variants of Islamic practice and belief. The Islam of illiterate tribal pastoralists was necessarily different to that of urban merchants. For this reason it is difficult to generalise about folk Islam and, therefore, about traditional Islamic education.

Generalisation is, however, necessary and only dangerous when the limits to it are not carefully understood. The knowledge that Islam contains both a great and a folk tradition is one limit which can be imposed on generalisation. So too, as part of it, is the knowledge that the urban Islam of the literate *Ulema* was different to that of the rural pastoralist in the conditions under which its central tenets were made legitimate.

Traditional religious authority and scholarly understanding of the Koran, Hadith and Sharia is based on a training which was rooted in literacy and the study of texts. Within this, of course, there were extremes; a teacher at the al Azhar mosque cannot really be compared to a poorly supported Koran teacher or prayer leader. But even the 'lesser ulema', to use Lapidus's phrase (Lapidus, 1967, p. 138) can derive their authority from the fact that they are men of the book.

The contrast with rural areas is marked. Ernest Gellner has made much of the fact that large segments of Muslim society look for guidance not to the literate *ulema*, but to other religiously significant personnel and groups connected with Sufism (Gellner, 1972, p. 308). The Word of God must, he claims, in tribal societies become flesh. Such societies, he writes, are

> cut off from the book by the fact that their members are illiterate (and, one should add, that they do not possess the means for sustaining or protecting a class of literate scholars), and in some measure cut off from the wider Islamic consensus by a relationship of hostility (and yet of economic interdependence) with those urban centres which are somehow the visible incarnation and centre of gravity of Muslim civilisation.

In this context there is a shift of legitimation away from the book towards the tribal lineage. Saints and tribal holy men become the key religious functionaries. Holy lineages of saints were believed to be descended from the Prophet.

In Gellner's analysis the political role of the saints is to link local traditions to the 'great traditions' of Islam thereby legitimating the legal claims of different tribes to be part of the Islamic community. Sufi practices and beliefs are part of these local traditions but not, Gellner argues, essential to them so that it would be false, without a proper understanding of the function of religious beliefs in different social contexts to claim that tribal Islam is necessarily mystical and inclined to Sufism.

Islam may have been the dominant religious form of the Arab Empire but there is much in Islam to divide men off from one another. Gibb and Bowen (1969) have made the point in this respect that Sufi orders and the traditional guilds of artisans in the towns may have played the vital role in bridging some of those differences. Differences of language, for example, made Turks and Arabs unintelligible to one another, and the Sharia - Islamic law - did not extend to all parts of the empire in the same way. But Sufist brotherhoods did spread throughout all ranks of society binding diverse elements into a larger community:

> Each village, each craft, each group had its own Sufi 'lodge' affiliated to one of the great *tarikas* and enrolled in its brotherhood. It was behind the banner of its *tarika* that each took part in the religious festivals (Gibb and Bowen, 1969, p. 78)

They go on to argue that the close connection between the craft guilds and Sufi orders was what 'in reality constituted the cement of the whole system'. For purposes of this discussion the main point to stress is that Islamic society was highly differentiated and that Islam itself meant different things to different people.

Even within the towns and ancient cities there were considerable differences between serious Islamic scholars and ordinary artisans and merchants. What matters for the purpose of this study is the fact that it was the theologians who defined standards of scholarship and learning, fixing all intellectual development into a strictly religious framework. Learning and scholarship was a question of interpreting the word of God as this was revealed in the Koran. Jurisprudence and the study of Arabic itself was the basis of this scholarship and the mosque its principal location. By the eleventh century a system of elementary schools (*kuttabs*) and of centres of higher learning (*maktabs*) and teacher training institutions (*madrasas*) existed throughout the Islamic world and students travelled from one centre to another to learn from the most famous scholars and *shaykhs*.

In Western accounts of this system two features are usually highlighted, the narrow range of subjects taught and the rigidly formal stress on memorisation which was the model of learning and teaching which the system perpetuated. Jacques Waardenburg (1965) for example, has suggested that the limited number of subjects taught 'had a narrowing effect upon the minds of educated Muslims'. Furthermore, 'the memorisation methods, becoming habits, made independent thought impossible in practice' (Waardenburg, 1965, p. 105). Nevertheless, it was a framework of learning and scholarship which helped consolidate over diverse people and cultures the essential tenets of the faith. It was this faith, already extensive through Anatolia, that the Ottoman warriors sought to defend and to expand. And the scholarship and learned men that were part of it came to play a central role in legitimating and running the Ottoman state itself.

OTTOMAN EDUCATION

Ottoman rulers saw themselves as defenders of Islam and their military victories throughout the second half of the fifteenth century, particularly after the defeat of Mamluk sultans in Egypt in 1517, established that position unequivocally. Religious law was of prime importance in the administration of the state and domination of the Arab lands gave the Ottomans total control over the world's richest centres of trade, doubling the revenues of the Palace treasury and facilitating further military adventures in the Balkans and South East Europe (Inalcik, 1973). Particularly in the Balkans the Ottoman

Empire was able to profit from political differences among feudal notables and religious conflicts between Orthodox and Western Christians with the former being more prepared to look eastwards for protection from the threats they felt came from the religious leaders of Italy.

The Ottoman state was thus in a position by the late sixteenth century to be a serious threat to Europe and to Russia. And within its own frontiers had achieved what Inalcik has described as 'harmony and equilibrium within its own systems and ideals' (Inalcik, 1973, p. 46). He writes:

> The Empire's ruling classes – the military and the ulema – had secure, lasting and sufficient sources of income. Their consumption of luxury goods increased. Not only sultans and viziers but even less wealthy persons, commissioned great works of architecture and created vakifs ... Thousands of people in government service – courtiers, teachers, soldiers, kadis and bureaucrats – received regular salaries or timar incomes, within a clear system of promotion. (Inalcik, 1973, p. 46)

The empire was self-sufficient in all basic commodities and the sultans were the centre of a political authority which was flexible enough to accommodate many religious minorities, to organise the administrative system of the state and wage successful war.

The absolute power of the Ottoman sultan was personal. It rested, as Inalcik (1973) has analysed it, on an old Oriental maxim that 'a ruler can have no power without soldiers, no soldiers without money, no money without the well being of his subjects, and no popular well-being without justice'. They achieved this position through forms of absolutism which were very different to those of Europe of the feudal period. They eliminated all aristocratic opposition in conquered lands. State administration was put entirely in the hands of a slave bureaucracy drawn from Christian minorities and trained and educated specifically for official status. The *ulema* were trusted with the administration of justice within a framework of Islamic law. The composition of the military class of the Ottoman state – the *askeri* – was defined by the sultan and the effective military arm of it, the janisseries, owed their allegiance directly to him.

Şerif Mardin (1969) has underlined three respects in which this system of domination was different to those prevailing in Europe. First, a patrimonial state controlled economic life directly and there were no feudal authorities intervening between the sultan and his subjects. Secondly, the Ottoman Empire lacked extensive intermediary institutions between the subject and the sultan which in the West have been described as 'civil society' and which were found particularly in the towns. Finally, there was a great cleavage between the 'great' culture of the elite and that of the rural masses on the other, a division rooted in language, status and even religion and certainly in social and political roles within the society and state.

The consequences of these features are revealed clearly in the social structure of Ottoman urban centres, in the forms of learning and of cultural transmission throughout the empire and in the economic structure of the state itself. These institutions defined a 'public sphere' in Ottoman lands essentially different to that which developed in Europe from the nuclei of independent towns and city states controlled by an urban merchant class with interests in trade, banking, industry and world exploration.

Education and learning were moulded into this social pattern reinforcing social divisions and legitimating political domination. What Mardin has referred to as the 'estranged cultures' of the palace and the provinces were maintained through the educational institutions of the Ottoman state. The elite culture was urban and its adherents felt superior to rural dwellers and nomads:

> A 'slave bureaucracy, a standing army, a treasury, a rich literature, books for interpreting the word of God – all these gave to the Ottoman elite the feeling that they were far superior to the always large contingent of newly settled or semi-settled Turks and could easily manipulate them. Indeed, the concept of *medeniyet* (city dwelling or civilisation) was the core self-image of the Ottoman ruling class and of its pretensions. (Mardin, 1969, p. 270)

What bolstered that self-image was a system of education appropriate to it. Mobility into elite status was possible through the remarkable mechanism of the *devshirme* system. Under this the sultan took annually boys from non-Muslim minority group families and subjected them to an extensive programme of training within the palace school to become civil administrators and political leaders, including viziers. Among other things this system promoted those with the greatest ability and prevented the consolidation of power in the hands of an hereditary caste. (Kazamias, 1966). It fashioned a well-trained and loyal cadre of warrior statesmen. They were men who had studied Arabic, Turkish, Persian and Muslim religion and culture. There were, too, the skills of riding and archery and mathematics.

Alongside this secular training school for the elite there was an extensive system of essentially religious education controlled by the *ulema*. At the lowest level were the *maktabs* or schools for teaching the Koran. Above these were the *madrasas*. These were higher institutes attached to mosques which provided the religious instruction necessary for the training of *ulema* and judges and teachers. These were positions central to the administration of the Ottoman state.

Ottoman scholarship was rooted in Islamic concepts of knowledge with religious study regarded as the highest of the sciences. While there were always some *ulema* who regarded sciences like mathematics and astronomy as contrary to religion, the Ottoman *madrasas* accepted al-Ghazali's view that these were tools to reveal religious truth. As a framework for scholarship within Islam this system fostered important work in theology, mathematics, astronomy and medicine and literature where a distinct genre, *Divan* poetic literature developed (Shaw, 1976). Theological scholarship was its strong point and this reflected the powerful position of the *Ulema* within the state.

Their religious status exempted them from taxation and conferred on them great authority and their functions as administrators and judges gave them a great amount of power. It was a system of learning, however, which inclined to nepotism and corruption. One writer has stressed the dysfunctional nature of this system for the Ottoman state:

> While the organisation of the learned hierarchy . . . at least for a period worked to the advantage of the state by providing it with a steady supply of well-trained scholars, the simple fact of the thorough-going organisation of the *ulema* carried with it seeds of considerable trouble for the state. The creation of a learned establishment tended to intensify the natural conservatism of the *ulema* . . . Likewise, the definition of success in the learned hierarchy in terms of money and power, a definition implicit in the very process of establishing a graded hierarchy, created the climate for precisely the sort of corruption – the sale of offices, the nepotism, and so on – that afflicted other governmental institutions. (Repp, 1972, p. 30)

In a similar vein Şerif Mardin (1969) has commented that Western views of the Ottoman scholarly meritocracy are often distorted by what he calls an 'Aladdin's lamp effect', i.e. by the appearance of the possibility of rapid social mobility based on merit. In fact, Mardin claims, such mobility could often be bought and the granting of certificates (*berat*) admitting subjects to the tax-free group of the Ottoman elite was a major part of Ottoman government business. The particular issue, that of corruption and inefficiency, will be examined in more detail in the next chapter when the decline of Ottoman power is described.

The culture of the people, the artisans of the cities, the peasants and nomads, non-Muslim minorities was different to that of the Ottoman ruling classes. City dwellers were the most privileged of the dependent classes since they were exempted military service. Since the taxation of cultivators in rural areas was a key element in the revenues of the state they were prevented by law from migrating to the cities although many succeeded in doing so (Shaw, 1976).

The life of urban artisans was framed by the organisation of his guild which regulated trade and training and whose rules the Ottoman state rigidly enforced. Inalcik (1973, p. 155) has suggested that this conservative system of guilds was one of the features of the Ottoman state which prevented the development of a strong Ottoman bourgeoisie and the growth of liberal ideas later in the eighteenth and nineteenth centuries.

Alongside the guilds were religious orders (*tarikats*) closely connected with Sufism. They fell into two groups, the established and famous with fixed rites and ceremonies including such well known orders as the *Mevlevis* (Whirling Dervishes) and the *Bektasis* and the secret orders such as the *Kalenderis*. Such orders are part of popular Islam. They functioned to give protection, help and religious fulfilment to those outside the ruling class and often, too, to provide a framework for political opposition to rulers. Shaw (1976) has suggested that these orders combined traditions of mysticism with the ideals of fighting for the faith against the infidel and emphasised the knightly traits of courage, generosity and nobility. Turkish nationalists were later to recall some of these traditions to give some coherence to their ideas of Turkey's national traditions and literature, but this is an issue for Chapter 9.

It remains only to note that the Ottoman Empire integrated successfully diverse cultures within the traditional framework of Islam and that the Ottoman state evolved structures radically different to and threatening to those of Europe throughout the medieval period. The modes of integration between the state on economic activity which in Europe facilitated the development of a capitalist spirit did not exist in the Ottoman lands. But for most of the period covered in this chapter it would not have been self-evident to anyone living in Europe that the social, economic and religious conditions prevailing there would have been any more favourable for the development of a strong state or economy or for a renaissance in scholarship and learning. Yet that is what happened in the course of the next two hundred years and it was a development which helped the demise of the Ottoman power.

EDUCATION IN EUROPE

Ottoman armies captured Constantinople in 1453. By 1481 when Mehmet the Conqueror died, Asia Minor, Greece and the Balkans were firmly under Ottoman control. By 1517 Egypt and the Levant were under Ottoman suzerainty. The capture of Constantinople gave the Turks easy access to the forests of Greece for boat-building and the capture of Egypt and Syria gave them ports from which to dominate the Eastern Mediterranean. Domination of the Balkans provided them with stable tax revenue from settled peasant populations and control of the Black Sea finalised their control of trade routes to the East and added more revenue to the treasury of the *Porte*.

During this period of Ottoman ascendency Europe was a battleground for competing feudal lords. The cultural unity which Christendom had achieved was no longer expressed as a political unity. Europe was an area of fragmented political authority and for most of the fourteenth century was ravaged by wars; there were peasant revolts, a steady decline of agriculture and plague.

Until the first half of the fourteenth century the institutions of medieval Europe, the industrial and commercial cities of Italy and the Netherlands, the papacy and the aristocracies and monarchies of northern Europe continued to benefit from a growth in population and an expanding economy (Holmes, 1972). From the mid-fourteenth to mid-fifteenth centuries, however, there was a long-term contraction in the economy and a decline of population through plague and famine.

The wealth of landlords, based on rents or sale of food produce to towns decreased along with their political authority. Well-to-do peasants and rural craftsmen benefited from this. The specific ramifications of these developments varied in different parts of Europe. In the east, for example, the *seigneurial* crisis was followed by a successful reassertion of lordly authority through the development of vast grain producing estates. In the west disused lands were taken over by freed peasant farmers. And the overall crisis affected towns and commercial centres in different ways.

The urban world did not decay to the same degree. There was a steady move throughout Europe to extend commerce and manufacture. Long-distance trade in silk and spices flourished from Italian ports. Commercial families like the Medicis reaped the rewards of this, extending their activities into banking and, of course, politics. The cities of north Germany formed into trade federations – the Hanseatic League – to regulate commerce and maintained trading links with the industrial cities of the Netherlands and the wool merchants of England.

It was from the cities that, as Tawney (1972, p. 77) so eloquently put it, 'in an age of political anarchy . . . the forces destined to dominate the future tried their wings'. And it is in the economic and political forms of the cities of the Occident that the contrasts between the societies of Europe and the Near East are most clearly visible. It was in the cities that a 'civil society' was created which, through control of urban government, banking and commerce, was able in the fifteenth, sixteenth and seventeenth centuries to direct the development of a new kind of society, capitalism, together with the social divisions which it created.

The towns organised taxation, public credit and customs; they organised industry and guilds, trading companies and accountancy. But there was civic struggle too. In the towns nobles vied with bourgeois, the poor against the rich, citizen against non-citizen (Braudel, 1981, p. 481). Their social forms were in sharp contrast to the cities of the Near East controlled by centralised patrimonial bureaucracies operating alongside and often through religious officials (Weber, 1978, p. 1249).

The contrast, in essence, is between two different complexes of domination, to use a phrase of Philip Abrams (1978, p. 31). In one the town is a set of opportunities for business increasingly dominated by social groups distinguishing themselves through trade from traditional power groups whose wealth was based on land. In the other, the town is a part of a larger complex of political domination without a corporate identity of its own in which opportunities for independent commercial development were severely circumscribed. The importance of this contrast will be examined in more detail in the following chapter. The point for the moment is that for much of the fifteenth-century Europe was politically divided and economically weak and threatened considerably by the seemingly invincible expansion of the Ottoman Empire on its south-eastern flank.

Intellectually, too, Europe, with exceptions which came later to have world-historical significance, was underdeveloped. The church was the dominant cultural influence but was itself a divided body unable to exert the political influence over monarchs that it had been able to in an earlier period. It was, too, a corrupt body prepared to sell indulgences and auction clerical appointments. It was the church, however, which was the provider of education and the most frequent lessons were sermons.

The institutional pattern of education comprised cathedral schools, some grammar schools and universities which dominated intellectual life. By the fourteenth century universities existed in Bologna, Padua, Paris and in Oxford and Cambridge. In the fourteenth century they were set up in Prague, Cracow, Vienna and Heidelberg. Theology was their main pre-occupation and within it a major challenge was to reconcile the pagan teachings of Aristotle with the bible. This was the intellectual frame of scholasticism, an attempt, assisted by Arab commentaries on Aristotle, to reconcile faith and reason and through careful logical argument clarify the basic tenets of the faith. Latin was the language of instruction and scholarship although it had long ceased to be a vernacular language. The purpose of education was to strengthen Christian faith and generally, boys who attended schools came from the ranks of people who lived in towns. It prepared them for professional employment as doctors and lawyers and priests. For the peasant mass there was no education beyond attending church. For town dwellers guilds of artisans organised the training necessary for the practice of their crafts.

Embedded in the teachings of the church and the practical pedagogy of schools was a whole social theory, a view of the world which sought to reconcile the authority of the church with the political power of lay notables whose power lay in a feudal land system. That theory asserted the unity of society in which different parts – lords and serfs, clerics and artisans – were like the parts of the body. It was a doctrine, argues Tawney (1972), which did not really change until the rise of theoretical individualism in England in the seventeenth century. The property of the feudal lord, the labour of peasant and craftsmen and ferocity of the warrior were brought under the same spiritual order. 'Baptized by the Church', he writes, 'privileges and power became office and duty' (Tawney, 1972, p. 36).

At the heart of this world view was a notion of a social order which was necessarily hierarchical. 'Medieval political speculation', writes the Dutch historian Huizinga (1979, p. 55), 'is imbued to the marrow with the idea of a structure of society based upon distinct orders'. Chivalry was the lynchpin of it. Chivalry reflected two ideas, that nobility was based on virtue and that all men were equal in the sight of God. As Huizinga has analysed it, this 'traditional fiction' became a 'sublime form of secular life' stressing piety and virtue as the essence of a knight's life, an idea which located honour and glory as the collective properties of particular social orders or estates.

The societies of Europe in the fourteenth and fifteenth centuries were organised into distinct social orders. The crude division between those who fought, those who prayed and those who worked, i.e. knights, clergy and peasants was a popular representation of what those orders were (Hay, 1966). The social structure was much more differentiated than this, of course. A full account would distinguish the clergy, the nobility and gentry whose land-holding was feudal and among whom there were further divisions of rank, and townsmen. This last category covers a wide range of groups and statuses from artisan to urban patriarch wielding considerable political and economic power.

To capture fully the character of the lives of people framed in this ordered universe would require a descriptive language which is far richer and subtle than is usually found in social science, and able to evoke the colour, violence and passion in their lives and one which appreciates what Huizinga (1979, p. 145) called the 'enormous unfolding of religion in daily life'. For the purposes of this study, however, it is not necessary to attempt such a description. The important issues for this analysis are the constraints and opportunities which define in the two social formations discussed – the Ottoman and the European – a range of attitudes and experiences which, as conditions for action, gave their future development such distinctly different twists.

2 Capitalist Development and Ottoman Decline

By the end of the eighteenth century and signalled above all else by Napoleon's invasion of Egypt, two great moments of historical change had transformed the world described in the last chapter. The first was the decline of Ottoman power. The second was the development in Europe of what Max Weber (1970, p. 17) called 'the most fateful force in modern life, capitalism'. The two are, of course, connected and their consequences are still evident in the social structures of underdevelopment in Turkey and throughout much of the Middle East. Those structures, discussed in detail in subsequent chapters, must be first understood historically.

The main theme to elaborate in this chapter is this: in the states of Europe changes through the sixteenth century took place which made possible self-sustaining economic growth within a capitalist framework. This did not happen in the Ottoman lands. In Europe scientific and technical knowledge was applied to business, industry and warfare. This also did not happen in the Ottoman lands. The development of bourgeois state forms in Europe created the political conditions for industrialisation from the eighteenth century onwards. Comparable conditions were not created in the Ottoman lands. There are no simple explanations for this. The causes of Ottoman decline cannot be reduced to the logic of oriental despotism or to the absence of a rational economic ethic in Islam. Nor does it help to see the empire as eclipsed by capitalism. These issues must figure in the explanation. The comparison between Europe and the Ottoman Empire when approached with an historical appreciation of their interdependence does, however, lead to a clearer understanding how these great issues must be ordered.

THE DEVELOPMENT OF CAPITALISM IN EUROPE

Tawney (1972, p. 78) has said of the medieval economy of Europe that, 'Tapping the wealth of the East by way of the narrow apertures in the Levant, it resembled, in the rigidity of the limits imposed on its commercial strategy, a giant fed through the chinks of a wall.' But the wall was being 'gnawed and fretted' by restless appetites. Prosperous peasants nibbled at commons and undermined manorial custom, guildsmen freeing themselves from the borough and their craft sought enterprise and profit elsewhere and the miners of Germany and the Tyrol were among those who, long before the great journeys of discovery and the flow of American bullion to Europe engineered an economic revolution which changed the world. Tawney summed it up in this way:

> Heralded by an economic revolution not less profound than that of three centuries later, the new world of the sixteenth century took its character from the outburst of economic energy in which it had been born. Like the nineteenth century, it saw a swift increase in wealth and an impressive expansion of trade, a concentration of financial power on a scale unknown before, the rise, amid fierce social convulsions, of new classes and the depression of old, the triumph of a new culture and system of ideas amid struggles not less bitter. (Tawney, 1972, p. 79)

Tawney was concerned in this famous analysis to track down the root of an idea and a process which he saw as 'the very tissue of modern civilisation', namely that economic motives and ends can be strictly separate from religion and acquire a moral purpose of their own. The idolatry of wealth was for Tawney the practical religion of capitalist societies. And in the course of their development the disciplined search for profit was made legitimate as the goal of economic life. Political thought became thoroughly secular and individualism its dominant motif.

Three interrelated facets of this development need to be highlighted to sharpen the contrast between what occurred in Europe and in the Ottoman Empire during the same period. The first concerns the development of the capitalist world economy from the sixteenth century onwards. The second involves the cultural frames which sustained a distinctly Occidental rationality in economic management, bureaucratic administration and, later, in the growth of science and technology. Finally, the political forms within which capitalist development took place, forms which by the nineteenth century had given shape to a distinctive bourgeois society need to be discussed. Each of these complex changes made possible the growth of a form of society capable of unparalleled economic growth and world domination.

Change in formal education, at least initially, played no role in this although state-provided mass education plays a critical role in its later stages. Without changes in attitude, however, outlook and modes of thinking and knowledge, which are evoked by the changes we now associate with the Renaissance, the Reformation and the scientific revolution of the sixteenth century, later developments made possible by the disciplined application of science to technology would not have been possible so these, too, must form part of the overall analysis.

For the period of the sixteenth and seventeenth centuries, however, a much broader notion of education must be used for the disciplined application of knowledge to economic affairs was in those fields as yet untouched by the schools of the church and the work of the universities; these include navigation, accountancy, warfare, mining and metallurgy and the creative skills of craftsmen.

THE WORLD ECONOMY OF CAPITALISM

Braudel (1982, p. 402) has insisted that long distance trade and extensive markets are a necessary but not sufficient condition for the development of capitalism. To look for its roots in a certain mentality, as he claims Weber and Sombart did, was simply a desperate device used to escape the conclusions of Marx. For Braudel capitalism cannot be explained either entirely by material factors; economic, political and cultural factors played their part. 'So too', he writes 'did history, which often decides in the last analysis who will win a trial of strength' (Braudel, 1982, p. 403).

The framework which Braudel uses rests on a distinction between three zones of economic life. The most visible is that of commerce and long distance trade, the market economy itself. Beneath this there is material life or civilisation, of production and local exchange. Constructed from both zones is a third, that of foreign exchange, of credit and the activities of great commercial houses. This Braudel (1981, p. 24) describes as 'the favoured domain of capitalism' and without it capitalism itself is unthinkable.

From such a starting point the task of explaining the development of capitalism in Europe turns on seeing clear connections between the growth in the mechanisms of long distance commerce – bills of exchange, banks, transport, merchant companies and accounting systems – and patterns of commodity production for markets.

One way in which to do this is to focus on the groups in society who fashioned those links into the scaffold of a new society. Tawney noted that the economic revolution of the sixteenth century, whose 'typical figure, the paymaster of princes, was the international financier', took place in the short space of two generations. International trade opened eastwards and westwards and south to Africa, and Antwerp became its financial centre. The commodities in which dealing occurred were both prosaic and exotic – sugar, wood and wool, silks, spices and bullion. But the consequences of such a trade were profound for they transformed the traditional structures of the medieval economy together with its social philosophies.

The contrast between the finance capitalists of the sixteenth century and the medieval middle class committed to the preservation of their corporate, yet local privileges, is stark. The capitalists of the Antwerp Bourse wanted free trade; they opposed the independence of the guilds and the schooling they sought for their sons was not that of the church or the university, rooted in theology and classics, but a schooling in finance and trade and the arithmetic of double entry book-keeping.

A secular education such as this had, of course, been available for a long time in Europe. The primary schools of Florence in the fourteenth century prepared their pupils for a distinctive secondary education for merchant apprentices. And some of these students went on to the University of Bologna to read law (Braudel, 1982, p. 408). And, as Braudel also notes, the background to this practical training was a solid cultural foundation. Italian merchants knew the *Divine Comedy* of Dante; many were Latin scholars; they read Boccaccio and patronised the arts; 'in short', writes Braudel (1982, p. 408), 'they carried on their shoulders an important part of the new civilisation that is conjured up for us in the word Renaissance.

The truth is that only through an artificial distinction is it possible to separate off that which is distinctively economic from that which is essentially political or cultural. Changing patterns of trade and of production were part of changing social values, structures of power and the ways of thinking with ramifications embracing the whole of Europe. Changes in education are only one small part of it.

The educational problem of the medieval period had been to combine the teachings of the church with the pagan philosophy of the ancients. The problem for the sixteenth and seventeenth centuries was how to cope with profound changes in religious outlook occurring simultaneously with a growth in scientific knowledge and a parallel demand for instruction in learning of a direct practical kind to facilitate trade, manufacture, navigation and war.

Some of the great technical achievements of the sixteenth and seventeenth centuries had little to do with the scholarship of the universities. The practical problems of guiding ships, draining pits, transporting coal and of producing iron – developments which, as Nef (1958) has demonstrated, made possible the industrial revolution at the end of the eighteenth century were solved by practical men. Christopher Hill (1965, p. 15) has shown that the science of Elizabethan England 'was the work of merchants and craftsmen, not of dons, carried on in London not in Oxford and Cambridge; in the vernacular, not in Latin'.

England in the latter part of the sixteenth century during the Tudor period was particularly well placed to incubate the new society. While continental Europe was torn by religious and dynastic conflict, England remained politically stable, a 'fortress against infection and the hand of war' as Shakespeare had John of Gaunt put it. The Reformation in England had stimulated popular literacy and economic change prompted 'a greedy demand for scientific information' (Hill, 1965, p. 16). Important practical advances were made in mathematics, navigation and cartography and Harvey got his ideas about the circulation of the blood from the action of pumps to drain mines.

Among the merchant classes of the sixteenth and seventeenth centuries there was a growing realisation of the need for practical and vocational learning. And the radicals of the English revolution imagined a network of national schools in which all young people should be instructed. As Christopher Hill (1975) pointed out, William Petty advocated in 1648 'colleges of tradesmen' and 'literary workhouses for poor children'. Indeed, the organisation of academies for the promotion of higher learning had been a feature of the Elizabethan age. Shakespeare satirised this in *Love's Labour Lost* when the King of Navarre says, 'Our court shall be a little Academe' and his lords 'have vow'd to study' and to live 'in leaden contemplation'. But, in less than forty years, the greatest scientist of the age, Francis Bacon, was to publish his *New Atlantis* in which he imagined an academy, Solomon's House, which would organise the pursuit of knowledge onto an experimental and practical plane.

The point is this: the opening up of international trade and the development of a commercial and legal infrastructure to promote it created some of the conditions for the development of the capitalist economy. Changes in attitude and outlook towards a secular and rational individualism was part of this although not in themselves sufficiently advanced to transform the older world of medieval Europe. As Braudel has noted, the seigneural regime of vast areas of European countryside, particularly in the peripheral areas of Europe, persisted for a very long time, holding on until the eighteenth and nineteenth centuries. Even at a time when Robert Boyle was turning alchemy into the modern science of chemistry, there were members of the Royal Society who still believed in witches.

THE SCIENTIFIC REVOLUTION

The growth of a distinctive rationalism was one of the forces defining the cultural framework of capitalist society and the growth of science was an integral part of this. The medieval notion of a flat earth with Jerusalem at its centre gave way easily early in the sixteenth century with Magellan's circumnavigation of the world. By the middle of the century Copernicus proposed his heliocentre theory of the universe in a major step to modern science as we know it. The precise observations of the Danish astronomer Tycho Brahe provided the mathematician Johannes Kepler with the data he needed to outline the modern theory of planetary motion. In Padua Kepler's contemporary, Galileo Galilei grounded, as Bronowski and Mazlish (1963, p. 146) say 'in the practical outlook of the trading Republic of Northern Italy' was working on the fundamental laws of mechanics and through precise observational and experimental work, was defining the main features of the scientific attitude.

Religious opposition to science, both in Catholic Italy but also in Germany where Luther opposed the Copernican system, explain why the vital thrust of modern science came from England where Bacon outlined its inductive logic and Newton demonstrated its fundamental laws. Newton was able to work in a religious environment in which no fundamental opposition was perceived between science and the works of God. Pope's famous epigram:

> Nature and nature's laws lay hid in night
> God said 'Let Newton be', and all was light

evokes that atmosphere humourously. And Newton's friend, Halley, greeted the *Principia* with the words:

> Here ponder too the laws which God,
> Framing the universe, set not aside
> But made the fixed foundation of his work.
> (Quoted in Hampson, 1968, p. 38)

It was a common enough viewpoint in the seventeenth century. Robert Boyle, in his last will and testament wished the Fellows of the Royal Society 'happy success in their laudable attempts, to discover the true nature of the works of God' (quoted in Merton, 1957, p. 576).

In this respect a close connection can be claimed between the Protestant Reformation and the Puritan ethos in particular, and the growth of modern science. Rationalism and empiricism are alike features of Puritanism and science; for science they are necessities and for the Puritan they are the essential tools with which to be serviceable in the world (Merton, 1957). Science could give rational weight to faith confirming in its results the notion that there is a necessary order to God's universe.

There are yet more direct connections. Merton (1957) notes that nearly two-thirds of the original list of members of the Royal Society were Puritans. And it was puritan thinkers who criticised the 'formal grammar grind' of schools and promoted a more utilitarian practical education of the sort favoured by Comenius and Hartlib, the continental educational theorists whose ideas influenced the protestant academics. The same sentiments are discernible in German pietism which was so important in the development of scientific studies in German universities, particularly Halle, the first German university to develop a training in science.

There were political and economic influences at work, too, to which the work of scientists in the seventeenth century was a response. Newton's mathematical work was directly relevant to the problems of navigation and ship design just as Galileo's work on ballistics was to the design and operation of cannon. Merton (1957, p. 626) in an analysis of Royal Society meetings between 1661 and 1687 has illustrated the relevance of science in England to practical problems of economic life for less than half of its investigations could be classified as pure science.

The importance of science extends, of course, far beyond either science itself or even its technical applications. It affects, too, philosophy. The bridge, at least in England, was built on the foundations of the work of Newton's friend, John Locke. In 1690 his *Two*

Treatises on Government attacked notions of divine right and absolutism to portray society as created by people freely entering into contracts with one another. This was the coherent statement of individualism; the forerunner in philosophy of many subsequent debates both in England and continental Europe about reason and rationality and political obligation. They were debates which through Voltaire, Rousseau, Hume and Kant were to define the eventual pre-occupation of the European Enlightenment and in a direct way, therefore, the political course of Europe's future.

STATE FORM AND CAPITALIST DEVELOPMENT

Growing trade and increases in production on which the growth of trade depended made possible the development of the modern state by opening up opportunities for taxation. Charles Tilly (1975, p. 31) has put it this way: 'The intermittent but substantial expansion of European trade and industry gave a competitive advantage to the political authorities who could devise means of diverting the resources to their own purposes.' It had been a tenet of medieval government that princes and king should live from their own resources. In any case, a largely agricultural economy meant that the potential tax base for a ruler was small.

Throughout the sixteenth and seventeenth centuries this changed. Absolutist monarchies in France, Spain and England developed. Anderson (1974) has suggested that these were the political responses of feudal regimes in crisis to bolster noble and aristocratic power. The logic of absolutism, however, with its central bureaucracies, extensive taxation and close links with trade and industry together with their rich veneer of courtly etiquette and culture, worked both to bolster feudal privilege *and* bourgeois interests. The centralisation of political power helped the development of a rational legal system building on the firm foundation of Roman Law and removed barriers to trade; it created the basis for a civil service of functionaries as well as for overseas colonial expansion. And the state's need for capital was met by the banker. In this sense the absolutist states can be seen as a vital phase in the development of capitalism in Europe.

Max Weber defined the state as that institution with a legitimate monopoly of the means of violence in society. However, the ability to maintain a capacity for violence turns, in the end, on the careful fusion of resources and technical knowledge. Both of these depend on a supply of competent and loyal personnel who can organise administration, collect taxes, organise armed forces and equip them with weapons and the know-how of their use.

The states of Europe, though each in different ways, solved these problems during the period from the end of the sixteenth century to the early nineteenth. The church and the universities supplied the states with legal and administrative personnel. In this respect, the theological and classical learning of the late medieval university was positively functional for public life. They supplied the state with notaries, excise officials, diplomats and the advantages of employing clerics in state office are primarily that they do not form the corps of an entrenched power group able to pass on their power to offspring.

The states of France, Spain and Hohenzollerin Prussia were much more centrally organised than Britain during the sixteenth and seventeenth centuries, but state building in each of these societies had to overcome common problems of finding and training specialist personnel. In comparison to the Ottomans each did so effectively with far-reaching consequences for their economic and political development.

Throughout the sixteenth century Britain relied often on foreign experts for its military, particularly naval strength. Fischer and Lundgreen (1975, p. 529) have pointed out:

> Fortification and ballistic experts from Italy, navigators from Italy, Spain and Portugal, astronomers, chemists and glassmakers from France, horticulturists, mill- and ship-wrights, and dyers from Holland, printers and miners from Germany and Hungary, warmongers from Sweden, brought their skills to England between the fifteenth and early seventeenth centuries.

The English iron ordnance industry which made guns for the navy was set up by Henry VIII and the Tudors developed their own naval dockyards and purchased the technical personnel to stock them. Merchant companies like the Muscovy Company sponsored development in mathematics and astronomy applied to the business of navigation.

In France at the end of the seventeenth century the Academy of Science was set up to apply science to improvements in navigation, warfare and technology for economic production. It has been said of France that it was 'the first nation to make scientific research a career and to recognise that the possession of highly skilled manpower was a basic factor in national power.' (quoted in Fischer and Lundgreen, 1975, p. 548). The point to be stressed here is that in the special circumstances of the growth of nation states in Europe opportunities opened up to develop scientific and technical knowledge and to apply both in the interests of successful commerce, industrial production and military efficiency. By the end of the eighteenth century, however, the absolutist states of Europe, the *ancien régime*, were giving way to new state forms, those of the bourgeois state rooted, ostensibly, in a new set of political concepts concerned with rights of individuals and their freedoms and the constitutional bases of state power.

The roots of the bourgeois state are too complex to trace here; a full account of them, however, would lead through a discussion of the English Civil War, to the American War of Independence, the French Revolution and the revolutionary movements of the nineteenth century which followed it. The ideological threads to be unpicked in such an account, tangled as they are with the growth of modern science and protestantism, include those of democracy, equality and individualism. In the economic realm the idea that free trade and the market were the cornerstones of the public good replaced mercantilist doctrines. The state, given the labours of Hobbes and Locke and Rousseau, is seen as reflecting a general will and not the interests of a particular class; it becomes a guarantor of individual freedoms subordinate to the interest of civil society. Barrington Moore (1967) has summarised all this as a 'bourgeois revolution', a continuation of capitalism with various forms of parliamentary democracy.

This same period saw the early stages towards the development of national systems of education. Indeed, an important concern of the French revolutionary government in 1789 was to devise a system of education to consolidate the idea of the revolution (Bowen, 1981). In particular they sought to reduce the influence of the church. Napoleon, who regarded church hostility to state supremacy as a facet of 'clerical ambition and medieval backwardness' set up the Imperial University with its *lycées* and *corps enseignant* (quoted in Bowen, 1981, p. 253). In Prussia during the early decades of the nineteenth century reforms were achieved in the *gymnasium* and the universities reformed under the guiding hand of Wilhelm Humboldt; the aim of the reforms was to revitalise the Prussian state, to create an intellectual elite to fill the offices of the bureaucracy.

In England from the beginning of the seventeenth century Anglican control of education was challenged in the dissenting

Puritan academies attractive to a growing lower middle-class clientele connected with trade. During the early part of the eighteenth century and reflecting bourgeois fears of the urban mob, the charity school movements laid the basis for a future system of mass elementary education.

It is impossible to give a precise assessment of the contribution of such changes to the development of industrial capitalism. That they played their part in nurturing the appropriate attitudes and dispositions towards productive wage labour in a market economy is unquestionable (Flinn, 1967). Changes in education played their role in defining the class structure of the new society and in fashioning a supportive institutional base for further development in science, technology and social control.

The growth of this bourgeois state provided the political frame in the eighteenth and nineteenth centuries for the development of industrial society; indeed industrialisation can be seen as its culmination. The development of factory production, the full commercialisation of agriculture, the growth of industrial cities and the birth of new kinds of class divisions are its hallmarks. This development profoundly transformed the economy of the whole world, defining northern Europe as its centre, and confining major areas of the globe, including the Ottoman and Arab lands, as well as Africa, the Far East and South America, to its periphery (Wallerstein, 1980).

THE DECLINE OF THE OTTOMAN EMPIRE

The experience of the Ottoman Empire to the growth in trade and science and to change in government was very different to that of Europe. The difference points to a contrast between a form of society organised to grow economically and one unable to resist its own decline. As early as the seventeenth century this contrast was recognised. Dr Bernier, a travelling French physician reported in 1685:

> How insignificant is the wealth and strength of Turkey in comparison with its natural advantages . . . I have travelled through nearly very part of the empire, and witnessed how lamentably it is ruined and depopulated. (Quoted in Anderson, 1974, p. 39)

Three issues stand out in explanation of the decline of Ottoman power from the sixteenth century onwards. They are, first, the failure of the Ottoman ruling classes to modernise their institutions of government effectively. Secondly, the development of Europe and of Russia to the west and the north of the empire and of Persia to the east constrained its further military development and through that, its economic development. Finally, intellectual stagnation in Islamic scholarship deprived the Ottomans of the scientific and technical skills upon which modernisation could be built and forced them into a dependence on European expertise.

These issues are interconnected and the way they interacted with one another was to confine the Ottoman Empire and its economy to the periphery of a world economy whose centre of gravity was western Europe and to hold back the development of those areas of the Middle East under Ottoman control.

ISLAMIC SCHOLARSHIP

Kemal Karpat (1972, p. 243) has noted that it is necessary to recognise that 'the Balkan and Middle Eastern Societies, and their sociocultural-economic structure in the Ottoman era, were subject to transformation through the impact of internal forces long before massive European influence accelerated this transformation'. One of the internal forces to consider in Islam itself. Without imposing a culturalist interpretation on the economic decline of Ottoman lands, the failure of Islamic scholarship after the medieval period to respond to new learning has to be acknowledged as having political and economic consequences of a profound kind. It was not, in fact, until the sixteenth century that any Latin or Western work of scholarship was translated into any Muslim language. The medieval Muslim view that Europe – the House of war – was barbaric, a culture from which Islam had nothing to learn, persisted into the sixteenth century (Lewis, 1968, p. 34). This is a frequent observation and not just for the Turkish heartland of the Ottoman Empire but for the Islamic world as a whole and particularly of its educational traditions.

Tibawi (1972, p. 45) has summed it up this way:

> From the Renaissance down to the industrial revolution the general trends in Islamic and European education and learning in

> general are discernible in formalism and stagnation on the one side and re-birth and development on the other: at a time when Europe was semi-barbaric and Charlemagne could hardly write his name, the Islamic world enjoyed a high degree of civilisation and its educational institutions were unrivalled. The forces that shaped European development were on the whole internal, springing, to start with, from the Greco-Roman tradition and Christianity. By comparison Islamic development or stagnation was greatly influenced not merely by the conservatism of theologians but also by formidable external factors.

Gibb and Bowen (1969) emphasise this same point in a discussion of *madrasa* education in the sixteenth and seventeenth centuries. Corrupt teaching appointments to Al-Azhar university and utterly uncommitted students were just two aspects of a general decline. But far more serious was a narrowness of outlook where, 'Neither teacher nor pupil regarded it [their training] as anything other than the acquisition of a certain amount of knowledge, all such knowledge being a considerable quantity with strictly defined boundaries' (Gibb and Bowen, 1969, p. 160). These authors continue:

> The inevitable result of such a system, over which no quickening breath had blown since at least the beginning of the sixteenth century, was to intensify with the narrowness of the educational range itself and its narrowing effect on the minds of the educated. (Gibb and Bowen, 1969, p. 160)

The failure of education to adapt to changes in knowledge, particularly in Europe, in a large part accounts for the failure of Islam to respond creatively to developments in medicine, law, science and economic life.

> If the dead point of a society is reached when the educational forces are no longer effective to influence or to direct its development, it must be admitted that the dead point has long since passed in Islamic society. Education had ceased to set before itself the hope of moulding society in the direction of its ideals, and had sunk to the level of merely holding society together by the inculcation of tradition. (Gibb and Bowen, 1969, p. 160)

Reuben Levy (1969, p. 501), making a similar point in a discussion of Islamic attitudes to science, lays the blame for this during and after the fifth century of Islam, i.e. through the medieval period, to 'the growing influence of the *Ulama* and the hardening of dogmatic feeling in the various 'schools' of faith'. In this account the doctors of Islamic law, as the upholders of the central traditions of Islam, were the group who sought to guard their faith from modern developments in science and philosophy.

The theme of the stultification of Islamic higher learning in its rigid religious mould is paralleled in the case of the elementary school (*kuttab*) or mosque school, in the narrow range of what it taught and the severe rigidity of its discipline.

In the early centuries of Islam the mosque schools were centres which helped consolidate the position of Islam itself among diverse peoples. But through an almost total preoccupation with a narrow curriculum based on the learning of the Koran (though not understanding it) and a reinforcing of the view that the only knowledge worth acquiring was that contained in religion, their schools pre-empted the development of other faculties of understanding and the growth of a desire, except in a few exceptional cases, to study (Szyliowicz, 1973).

In such accounts of the stagnation of Islamic learning the root problem is seen to be part of the cultural system of Islam itself. The obvious contrast to it is, of course, Europe and the growth of scholarship during the Renaissance and, later, the development of science.

In the specific case of the Ottoman state the root problem was decay in the *devshirme* system of elite recruitment and corruption among the *ulema*. Religious scholarship was regarded as the true science with résumé, compilation, annotation and commentary on the Koran as the main forms of scholarship (Inalcik, 1973). Progress through the ranks of the *ulema* was based in theory on ability: in practice the system inclined to nepotism in its higher ranks and fanaticism among those *ulema* who preached and taught in the mosques. The outcome was an intellectual inability to conceive of the necessary adjustments which the modern world required of the Ottoman state.

THE IMPACT OF EUROPEAN DEVELOPMENT

The development of capitalism in Europe and the opening up of the Far East to European trade directly affected the Ottoman Empire by eroding the fiscal revenues of the state, testing severely its military capability and foreclosing its industrial development through trading concessions (capitulations).

Up to the end of the sixteenth century Ottoman control of trade patterns from the Far East, Egypt and Sudan through the Eastern Mediterranean to Europe was strong and the state gained greatly from taxes and excise revenues in silk, spices, sugar, dyestuffs and grain from Egypt. It benefited, too, from Ottoman control of the Black Sea and its trade. The cornerstone to it all was Ottoman maritime control of the Eastern Mediterranean. But this was decisively overcome at the battle of Lepanto in 1571 and invasions of Cossacks threatening the Black Sea ports weakened Ottoman power further. The defeat of Lepanto revealed the superiority of European naval technology and strategy over that of the Turks.

The opening up of the cape route to India and the Far East further undermined the empire by cutting its revenues from excise duties leaving Turkey, as Lewis (1961, p. 28) has put it as a 'stagnant back-water through which the life giving stream of world trade no longer flowed'.

Two features of Ottoman economic policy facilitated a growing European domination of the economic life of the empire. The policy of encouraging manufactured imports from Europe for excise purposes and to create material prosperity did little to encourage industry in the empire itself. Secondly, the policy of leaving all matters of trade and commerce to non-Muslim minorities acted as a block on Ottoman statesmanship to think of ways of improving primitive methods of production and transport (Lewis, 1961, p. 35).

Perhaps more seriously, by denying the Jews, Greeks and Armenians who were involved in commerce the political rights and opportunities to build up an effective system of banking and credit, the state, unlike its counterpart in Europe, denied itself a source of credits and its economy an efficient mechanism of capital formation.

OTTOMAN GOVERNMENT

Fortunes could be made in the Ottoman lands but were more likely to arise through the sale of government offices, corruption and the con-version of tax revenues than from trade or industry. From the middle of the sixteenth century onwards processes of sub-infeudation occurred in which local nobles, particularly in the Balkans, could claim autonomy from the sultan. The flow of Mexican silver into the European market fuelled price increases causing inflation in the Ottoman market, reducing the incomes of *timar* holding troops and creating difficulties in paying the army. Army rebellions, brigandism in Anatolia and administrative inefficiency and factionalism in Istanbul compounded the failure of the state to keep abreast of modern military technology and sapped its strength from within. From the second half of the sixteenth century, unable to devise a coherent economic policy for the empire, Europeans through capitulation, began to control its Mediterranean trade. The result in the long term was further decline. The Ottoman failure to capture Vienna at a second attempt in 1683 was a measure of it. Lewis (1961, p. 36) sums it up this way:

> Fundamentally, the Ottoman Empire had remained or reverted to a medieval state, with a medieval mentality and a medieval economy – but with the added burden of a bureaucracy and a standing army which no medieval state had ever to bear. In a world of rapidly modernising states it had little chance of survival.

Reforms were attempted during the eighteenth century. Grand Vizier Damad Ibrahim Pasa in the period 1718 to 1780 commissioned a study of French military technology and recruited French experts to reform the army. A school of geometry was set up in 1734 to help train bombardiers and later in the century a similar school was opened for the navy. Outside the military field developments took place in printing. Military reforms by Selim III at the end of the century have to be seen as part of a growing influence of European thought in the empire particularly from France. Many reforms were effected as part of Sultan Selim's 'New Order' (Nizam-i Cedid) and these helped to define a new corps of Western-created army experts. French influence in Instanbul actually increased after Napoleon's invasion of Egypt although there was a reaction to this in the early years of the nineteenth century when Sultan Selim was deposed under the weight of army mutiny against his military reforms.

Pressure for reform was reasserted throughout the nineteenth century. But this was during a period when European economies took their decisive steps to industrial society and the Ottoman regime itself was severely challenged from within the Balkans and in Egypt.

3 Industrial Capitalism: Modernisation and Change in Education

By the end of the eighteenth century capitalist society in Europe, and particularly in Britain, had entered its industrial period. The populations of the states of Europe were at this time still largely rural. And, as Eric Hobsbawm (1962) has noted, the profound consequences of the industrial revolution were not fully grasped until late in the middle years of the nineteenth century. 'It is only in the 1830s', he writes, 'that literature and the arts began to be overtly haunted by that rise of capitalist society, that world in which all social bonds crumbled except the implacable gold and paper ones of the cash nexus' (Hobsbawm, 1962, p. 44). But the shift to industrialism was inexorable and the world economy of capitalism developed around competing nation states, each one of which was divided within itself along lines which were increasingly those of class. And the economic and political divisions of class became simultaneously those of culture, learning, ideology, experience and power.

The changes wrought in the social structures of European societies by the development of industry by increasingly powerful groups of bourgeois entrepreneurs is something which can only be discussed properly in the light of the specific experience of particular states, industries and communities. For industrial capitalist society emerged in Europe in different ways and within different ideological guises. Differences in the spread of industrialism, in the role which states played in its development, in the character of the social and political divisions which accompanied it and how those divisions found concrete expression in the particular politics of each European society is something which must be held in view in order to understand what took place in the Middle East.

While it is convenient to analyse changes in the Middle East during the nineteenth century as being influenced in a fundamental way by 'the West' it is not entirely satisfactory to do so. 'The West' is a mighty abstraction embracing diverse societies and systems of belief; and from the end of the eighteenth century onwards the industrial

West was a network of states locked into an international economic and political order which generated class conflict within its component states and war between them.

The Middle East was, indeed, profoundly influenced by the West. It was an area of the globe in which European nations, particularly France and Britain, fought out their conflicts of interests. The ideas and the material culture of the West penetrated and transformed the societies of Islam. The Western economies set the constraints within which the economies of the Middle East could develop and military might secured that dominance. And the secular political philosophies of the West influenced how new elites in the Middle East came to conceive their own notions of what development for their own societies should mean. In this way the contradictions and conflicts of Western societies were transferred to the Middle East with clear consequences for how those societies developed in the nineteenth and twentieth centuries.

Education played a vital role in this process for a narrow view of what the real achievements of Western education had been was seized on by reformers throughout the Ottoman Empire as the key to their own efforts to halt its decline. The development of specialised state schools in military science to train modern officers for the armies of the sultan was the start of it. Foreign advisers, particularly from France, helped to form the institutions which later became important agencies in the dissemination of Western political ideas throughout the Ottoman Empire.

Western ideas, as Bernard Lewis (1961, p. 54) has pointed out, affected patterns of identity and loyalty and fashioned new aspirations. 'These new ideas', he writes, 'may be summarised in three words: liberty, equality and – not fraternity, but what is perhaps its converse, nationality. These same ideas, of course, were to transform Western societies themselves. The French Revolution of 1789 was the decisive moment of change for the new concepts of citizenship which it articulated and the political reaction it provoked from threatened aristocracies defined the contours of political conflict in Europe for over a century.

The specific educational ramifications of these 'new ideas' throughout Europe can only be hinted at here but two themes stand out. Both concern the structuring of the class relationships of a burgeoning capitalist society. The first is the legitimation of the emerging position of the bourgeoisie was the one coherent and powerful class in Europe in the early decades of the nineteenth century. Throughout Europe, however, it was as James Bowen has pointed out a religiously conservative class for which a classical grammar school education became a mark of social and political legitimacy:

> The result was that in England, France and Germany, and to a considerable extent in the United States, nineteenth century bourgeois schooling followed the traditional conservative model of the preparatory school, grammar school (or *lycée* or Gymnasium) and if possible humanities, liberal arts or philosophy at the university. (Bowen, 1981, p. 285)

Within this curriculum the classical languages were central; science and technology were almost completely ignored although this was a period of considerable scientific innovation and development and one on which some middle class people influenced by utilitarian social theory and empirical philosophy clearly understood the importance of science and technology in education.

Revolutionary France seized the initiative in science and education and political and social theory; and developments in France prompted change throughout Europe. France mobilised science and technology for warfare. The revolutionary government set up the *École Polytechnique* in 1795 and drew up plans for the *École Normale Superieur*. Under Napoleon the *Polytechnique* flourished and as a model of a higher education was copied throughout Europe almost everywhere except Britain.

In Britain during the period following the Napoleonic wars there were a number of middle-class supported bodies to encourage the development of science and technology and considerable radical criticism of the traditional universities of Oxford and Cambridge. Such criticism led among other things to the setting up of the University of London.

This is not the place to describe such developments in any detail and in any case, the listing of institutional developments in education only begins to hint at the profound transformations in science and social theory taking place at this time which were together defining new forms of consciousness for the modern world.

Between the French revolution of 1789 and the revolutions of 1848 there was something of a scientific revolution in Europe. Major developments occurred in electricity and electromagnetism, in chemistry – the atomic theory and the development of organic chemistry – both of which stimulated advances in biology. In mathematics developments took place in the theory of groups, of vectors and the functions of complex variables. In the field of social science this is the period in which writers sought the laws of political economy and positivism as the philosophical base of the human sciences was outlined.

Hobsbawm (1962) has suggested that these developments in science and technology were inextricably bound up with revolutionary changes in the structure of society. The point is worth stressing to underline the fact that science and technology *as we know them* are inseparable from the economic and political and cultural characteristics of the societies in which they developed. The French mathematician Carnot was led from a study of the steam engine to the laws of thermodynamics and developments in palaeontology and geology, writes Hobsbawm (1962, p. 343) 'owed much to the zeal with which industrial engineers and builders hacked at the earth, and the great importance of mining'. Darwin derived the notion of natural selection by analogy from the logic of capitalist competition theorised by Malthus as 'the struggle for existence'.

Such ideas - evolution, science, progress, rationality - were refashioned into powerful and essentially bourgeois social philosophies like positivism and utilitarianism which strengthened further the political and ideological position of the increasingly powerful bourgeois classes in Europe. In the course of the nineteenth century bourgeois education came increasingly to reflect them.

Science and technology were not responsible for the industrial revolution although they subsequently became an indispensable part of it. Of much greater significance in the early phases of industrialism was the availability of market opportunities and a good supply of labour which could be exploited cheaply and kept under control.

Britain had secured a dominant position in world markets throughout the eighteenth century and it can be noted in passing that Britain's naval strength had done much to prompt industrial developments in the eighteenth century in iron manufacturing related to naval contracts for cannon and ammunition. The labour supply problem in Britain, together with the problem of feeding a growing population had been solved throughout the eighteenth century by agricultural reform and the growth of towns and cities.

The problem of labour control was, however, a fundamental one. The social history of it is well enough known to require no repetition. The appalling social conditions of the industrial centres of Europe, particularly Britain, spawned, on the one hand revolutionary responses among the emerging working classes and, on the other, acts of severe repression by governments fearful of a breakdown of social order. Alongside the repressive apparatus of the militia and of labour laws prohibiting workers' organisations, of ruthless discipline and exploitation in factories and mines and farms, education took its place as an instrument of social control. The central themes around which the development of mass education in the nineteenth century had to be written are those of social control and industrial acculturation.

Both are manifest in the institutional form of the school itself. The model for the elementary schools which developed later in the century was provided by the monitorial system of Lancaster and Bell. It was a cheap and efficient system of mass schooling based on a hierarchy of monitors and children were encouraged through a merit system to succeed in their work. Its emphasis was on order and discipline. Several writers have drawn attention to the close parallel between the methods and form of the schools and the factories for which they prepared their pupils (see e.g. Johnson, 1976). Behind such provision was deep-seated fear for what was perceived as the morality and what Richard Johnson (1976, p. 49) calls 'the obstinately ungovernable behaviour' of the working classes.

It was not only firm discipline and strict religion which was mobilised to education in this way; so too was the new science and technology, in the Mechanics' Institute movement in the early decades of the nineteenth century. There were about 600 such institutes by the middle of the century with more than 100 000 members (Bowen, 1981, p. 344). They were organised throughout Britain by middle-class reformers of various kinds to provide scientific and technical training to artisans. As Shapin and Barnes (1976) noted, this class was already literate; the problem was to control what they were reading, to focus their minds on the factual order of the world as it is rather than on speculation about how it might otherwise be so that this nascent labour aristocracy would co-operate with its masters rather than challenge them.

The monitorial system spread through Europe and into the United States and in an attempt to utilise science to industry there was throughout Europe attempts to set up schools and colleges (e.g. the *écoles* of the Napoleonic period) which would train mechanics and technicians for both military and civilian employment.

These developments can be seen, then, as part of a long process of fitting out the new society with the rudiments of a system of education which would help to stabilise it politically. With the exception of some radical education thinkers who could conceive of education as a fundamental human right and something to be developed for the common good, the concepts of education which emerged in Europe stressed, for the middle classes, the cultivation of individual sensibilities and for the workers, respect for authority. Different social classes received very different forms of education and it was not until much later in the century that working-class people could countenance more for themselves than elementary education. The irony then was, of course, as will be shown later (see Chapter 4), that the education they demanded was that which had been given to middle-class youths and from which they themselves had been systematically debarred. Moreover, their exclusion had been justified on grounds they were intellectually ill equipped to benefit from it, that the social divisions of society reflected natural differences of ability. Modern education developed in Europe then in a framework of competing nation states in which the states dominated by *bourgeois* interests either directed (as in France and Prussia) or condoned (as in Britain) the development of educational institutions fitted to the social and economic framework of the new capitalist order of society. The institutional forms of education for the economic development of Europe during the early part of the nineteenth century is not something which can be precisely measured. Its ideological importance, however, was profound. It legitimated the inequalities of a society which was in the normal course of its functioning necessarily and deeply inegalitarian.

OTTOMAN REFORMS

Bernard Lewis (1961, p. 55) argued that the French Revolution had a profound impact on the House of Islam and its secular character was for Muslims its most important feature; for it was this which pointed to the importance of representative governments, the rule of law and strong secular political authority as the best defence against domestic despotism and foreign imperialism. This was an attitude which was to grow throughout the nineteenth century and to culminate in the revolution of the Young Turks. Changes in Ottoman thinking began, however, with the military reforms of Sutan Selim III and his attempt to build a modern military machine (the Nizam-i Cedid) separate from the Janissaries. His efforts were unsuccessful but by the late 1820s janissary power was broken and with French help the army was reformed. So too were many aspects of Ottoman government and education. Naval and military engineering schools (set up in 1773 and 1793) were followed in 1827 by a medical school. In 1838 Sultan Mahmud encouraged the setting up of two grammar schools (*rüsdiye* schools) to train officials and translators. The impetus behind such reform was to protect the Ottoman state against the challenge of Europe but also from that of Muhammad Ali in Egypt who had begun a programme of rapid modernisation. The constitutional reforms of 1839 – the Noble Rescript of the Rose Chamber – have to be seen in this light. This was the first edict in a series of reforms throughout the nineteenth century known as the *Tanzimat* reforms. The Rescript endorsed a number of rights of citizenship – such as the right to private property – which had not existed in the Ottoman Empire – fair trials and the abolition of tax farming. These were a response to a foreign minorities but they reflected, too, a deep-seated concern in the Ottoman ruling class to modernise its institutions. Further reforms followed in the 1840s and early 1850s, in legal codes, commercial practices, and education. The long-term importance of the Tanzimat reforms lay above all in giving shape to a new educated elite which late in the century was to define a movement of reform and, later, revolution to westernise the empire in the framework of a constitutional state.

In the early part of the century, however, the main challenge to Ottoman power came through events in Egypt, events which were brought to a critical point with Napoleon's invasion in 1798. This has been described by P. M. Holt (1968, p. xv) as 'the first large-scale and effective European attack on the Arab provinces of the Ottoman Empire and was to initiate a century and a half of growing political domination'.

MUHAMMAD ALI'S EGYPT

Napoleon invaded Egypt in July 1798. He took an armada of 400 ships and 40 000 men and successfully stormed Alexandria on 2 July. He pressed on immediately to Cairo to defeat a Mamluk army in the battle of the pyramids. Within a month, however, his strategic position became desperate because a British force under Lord

Nelson destroyed the French fleet at anchor in the Bay of Aboukir on August 1st.

Napoleon's attack on Egypt was part of his struggle with Britain. Lacking naval superiority in the West his strategy was to choke off Britain's supply route to India thereby, in the longer term, undermining British strength in Europe. There was, too, a strictly commercial purpose to it. Napoleon saw Egypt as a potential rich source of grain to feed southern France and French control of the country would have facilitated French commerce and merchant shipping throughout the region (Lutfi al-Sayyid Marsot, 1984).

Egypt was at this time legally part of the Ottoman Empire but was in fact under the precarious control of the Mamluk Beys and in a state of considerable economic decay. It was a poor society with a peasant economy, considerable political disorder and one in which the *ulema* played a role as representatives and protectors of the people.

The wealth of the Mamluk rulers and their power was based on tax farming (*iltizamat*). Turkish speaking, the ruling families were culturally set apart from the *fellaheen* on whom they ultimately depended and conflict among the ruling families reduced the country by the 1780s to a state of 'quasi-permanent civil war' (Lutfi al-Sayyid Marsot, 1984).

Culturally and intellectually Egypt was stagnant. Al-Azhar was an important Muslim institution but little scholarship took place there. And according to one writer, the growth of Sufism made matters worse: 'Sufism became a kind of form of hallucination, and people believed greatly in the occult science and superstitions. Lunatics were taken for saints, imbeciles for respected Shaykhs' (El-Din El-Shayyal, 1968, p. 119).

The French invasion and occupation began the process which transformed this state of affairs. Napoleon took with him not only soldiers but a corps of scientists, too. This was the *Commission des Sciences et des Arts*. Its job was to survey Egypt's resources. Inspired by St Simonian ideas about science and progress the Commission included mathematicians, a chemist, a mineralogist, a naturalist, a civil engineer and many others. From this body Napoleon formed the *Institute of Egypt* with the aim of spreading scientific knowledge and advising the government he had set up. Their work led to the publication of the *Description de l'Égypte* which appeared between 1809 to 1828. This document in its several volumes laid the foundations of modern Egyptology and inspired, too, the decorative arts of the First Empire itself (Richmond, 1977, p. 22).

Napoleon's occupation lasted three years and while, as Vatikiotis (1969, p. 39) has underlined, it must be judged a military failure, 'the scientific and educational consequences of his adventure for both Egypt and Europe were monumental'. The Commission undertook studies of the country's basic mineral resources, population and water supply; it set up laboratories for chemical analysis and initiated archaeological excavations. The French planned schools, too, but little was actually done to educate Egyptians. Indeed, the invasion may have had an adverse effect on Egyptian learning since the *madrasas* were disrupted and traditional relationships between students and *sheykhs* were transformed to the latter's disadvantage. From being almost revered, *sheykhs* lost both wealth and prestige. The English traveller, Lane, commented in 1836 that: 'The condition of a man of this profession is now so fallen, that it is with difficulty he can obtain a scanty subsistence, unless possessed of extraordinary talent' (Lane, 1917, p. 219).

The longer term significance of Napoleon's invasion lay in the way it opened up opportunities for European ideas to influence intellectual life in Egypt for the remainder of the century. Its immediate effects on Egyptian culture and learning and scholarship were very limited. J. Heyworth-Dunne (1968, p. 96) notes that 'the invasion was an act of aggression and it was not in the nature of things that the Egyptians should take an interest in any of the aggressor's institutions'. Prominent Egyptian scholars like al-Jabarti and Sheykh Bakri visited the French Institute and were given demonstrations of scientific experiments. This was part of a programme to win over leading *ulema* to support French occupation but the demonstrations they witnessed 'did not elicit from them any symptoms of surprise. They witnessed . . . the operations . . . with the most imperturbable indifference' (Heyworth-Dunne, 1968, p. 97).

The traditions of Islamic scholarship of which they were a part attached no importance to scientific and technical skills. Tradesmen were often illiterate. Medical practitioners were mostly barbers and in illness people relied on the help of Providence and the efficiency of charms. Lane (1917, p. 222) noted that the magnetic needle was used only to discover the position of Mecca and that 'Those persons in Egypt who profess to have considerable knowledge of astronomy are generally blind to the true principles of the science: to say that the earth revolves round the sun, they consider absolute heresy.'

European ideas seeped into Egypt slowly and not through the general education of the people but through military influence and Muhammad Ali's programme to build a state and an army capable of effective warfare. The educational strategy which he evolved during the first half of the nineteenth century aimed to train technicians for state service but the system created to achieve this lacked firm roots in the wider education of Egyptian *fellaheen*. Indeed, by linking the idea of education so closely to military service the unintended consequence of his reforms was to encourage peasants to avoid educating their children in the *kuttabs* for fear of them being drafted to the army. In addition, the failure to develop a general education to form the basis of specialist training later compelled Muhammad Ali to rely on outside assistance, particularly from France, for help with the training of the experts his state system required. This assistance became one element of a larger European intrusion into Egyptian affairs setting the early parameters of Egyptian dependency and underdevelopment. Muhammad's own plans were, of course, quite the opposite of this. The period of his rule was one in which a programme of industrialisation was attempted on the basis of import substitution and one in which the political framework for a nation state in Egypt was established.

Muhammad Ali arrived in Egypt in 1801 with a detachment of Albanian troops to attack the French and restore Ottoman authority in the country. By 1805 he became the effective ruler (or *wali*) of the country having destroyed Mamluk power in lower Egypt. And in 1811 in a famous bloodbath he destroyed all Mamluk opposition in the Citadel Massacre. In the following twenty years he built up a military machine and a state system which enabled him to challenge seriously the Ottoman government in Constantinople and for him to be perceived by the major powers of Europe as a threat to their interests in the eastern Mediterranean.

His achievement was to exploit the economic and military weaknesses of the Ottoman central government and to claim Egypt as his own possession (as a *mulk*) to be developed in the interests of his own household. The ethnic background of Muhammad Ali and the elite of his administration was Turco-Circassian and Albanian and they regarded themselves as different from and superior to the Egyptian population they ruled over. The language of government remained Turkish and, at least at the beginning of his rule there was no concept of or intention to develop an independent nation state in Egypt which would be free of Ottoman authority. Muhammad Ali's commitment was to his own profit and power within the framework of an Ottoman and Islamic political order.

He was, however, a moderniser who had been influenced by the

Ottoman reforms of Sultan Selim and who had absorbed through foreign advisers, particularly from France, some of the ideas of St Simon. He consulted foreign consular staff on military affairs and picked the brains of foreign merchants for ideas about machinery and trade (Lutfi al-Sayyid Marsot, 1984, p. 78). What unfolded was an essentially mercantilist vision of a strong state deeply involved in the control of the economic life of the country and on the basis of increasing agricultural exports being in a position to help the industrialisation of the country and establish the basis for a strong and modern military machine.

Muhammad Ali perceived the necessity of economic change not only in relation to the military requirement of an efficient army and navy but also in the light of opportunities which clearly existed to supply the European powers products (initially grain) which Egypt could easily produce. He had sold grain to the British during the period of the Napoleonic wars and during the period of food shortages which followed them. The longer term unintended consequence of these policies was to bring the Egyptian economy closely into alignment with the more powerful area of continental Europe and to fuel European fears of competition for European industry. The economic thrust of his reforms was to appropriate as much as possible of the agricultural surplus as state revenues (see Owen, 1981). The mechanisms he created to achieve this goal involved tax reform, including the taxation of *waqf* lands, the creation of centralised administrative bureaucracy and the setting up of state monopolies to control imports and exports. He began, too, behind the protective wall of import controls a programme of industrialisation beginning with factories set up for war production. The history of these developments is that of what is known as a 'military-industrial complex'. In parallel with changes in industry Muhammad Ali engineered profound changes in agriculture; he developed irrigation networks, stimulated cotton growing and agricultural exports. Complex social changes followed. A new landowning class emerged; Muhammad Ali successfully settled Bedouin tribesmen in rural areas; new patterns of rural social differentiation emerged and Egyptians rather than Turks began gradually to occupy the lower administrative positions in the state. The number of Europeans living in the country increased as commerce expanded, yet another channel of Western influence in Egypt (see Baer, 1969).

Of great long-term significance was the strategy of education which accompanied the modernisation plans. For what developed was a system of specialist training to produce the technical and military personnel Muhammad Ali's factories and army required. Elite modernisation rather than the general educational development of the people of Egypt was his main concern. Indeed, his early views of the educational potential of Egyptians were very negative. He apparently had responded to the suggestion that Egyptians should be sent to France for education – a suggestion put to him by the French geographer and engineer, Jombard, editor of the *Description de L'Égypte* – with the comment that 'his subjects were too ignorant to benefit from European travel' (quoted Silvera, 1980, p. 6). That was in 1811. In 1826, however, he sent a student mission to France.

It was not the first time Muhammad Ali had sent students abroad; from as early as 1809 he had sent students to Italy to study military science, printing and shipbuilding. In 1816 he set up a military school in the Citadel and others were to follow. In 1821, with French help he set up a military school at Aswan and from this time on received much French help in the training of his army. In 1827 a medical school was started under the French physician Dr Clot with translators in the classroom to translate the French of the teachers into Arabic. The students were all Egyptians and there were, among all other technical difficulties, some cultural obstacles to be overcome for successful teaching. In particular the school had to ignore the views of the *ulema* that it was against the Islamic faith to dissect dead bodies. To facilitate the progress of students Dr Clot opened an annexe to the school where students could be taught French and be given help with their general education (Heyworth-Dunne, 1968, p. 128).

In 1829 a school of pharmacy was opened and from 1827 a school of veterinary studies was developed. Within the military several schools were opened up: there was a cavalry school, a music school and schools for the artillery and infantry and navy. Technical schools for mineralogy, engineering and applied chemistry followed. The engineering schools were much influenced by St Simonians with the help of students who had returned from missions to France. Muhammad Ali developed civil schools to improve the skills of his administrators and several other specialist institutions developed, e.g. a school of agriculture and a school of irrigation. The whole system of schools was co-ordinated by a central educational administration – the *Diwan al-Madaris* – although, perhaps, not very effectively (see Heyworth-Dunne, 1968, p. 226).

Designed for state purposes the system by-passed the traditional educated elites of Egypt and nurtured what Vatikiotis (1969, p. 62) has described as 'a state trained, European-influenced native elite of public officials, teachers, technicians, scientific and administrative officers'. Those who had been on missions abroad provided the officials for government posts and created a new status group in society which Heyworth-Dunne (1968, p. 170) describes as 'the cultured aristocracy' clinging to the idea that 'training and specialisation abroad was the hallmark of education'. 'It was through their training', he continues, 'that they were enabled to take over posts that led to high salaries, gifts of land and titles.' How far that training influenced their basic outlook, however, is not absolutely clear. The traveller, Lane, noted in 1836 that the 'lights of European science' were 'almost exclusively confined to those servants of the government who have been *compelled* to study under Frank instructors' and that 'European customs' were adopted 'by scarcely any persons except a few *Turks*.' (Lane, 1917, p. 228). And he added: 'Some Egyptians who had studied for a few years in France declared to me that they could not instill any of the notions which they had there acquired even into the minds of their most intimate friends.'

General education, as already noted, was poorly developed during this period and students had often to be conscripted into schools. In 1837, following the reorganisation of school administration, forty-one schools (*maktabs*) were opened but shortages of modern teachers meant that they had to be staffed by graduates from Al-Azhar. The emphasis in these schools was on reading and writing Arabic, a continuation, in fact, of the traditional *kuttab* system.

Heyworth-Dunne portrays these schools as very ineffective institutions in which students relied on traditional methods of rote learning and valued their schooling only in terms of the employment opportunities it would open up. For the *fellaheen* in the villages work on the land took precedence over schooling. The English traveller, Bayle St John, noted in 1852 that 'When a boy reaches the age of seven or eight years, he is, even in the villages, sometimes sent to school, where he learns to read and write a little, but rarely enough to be of much use to him in after life' (St John, 1973, p. 197). Looking after cattle and scaring birds from the crops in the fields or being drafted onto canal work had priority over schooling in what was still, essentially, a peasant society. Muhammad Ali's school system, however, tied as it was to the needs of military training, did not survive the collapse of his industrial and military ambitions in the 1840s; and from this period on, European influence over Egyptian affairs steadily increased.

The extent to which Muhammad Ali succeeded in his plans should not, however, be underestimated. He doubled Egyptian cotton exports between 1820 and 1845 and developed an Egyptian textile industry (Owen, 1981). He built arsenals, sugar refineries, rice mills and tanneries; his irrigation schemes and agricultural policies all combined to transform peasant agriculture and working conditions as well as the traditional handicraft industries of the urban areas. It has been estimated that by 1840 there was a labour force of over a quarter of a million in the industrial enterprises (Vatikiotis, 1969, p. 64).

The Egyptian strategy of industrialisation revealed, however, the severity of the constraints on independent development in a poor country faced with an international economic and political framework dominated by European powers superior in economic *and* military power. Muhammad Ali imported machinery; he relied increasingly on foreign loans and technical assistance and European merchants and ethnic and religious minorities - Greeks, Armenians and Jews - grew in importance in the economic life of his state. They set up their own schools and in Heyworth-Dunne's (1968) assessment of it, this was to the considerable disadvantage of Egyptians who, from the 1840s onwards were faced with a collapsing system of already inadequate schools. These foreign communities became important vehicles for further European cultural and economic influence on Egyptian society and, later, of direct control.

The collapse of Muhammad Ali's state system has to be seen as part of a larger moment of change involving the European powers (particularly Britain) seeking to protect both what they saw as their own interests in the eastern Mediterranean against what they understood as the threat of Muhammad Ali, and the balance of power in Europe itself. There were, of course, features of Egyptian society itself which contributed to his failure. He over-extended himself militarily; the technology of his factories was inferior to that of those he sought to compete with in Europe and Ottoman-type control of decision making created considerable problems of economic management (Owen, 1981). It would be wrong, therefore, to claim that had Britain and France not intervened to clip his wings, Muhammad Ali would have led Egypt down the path of industrialisation to become a modern industrial state.

Nevertheless European intervention to curtail his power was

decisive. Ottoman decline in the region was the background to it; but so, too, was the development of national independence movements in the Balkans. Egyptian forces had fought in the 1820s to suppress the Greek independence movement and this intervention had profoundly alienated public opinion in Europe, particularly among those groups at the centre of political life who had received a classical education and who had come, much influenced by Romanticism, to regard Greece as the fount of European civilisation.

Muhammad Ali's military sweep through Syria in the 1830s was what prompted European intervention to support the Ottoman government. In the case of Britain there were great fears of Russian influence in Constantinople and of the opportunity the Syrian occupation gave Muhammad Ali to exert military and commercial influence right through to the Persian Gulf. Egyptian control there was perceived by Palmerston as threatening trade with Syria and the overland route to India.

These British concerns developed at a time when, through domestic economic difficulties and high tariff barriers to British goods in Europe and America, British merchants were seeking new markets. Manchester manufacturers were obliged to live, as one writer put it, 'on shirts for black men and brown men and for the Muslim world' and some voices in Britain were calling for colonies to secure more markets to fend off revolution at home (Lutfi al-Sayyid Marsot, 1984, p. 236).

Treaty arrangements with the Sultan lowered tariff barriers to British trade and effectively undermined Muhammad Ali's monopolies in Egypt and opened the country up to cheaper British goods. The long-term effect of this was, of course, to transform Egypt into a supplier of raw materials and an importer of European manufactures; to define, in short, the economic parameters of dependency.

By 1841 the European powers, for different reasons and through a complex diplomatic process, had agreed to co-operate politically and militarily (with a British naval force blockading Beirut and Alexandria) to expel Muhammad Ali from Syria, reduce his armies but accept that he would remain lifelong Pasha of Egypt. Egypt's war industries contracted as did her textiles; state debts increased as the scope for earning revenue from trade and taxation declined. To raise revenues Muhammad Ali began a process of privatising land, largely through grants to members of his own family, but this was to lay the basis in Egypt for the emergence of a landowning class. Change in the countryside prompted partly by irrigation schemes facilitated the emergence of richer *fellaheen and* wage labourers. In short, the period from the 1840s onwards was one in which an internal division of labour emerged in Egypt to be a central component of the country's state of dependency *vis-à-vis* the stronger economies of Europe.

Muhammad Ali's plans to become independent of the Sultan in Constantinople landed Egypt, ultimately then, into a position of dependency on Europe. It cannot be claimed that this was the particular intention of any of the great powers or of powerful groups within the European states. But it is something which can be explained as the outcomes of different states (and dominant groups within those states) seeking to realise their strategic aims and optimise their economic interests in a rapidly changing commercial and political environment.

The new framework of constraints imposed on Egypt by treaty arrangements among the European powers and the Ottoman government, together with those that were already woven into the fabric of a peasant society legally and militarily subservient to stronger external powers, were not of a kind preventing further rapid social change in that society.

Dependency does not mean stasis. Muhammad Ali had fashioned a society in which the conditions had been created to sustain growing demands for further modernisation of the economy along the lines of those in Europe; in which the essentially political demand for independence from Constantinople would grow to become inexorable. The steady Egyptianisation of the state bureaucracies nourished among the bureaucrats a distinct *national* identity and one influenced in no small way by the growing use of Arabic as the language of government gradually allowing Egyptians access to authoritative positions in the state. The longer-term results of these developments were to define the characteristics of nationalist political movements in Egypt against foreign domination and to mark out the social character of a society in which strong links were forged between private ownership of land, modern education and political power within the state.

Egypt became a society in which an educated elite (many of whom, later, were to be further educated in foreign schools in Egypt) were able to dominate a society in which, as late as 1850 only 3 per cent of the population were literate and capable of access to Western values in the way their rulers were. Gabriel Baer (1969, p. 228) has noted that, while at the beginning of the nineteenth century 'there were no significant cultural differences among Egyptians, the impact of the West created a gulf between the Europeanised and educated

Egyptian officials and other parts of the upper classes and the great mass of *fellahs* and town dwellers, including the lower middle classes.'

But with the growing urbanisation of the society together with further social differentiation on non-traditional lines, opportunities for social mobility opened up in ways that required education, for they were dependent on state employment. The roots, therefore, of powerful expectations about education and national independence can be traced to the period of Muhammad Ali's reforms and the changes they unleashed in Egyptian society. A full understanding of how these changes worked out, however, required close attention to what was happening elsewhere in the Middle East, particularly in the Turkish homelands of the Ottoman Empire and in Europe. From mid-century onwards in Europe, the powerful momenta of industrial capitalism, political competition among states and the buoyant growth of a liberal imperialism snared the whole world in the interests of trade and profit, creating an entirely new set of constraints on what was possible in Egypt itself.

4 Imperialism, Modernisation and Revolution

Just over thirty years after the death of Muhammad Ali, Britain invaded and occupied Egypt. That was in 1882. It was an action ordered by a Liberal government under Gladstone and one which, as the historian A. J. P. Taylor (1957, p. 68) has put it, 'launched Great Britain on the course of Imperialism'. The consequences of the occupation for the economic and political fortunes of Egypt were, of course, profound. Egypt's economic dependency on Europe was brought under tight political control and in the years which followed the cultural, religious, and intellectual life of the society developed inextricably with the policies and attitudes of the occupying power. Opposition to British rule was widespread but the ideas which informed it were diverse and reflected the deep cultural and political divisions of Egyptian society itself.

Britain's occupation of Egypt did not command full support in Britain itself. Why it happened, therefore, is something to be explained by reference to the political divisions of British society and to the growth, in both Britain and Europe, of imperialist ambitions which were themselves, in part, a response to the evolving structures of class divisions and awareness characteristic of capitalist society at that time.

The conflicts of interest which divided the advanced European states in the second half of the nineteenth century must also figure in the account of Egypt for they related directly to the position in Europe's *realpolitik* of the Ottoman Empire and of the changes which were taking place within it. For the Ottoman state retained its legal title to Egypt throughout the British occupation. Turkey remained, too, the political home of the caliphate and as such could claim the loyalty of Muslims throughout the Middle East. But it also was a society undergoing rapid change and from the 1860s onwards the direction of the change was set increasingly by reform-minded elites in the bureaucracy and in the army who gave Turkish nationalism its distinctive shape. It led eventually to the Turkish involvement in the First World War and the final collapse of the empire.

The aim of this chapter is to examine the educational ramifications of these complex developments. The essential thread to what follows is this: the individuals and groups who, both in Egypt and Turkey, articulated most effectively the decisive reformist ideas of their era – ideas about constitutional government, national independence and modernisation of Islamic institutions – owed much to essentially Western ideas filtered through to them by their education. As the economic and political ties binding the two societies to the stronger states of the West tightened, demands in the Turkish case for reform and in that of Egypt for independence increased. They were demands reflecting new forms of both social and self-awareness which broke free from the traditional forms of thought which were defined both by Islam and the Ottoman social formation.

CAPITALISM, IMPERIALISM AND SOCIAL REFORM

Imperialism and imperialist rivalry among the great powers of Europe were the great episodes of modern history against which the transformations of the societies of the Middle East at the end of the nineteenth century have to be understood. Imperialism itself, moreover, has to be seen against the social and political divisions of the capitalist states themselves.

The key notion to be stressed for the purposes of this account is that 'liberal imperialism' was a solution to a crisis, that of maintaining secure markets for the factories of Britain *and*, through the political ideas which were part of it, binding the interests of an increasingly powerful (though diverse) labour movement to the fortunes of capitalism itself. The rival imperialisms of Russia, the United States, Germany and the Austro-Hungarian empire stemmed from a world perception that the future would be dominated by blocs of empires and that nations which did not acquire them would be seriously disadvantaged (Semmel, 1960; Lichtheim, 1971).

This is, of course, far too simple a summary of what was (and is) a complex phenomenon and one which cannot be reduced to purely economic causes. Imperialism was inspired by economic interests; but it was propelled and justified by visions of national glory, racial superiority and straightforward political judgements about the balance of power in Europe. It is not something which can be explained, therefore, without taking into account the perceptions and intentions and actions of those groups in Europe which actively and successively promoted it, often against opposition from within the ruling groups themselves.

Four issues will illustrate the argument. They concern the changing class relations of the capitalist states of Europe, changes in the role of the state in regulating social conflicts, changes in political and ideological thinking in the second half of the nineteenth century and, finally, changes in the position of Britain *vis-à-vis* the other powers of Europe. These interrelated issues each underly the relationships, the connection, the essential interdependence of what was taking place in Europe and what occurred in the colonial world and which bound the fortunes of both.

By the final quarter of the nineteenth century the British economy was fully established on a base of large capital goods industries; by 1880 four out of five citizens were living in large towns and agriculture accounted for only about 10 per cent of the country's gross national product. Britain had, in short, a fully industrialised economy and as early as 1870 British investors held nearly £700 million of assets abroad (Hobsbawm, 1971; p. 118). It was a society dominated economically by a confident middle class whose battles with the older landed aristocracy with its roots in Toryism had successfully extended the franchise and through that its representation in Parliament through the Liberal Party. It was a society in which three-quarters of the population belonged to a class of manual labourers who, from the 1870s onwards, were organising themselves into trades unions and among whom many were becoming aware of themselves as a class of exploited workers in whose interests the overthrow of capital was a pressing need.

In the main, however, the ideological fissures of the society were not of a kind to create the conflicts of class that the socialist theorists of the Labour movement expected. In fact, significant numbers of working class people were attached, through the Liberal Party of Gladstone to a philosophy of gradual social improvement and co-operation between classes.

Among the ruling classes of this society there was a firm self-confidence rooted in wealth and a social distinctiveness, and rooted in education and bolstered by social-Darwinist philosophies underlining their sense of progress, racial superiority and tradition (Semmel, 1959). For the middle classes opportunities had opened up for public careers after the Northcote–Trevelyan reforms of the civil service and the growth of the liberal professions, with entrance based on examination performance, had opened up many more opportunities for social mobility.

The ideological cross-currents of this society are well enough known not to require detailed recapitulation; they focused in the years up to the end of the century on the position of the established church, on socialism, on Irish Home Rule and, of course, on empire – each of these issues which were seriously divisive and cut across some of the more basic divisions of social class which were the hallmark of Victorian Britain. The relevance of this for the argument being developed here is that imperialist expansion into Africa and the Middle East was something which refocused social conflicts in Britain and did much to stabilise late Victorian society politically. The key to it was to secure working-class commitment to imperial goals. This was the real achievment of the liberal imperialists.

One element in this momentous achievement was education; it served both to differentiate the social classes from each other by offering qualitatively different schools for them. But in so far as schooling came gradually, after 1870, to be associated in the minds of skilled workers with their claims for social respectability and for greater opportunities for social advancement, it secured the commitment of a growing number of working people to the politics of reform rather than revolution.

Elementary education for working-class people remained throughout the 1870s and 1880s geared directly to producing pliable workers aware of their status in life. For middle-class people and in particular the wealthy and powerful of Victorian England, the public schools, reformed during the second half of the century, offered an education for leadership in politics, the professions, commerce and the armed forces and, of course, for the administration of Britain's vast colonial empire. Such schools played their part in grafting onto the mundane business of exploiting colonial possessions a moral purpose which could transform appalling violence into a justifiable necessity.

James Morris (1979, p. 220) noting that the public schools 'lay somewhere near the heart of the imperial ethic' emphasises some of their features which allowed them to play this role. They include 'celibate discipline', 'classical loyalties', and an 'emphasis on self-reliance, team spirit, delegated responsibility, Christian duty and stoic control'. An intellectual narrowness combined with a strong sense of separateness and of chauvinism produced a type of man possessed of what they themselves understood as *grit*; but as Morris (1979, p. 220) has underlined, 'the rarest of his virtues was human sympathy'. The character of British colonial administration, particularly of education, shaped the responses of those who laboured under it and must be seen therefore against this background.

The techniques of colonial administration which Britain brought to bear on the Middle East had been perfected in India. As will be illustrated shortly, the Anglo-Indian tradition of treating orientals as inferior beings soured relations between British officials in Egypt and the Egyptian officials whose work they supervised. The British were, in addition, very careful in their Egyptian policies to avoid allowing Egyptians to acquire aspirations beyond their status. They failed in this but it was none the less one of their central aims.

EGYPT IN 1882

Egypt was, in 1882, close to the centre of the Great Power rivalries of Europe. Britain was suspicious of French involvement in Egypt and North Africa and fearful that its strategic interests in the area and its routes to India were in jeopardy. The Ottoman Empire retained legal title to the country but was itself embroiled in conflicts in the Balkans and with Russia. To the British Foreign Office the continuing decline of Turkey was an added reason to secure a strong British presence in Egypt. Not least among the other reasons for this was a strategic perception that Ottoman decline could open up opportunities for Russian advances into the Balkans and eastern Mediterranean and for the growth of Islamic movements in Arabia and the Sudan.

Decline and political instability in Turkey was the thread which entangled the disparate interests of the Great Powers. The instability at the centre of the Ottoman Empire was itself, of course, the product of change and modernisation. A full account of what these changes were would include discussions of the growth of the Ottoman bureaucracy during the *Tanzimat* period, the further extension of economic rights to foreigners trading in the empire through the Capitulations, the emergence of Westernised elites in the army and through the schools who began to define the outlines of an Ottoman nationalism and oppose the corruption of the central government and the higher religious officials.

Under the leadership of men like Mehmed Bey, Namik Kemal and Mustafa Fazil Pasa, the brother of the Khedive of Egypt, the young Ottoman movement pressed from the 1860s onwards for constitutional reforms and modernisation. Their opposition to the *Porte* has complex roots in the social changes of Ottoman society, e.g. the growth of a secular schooling and the spread of European political ideas. But it was also related to distinctively Islamic conceptions of the just state and to a sense of frustration borne of their experience of corruption in the bureaucracies which they themselves served (Mardin, 1962).

Considerable changes, therefore, were taking place within the Ottoman Empire, particularly in the attitudes and ideas of some sections of the governing class. Their concern for modernisation was also a reflection of deepening economic difficulties after the Crimean War. Turkey imported more manufactured goods from the West, particularly military equipment to bolster a military policy which the state had not the resources, in fact, to fund. Turkey imported Dreadnought battleships from Britain, field guns from Krupp in Germany and by 1877 (the time of the Russo-Turkish war) had the third largest navy in Europe (Owen, 1981, p. 105).

The Capitulations policy facilitated further European imports and hindered the development of Turkish manufactures. Young Ottoman critics seized on the policy of state borrowing which was necessary to fund such policies as one of the fundamental causes of the decline of the empire. Ottoman debt was, of course, an opportunity for the financial houses of Europe seeking new sources of investment to penetrate further into the financial life of the empire and reap enormous rewards. The *Porte* found itself in the early 1870s in the classic debt trap of having to borrow short-term funds to finance interest charges on long-term debts (Lewis, 1961).

The weakness of the Ottoman government in Instanbul was an opportunity for Ismail, the Egyptian Khedive, to press dynastic claims on the Sultan and to assert a greater autonomy and create a base for his modernising programme and his own plans for an empire incorporating the Sudan. Ottoman debt servicing depended in part on Egyptian tribute but Ottoman weaknesses, made worse in Egypt by the earlier reforms of Muhammad Ali made the *Porte's* claims on Egyptian taxation tenuous.

At the same time, any crisis in Egyptian state finance was likely to have serious consequences for the overstretched resources of the Sultan in Istanbul. This was the factor, above all others, which ensured that the governments of France and Britain would be vitally concerned with Egypt's financial affairs. By the end of the 1870s those affairs were in serious disarray and Egypt itself was seriously in debt to European banks and bond holders. The complex problems of the Middle East cannot be seen apart, therefore, from the network of changing relations both within each of the principal powers with interests in the region or from the character of relations among them.

Imperialism injected a dynamic of change into an Egyptian society which was itself changing rapidly. Land reforms in the years following Muhammad Ali's death laid the basis for the emergence of a strong class of landowners in Egypt. This took place during the reign of Said Pasha as Viceroy of Egypt and was made possible by legal changes permitting private property in land. The growth of an export-oriented cash crop policy based on cotton consolidated the position of these large landowners and transformed the nature of the Egyptian village community; individuals rather than communities became the unit of tax collection. As part of this change landowners gradually increased their social status and gained increasing access to official positions. Gabriel Baer (1969, p. 225) has noted a profound consequence of these changes for the social structure of Egypt: 'no urban *bourgeoisie* in the European sense emerged in Egypt. There was no social class of Egyptians whose principal interest concentrated in the towns and in the promotion of urban economy.' This had particular consequences for the character of Egyptian nationalist politics in that the landowning class came to see constitutional government, and later independence from British rule, as a way of strengthening their position and not as something which would liberate peasants (see Pelletiere, 1979).

The development of the cotton and sugar crop for export also opened up rich opportunities for European and Egyptian merchants and money lenders in the finance of agricultural production. Europeans were particularly favoured since they operated under the tax concessions of the Capitulation arrangements (Owen, 1981) and cotton gradually transformed peasant working conditions, tying them to tighter schedules, harder work and tighter management on large estates to secure a reliable crop for the cotton mills of Manchester.

The cotton boom brought with it a massive increase in the numbers of foreigners in Egypt. Since the foreign communities established their own schools which were also attended by Egyptians, the influence of Western ideas and values spread throughout the educated groups in Egyptian society. Educational provision of all kinds increased steadily during the second half of the nineteenth century and French influence on Egyptian professional and technical education was particularly marked. The school of engineering which was set up in 1844 was modelled on the French *Polytechnique* and the influence of those Egyptians who had been sent on study missions abroad increased steadily. The professional schools which Muhammad Ali established continued to produce Egyptians who entered state service as teachers, translators, and technicians.

Alongside foreign schools such as those of the Greek community in Alexandria which was said to have maintained some of the best schools in the history of Greek education as a whole, foreign mission schools increased in number (Vatikiotis, 1969). French support for Catholic missionary schools in Egypt was aimed at achieving a controlling interest in the welfare of Catholics not only in Egypt but throughout the Levant and the English missions aimed their efforts at the Copts (Heyworth-Dunne, 1968). The presence of such schools served to facilitate the job prospects of the children of Europeans in the banks and business houses which their parents controlled and to point up the inadequacies of the schools provided for Egyptians.

The rulers who followed Muhammad Ali – Ismail (1848), Abbas (1849–54) and Said (1854–63) were not strongly committed to developing a state education system. Said is reported as saying, for example, 'Why open the eyes of the people, they will only be more difficult to rule' (Heyworth-Dunne, 1968, p. 313). There may not have been a strong popular demand for Western-type education during this period but changes in the perception of educated Egyptians were considerable. Notable Egyptian educators like Mubarak and Tahtawi, both of whom had been students abroad in France, were active in developing Egyptian education. Mubarak, who had been Director of the School of Engineering until Said closed it, became, under Ismail Pasha (1863–79) a senior figure in schools administration, taking an active interest in the development of school curricula, text books and teaching methods. From his position in the *Diwan al Madaris* he was able to reform *kuttabs* to be the base of a state system of elementary education. Mubarak was a central influence in the setting up, in 1872, of the *Dar al Ulum*, the teacher training college.

Mubarak's career is paralleled by that of another French-trained Egyptian, Shaykh Rifaa Rafi al-Tahtawi. Through his work in the School of Languages from 1835 onwards Tahtawi made European science and philosophy and literature available in Arabic. Vatikiotis (1969, p. 116) says this of him: 'He was the first Egyptian to report fairly systematically and intelligently to his compatriots on the general outlines of European political institutions, the ideas of the Enlightenment and the French Revolution which underlined them'.

His translation of European, particularly French, legal texts had an important bearing on the development of the Egyptian legal profession and legal system.

Neither of these men were radicals in their educational or political outlook. They did not seek to remove the ruling dynasty of Egypt which was of foreign origin with one which was Egyptian and their interest in European political ideas did not turn them against the rulers of their own society. Vatikiotis (1969, p. 119) stressed that distinctively Islamic concepts of community and country shaped the views of Tahtawi and that Egyptian nationalists of the twentieth century were not inspired by him. Their importance at this stage in Egyptian history and education was that they were the filters through which Western influences were refracted into Egypt's cultural and intellectual life. There were different currents, however, running from Islamic sources and represented by the reformer and political activist, Jamal al-din al-Afghani. Arriving in Egypt from Istanbul in 1871 he articulated a strong sense, particularly among some sections of the educated classes, of the need for reform within Islam to strengthen the opposition of the whole Muslim community against foreign influences. Afghani even urged Egyptian *fellaheen* to throw off the yoke of their Turkish-Egyptian rulers who had oppressed them and to lay claim to Egyptian independence.

Afghani had considerable influence in Egypt through the work of one of his student disciples, Muhammad Abduh (1849–1905). Abduh was a *sheykh* at al-Azhar and his contribution to Egyptian cultural and political life lay in his insistence that Islam was a faith which was relevant to the modern world, that freed from some of its traditional rigidities of belief and practices, particularly an uncritical acceptance of religious dogma, it gave a special place to the exercise of reasoned thinking. Muhammad Abduh sought to improve teaching methods in mosques and at al-Azhar itself; he actively promoted the teaching of modern scientific subjects and in the course of his career he incurred the opposition of some of the traditional *ulema*.

On the other hand his ideas proved attractive to a growing class of educated Egyptians for they nurtured a nationalism and an interest in Egyptian literature which fuelled what Heyworth-Dunne (1968, p. 402) has called a 'literary revival' but which other writers have been bold enough to describe as a renaissence or even a 'cultural revolution' (see Cachia, 1956). Certainly some of Abduh's supporters had influence in the Egyptian army since modernisation and reform within the precepts of Islam was one of the ideas attractive to those who supported Colonel Arabi in his revolt against the government of Khedive Tewfik and what many Egyptian officers in the army understood as foreign interference in Egyptian affairs following the bankrupting of the country by Khedive Ismail and foreign intervention from France and Britain to take control of the government debt. With the help of Muhammad Abduh, Colonel Arabi drew up a programme for a Nationalist Party in Egypt but one which fixed its hopes on constitutional government for the country.

By the 1880s, therefore, a political arena had been cleared in which distinctively Egyptian political claims could be articulated against those of the *Porte* and the ruling dynasty and the influence of foreign consuls and business interests who were the effective controllers of the country's finances. A full understanding of what made this all possible would give a central place to the influence of the schools and the central role they played in filtering ideas about modernisation to the emerging elites defining themselves a place at the centre of Egyptian society.

The British invasion of 1882 provided Egyptian nationalists with a very precise target for their movement but prevented that movement developing any real coherence or any precise vision of what independence might mean. Preceded by a financial crisis which was brought under control by a joint agreement between Britain and France to manage the Khedive's debts, the invasion was finally prompted by British fears that the growing opposition from the supporters of Arabi to the Khedive, an opposition which brought with it street disturbances in Alexandria in which foreigners were attacked, might actually succeed in deposing him. On 11 July 1882 Admiral Seymour's ships bombarded Alexandria and troops landed at Suez and Alexandria on 2 August. Egyptian forces could not contain the advance and were decisively beaten at the battle of Tel el Kebir on 14 September.

THE BRITISH OCCUPATION OF EGYPT

The British entered Egypt without any clear idea how long they would stay and justified the action both at home and abroad, partly at least, on the grounds that it would be temporary. The government's insistence on this was, of course, contrary to its actions and the growing gap between the two was a constant theme of the critics such as Wilfred Scawen Blunt and the radical Liberal J. M. Robertson, one of the Members of Parliament for Newcastle upon Tyne. But occupation carried its own logic and even some of the critics understood that withdrawal was not such a simple option unless political conditions consistent with Britain's interest in Egypt could be secured. Even men like the radical Liberal MP, Joseph Cowen, who opposed Britain staying in Egypt, was careful in his views about how the occupation should end. He did not believe that the 'nomadic, dreamy, fatalistic Asiatic, and the pushing, practical, and progressive Englishman' could really mix on equal terms (Cowen, 1909, p. 150). But withdrawal was almost unthinkable to him. 'If we do', he wrote,

> woe betide the hapless Fellaheen. Chaos would indeed return. The finances would be fastened on by harpies, the taxes would be enforced by the curbash, justice would be bought and sold, the group of slothful and mendacious pashas and unprincipled and greedy usurers, who constitute the entourage of the Khedive, would revel in their regained liberty to rob and ravage. (Cowan, 1909, p. 150)

This is the authentic voice of liberal imperialism combining in an acute sense of national interest with a strong sense of mission to civilise the colonies. It was a view shared by Liberal and Conservative governments and by their representatives in Egypt itself. And it was a reflection, too, of a much more diffuse and popular belief which gathered strength in the last decade of the century, that the advanced societies had a moral responsibility for the rest of the world; it was an ideology of imperial paternalism.

The British authorities in Egypt and particularly Evelyn Baring (Lord Cromer) justified their actions very much in these terms. And they justified their sense of mission by seeking to cultivate the view that the backwardness and financial chaos of Egypt was something attributable to the failings of the Egyptians themselves. The British tried to reject the view that the people who lived in Egypt constituted a nation and Lord Cromer, who became until 1906 the virtual ruler of Egypt, thought of Egyptians as morally inferior people, 'the rawest of raw material' on which the 'Englishman' could work (Cromer, 1908, p. 131). In contrast to the European who was, in Cromer's view, 'a close reasoner', someone who 'loves symmetry in all things' who is 'by nature sceptical and requires proof before he can accept the truth of any proposition', he regarded 'the Oriental' as only capable of slipshod thinking. 'Want of accuracy', he wrote, 'which easily degenerates into untruthfulness, is, in fact the main characteristic of the Oriental mind' (Cromer, 1908, p. 146).

In a passage dealing with education and one clearly intended to deflect criticism that he could have done more for Egypt, Cromer (1908, p. 526) bridled at 'the unpromising nature of the raw material on which the English had to work' so that the surprise was that so much had been done for them. The Egyptians might be trained to manage their own affairs in a relatively short period of time is something to be regarded as a 'sheer absurdity'.

Given these views it is hardly surprising that Cromer attached a low priority to the development of education. His colonial experience in India (and, indeed, his family connections) had been in banking and finance. He saw his main role in Egypt as stabilising the finances of the country to pay off its debts and building up slowly a capacity for the economic and social improvement of the country. His education policy was therefore just one component of a whole series of policies concerned with finance, local government, law, agriculture, irrigation and the military.

But the assumptions upon which it was based permeated the whole British presence in Egypt. It was the contradictory features of that presence, e.g. a public commitment to pull out while each year that passed saw a yet deeper encroachment into the country, which contributed so much to defining the character of Egyptian opposition to it. It is necessary, therefore, to understand the development of Egyptian nationalism and its contradictions in relation to the character of the British presence in Egypt.

Lord Cromer defined his education policy as having four principal objects. They were first, to raise the general level of education in the village schools; secondly, to create an efficient civil service; thirdly, to limit access to secondary and higher education to avoid creating a group of people whose education, as he put it, 'unfits them for manual labour' so that they look exclusively to government for employment, and fourthly, to encourage technical education (see Marlowe, 1970, pp. 290–1). Cromer set out these aims in 1903, no doubt partly to answer criticisms about his policies both in Egypt and in Britain. The striking similarity between his views and those currently being expressed by some educational planners in Egypt is worth noting and will be discussed in more detail later (see Chapter 7).

Three features of British policy deserve emphasis. They are the devaluation and neglect of traditional education in Egypt, the poor provision of education and the strictly functional character of what was provided. The unintended consequences of these policies were almost the opposite of what was actually intended; instead of holding back educational aspirations in Egypt and containing the development of nationalism, the practical application of these policies inspired both.

Cromer clung to the belief that people only valued what they paid for and it was this which justified his policy of levying charges on parents for education. In addition he controlled education spending within the tight limits of what he thought the government could afford. The result was that throughout the 1890s education received only a very small fraction of the budget, and the result of this was paucity of provision. Even as late as 1910 there were only just over 2000 pupils in government secondary schools. (Tignor, 1966, p. 323). This was in a country with a population of about eleven million people in which, as the 1897 census had revealed, only 11 per cent of the male population above the age of seven could read (Tignor, 1966, p. 324). The critic, J. M. Robertson (1908, p. 142) noted that 'the only ones who are content with the existing condition affairs are the large army of English professors, inspectors and administrators who prosper on large salaries and meagre employment.'

Among other consequences three stand out as related directly to the poverty of education provision in Egypt. The first is that foreign schools flourished, meeting a demand for education which the goverment was not prepared to meet. This had the effect of strengthening French influence in Egypt, something which Cromer deplored, so that the School of Law became a very prestigious and important institution and a crucible for Egyptian nationalist sentiment. Wealthy Egyptians were also prepared to finance their children to study abroad and gain education this way and subsequently come to monopolise the prestigious positions in government service and dominate the professions. Cromer's policies contributed to social differentiation in Egypt.

The negative attitude struck towards the traditonal institutions of religious education, particularly al-Azhar which, it has been claimed, the British viewed as a hot bed of Muslim fanaticism, led them to emphasise more a secular education as the essential prerequisite of entry to government service (Reid, 1977). This generated opposition among students of al-Azhar since they felt that British legal and administrative reforms had closed off career opportunities for them both as lawyers (*kadis*) and teachers. Yet it prompted reform, too, particularly through the work of Muhammad Abduh, which fostered among his followers a sense of the necessity of opposing the British as a way of defending the Faith. Al-Azhar remained, however, a deeply conservative institution.

The functional character of British education was its main hallmark and the implementation of a strictly utilitarian education policy did much to galvanise nationalist opposition to the occupation itself and ensure that it was the educated classes and students which would emerge as the strongest oppositional force in Egypt.

Behind the scant provision of public education, particularly secondary education, together with the strict imposition of rules requiring examination passes as a conditon of entry into government service, was an essentially Anglo-Indian fear that educated Egyptians unable to find work would become a source of civil discontent. Cromer was eloquent on this point:

> The intellectual phase through which India is now passing stands before the world as a warning that it is unwise, even if it be not dangerous, to create too wide a gap between the state of education of the higher and of the lower classes in an Oriental country . . . the ignorance of the masses must be tempered *pari passu* with the intellectual advance of those who are destined to be their leaders. (Cromer, p. 534)

The danger of acting otherwise, he felt, was that 'the people should be left intellectually defenceless in the presence of the hare-brained and empirical projects [of] the political charlatan' who would prey on them with their 'perfervid eloquence and political quackery'.

Cromer's preference was for a basic technical education which would lead to employment. He wrote in his 1902 report:

> Any movement which tends to divert the natural inclinations of Egyptians from an office career to skilled industry is, therefore, calculated not only to benefit those who come under its influence, but to aid materially in furthering the development of the country. (Cromer, 1902, p. 42)

In 1904 he quoted with approval a comment from Lecky's book, *Democracy and Liberty* that the best education for the poor should be technical and industrial rather than literary, 'more concerned with the observation of facts than with any form of speculative reasoning or opinions.' Egyptian village schools, said Cromer, were designed 'to equip the pupil with sufficient knowledge to take care of his own interests in his own station in life, as small landowners, fellah, petty shopkeepers, handicraftsmen, weaver, village headman, boatman, fisherman etc.' (Cromer, 1904, p. 61).

His comments on technical education reveal a clear grasp of the relationship between education provision and the division of labour in society and one which echoed almost identical views to those being elaborated in discussions about the education of the working class in Britain at the time. He wanted more artisans and a 'restricted but better educated and more highly qualified class, capable of acting as designers, foremen and managers' (Cromer, 1904, p. 63). He failed to achieve this, of course. The village *kuttabs* which he supported did little more than teach the three 'Rs'. (Tignor, 1966, p. 330).

Cromer's policies also required a degree of anglicisation of the curriculum of the secondary schools to produce administrators with good English. English gradually came to replace French as the principal foreign language but the devaluation of Arabic was seen by nationalists as another indignity inflicted on them by the British, and this sense of indignity was clearly reinforced by authoritarian teaching methods, a lack of contact between English teachers and their pupils and the way in which the British cut themselves off socially from the Egyptians they governed.

Cromer was, however, struggling hard against a tide for it was within the logic of the system that he supervised that resentment against British rule was coupled with a strong sense of frustration among Egyptians, particularly those from wealthier backgrounds, that the system was denying them proper opportunities for their own advancement. Critics in Europe opposed to Britain's policies in Egypt endorsed such criticisms (see Robertson, 1908; Rothstein, 1910).

Most damaging of all, however, as a summary of the failure of British education policies in Egypt was the report of the mission of inquiry led by Lord Milner in 1921 which examined the causes of what in Britain were known as the 'disorders' but to Egyptians the 'revolution' of 1919. Milner, himself an arch imperialist and former civil servant in Egypt, summed up his criticisms of education in this way:

> Another contributory cause of the general discontent was the manifest unsuccess of educational policy resulting in the production of an unnecessarily large and ever increasing number of candidates for official posts, provided with examination certificates, but destitute of any real educational culture. It was necessary in the

initial stage to train a number of young men to such a standard of efficiency as would enable them to undertake clerical duties in State departments which had hitherto largely been performed by non-Egyptians, and to prepare pupils for the higher colleges of medicine, law and engineering. But here again, there seems, until quite recently, to have been little attempt to revise a system adopted under exceptional circumstances or to realise that changing conditions required new methods. Education, for which there is a real and crying demand among the people, remains atrophied. The mass of the population is not only still illiterate, but without social or moral training. (Milner, 1921, p. 10)

NATIONALISM, WAR AND REVOLUTION

The British occupation of Egypt was opposed increasingly after the turn of the century and particularly from 1906 onwards, in nationalist terms, which took the form of a demand for constitutional government. Egyptian nationalism, however, was never a coherent body of thought or opinion; its cross-currents reflected the social and economic divisions of Egyptian society as well as differences in strategic estimates about how best to wrest power from the British.

It was during the period before the First World War that the directions in which nationalist opposition would subsequently go were first indicated. The first point to stress is that it was a divided movement. A feeling of resentment against foreign rule was basic but there were sharp differences among nationalists about tactics for removing the foreigner. Those associated with the young lawyer Mustapha Kamil sought to unite Egyptians and to rouse public opinion against the British. Appalling actions like the execution of peasants who had objected to British soldiers trampling over their land while shooting pigeons and who, in the confusion which resulted, inadvertently caused the death of one of them – the famous Dinshwai affair – assisted Kamil enormously. Using the extensive popular press he was able to capture the imagination of young educated people, particularly school students and graduates from the School of Law.

His newspaper *al-Liwa* campaigned hard against the British; it demanded, among other things, a national system of education and supported students in the Law School in 1906 who went on strike against changes in examination arrangements. Students were, of course, a fertile ground for support since they were directly threatened by a British policy which seemed to prevent Egyptian access to government employment. Kamil referred to the striking students as 'the flower of Egypt's youth', 'the men of tomorrow' (Pelletiere, 1979, p. 186). The landowning class of Egypt, moreover, was prepared to support and use students as a political instrument to press change on the British. It was at this time that nationalist leaders began to press for an Egyptian university, a demand that Cromer rejected by insisting it would be better for the country to strenthen its elementary education.

Nationalists differed on several issues; on Egypt's relationship to Turkey, on the relevance of pan-Islamism to the Egyptian struggle, on how best to force the British hand and on their attitudes towards the Khedive. By 1907 different sections of nationalist opinion began to crystallise into political parties. The grouping of constitutionalists formed after 1907 around the newspaper *al-Jarida* and attracted such men as Saad Zaghlul, Ahmad Lutfi al-Sayyid, both of whom were lawyers. The Egyptian historian, Afaf Lutfi al-Sayyid (1968, p. 168) says of *al-Jarida* that its subscribers read like '*a Who's Who* of the notables of Egypt'. Suspicious of pan-Islamism, moderate and bourgeois in outlook, the *al-Jarida* group formed the People's Party (*Hizb al-Umma*) on a platform of constitutional demands. Some of these men, Saad Zaghlul, for instance, even approved of some aspects of the British attempts to reform Egyptian society and believed that Kamil's agitation was that of a 'lunatic baying at the moon' (Lutfi al-Sayyid Marsot, 1977, p. 47). Zaghlul became, in fact, the Minister of Education in 1905, appointed by Cromer as part of his plans to encourage the growth of a moderate Egyptian leadership.

Such divisions among the nationalists set the framework for Egyptian politics before the First World War. The basic demand which united them, however, was a form of constitutional independence for the country and constitutionalist ideas in Egypt and, indeed, throughout the Middle East were adopted enthusiastically in the wake of the Japanese defeat of the Russsians in 1904, the Russian revolution of 1905, Greek independence struggle and, of course, the Young Turk revolution of 1908.

Nationalist politics in Egypt, however, were very much the concerns of elite groups in the society. Behind them stood the Egyptian *fellaheen* and the relationship between elites and masses was a distant one and an exploitative one. Out of a population of about ten million, eight million people lived in villages and about two million peasants were landless (Baer, 1969). A growing number of peasants were migrating to the cities to swell the ranks of workers, petty traders and the unemployed, the nucleus of a new working class. Peasants and workers differed considerably in their outlook and education from nationalist elites. Charles Smith (1980) has suggested that the Egyptian leaders who sought to influence Egypt in the light of the European values many of them had acquired, particularly the group associated with *al-Jarida*, did so in an effort to protect the status quo of social relations in which they were the dominant group. Men like Muhammad Haykal (who became leader of the Liberal Party after the First World War) were opposed to mass involvement in politics. Their concerns in education, for example, have been characterised as focused more on the need for higher education than for the education of peasants and workers (Pelletiere, 1979).

The public sphere which they sought to construct was thus one free of foreign domination but one which envisaged no real role for the mass of the Egyptian people. The ambiguity implied in such a position carried over into the politics of the inter-war period and was only resolved, then only for a while, by President Nasser after 1952. It was not difficult, however, for the British authorities in Egypt to contain the nationalist movement. The well-tried techniques of counter-propaganda, imprisonment and exile worked well right through to 1919.

The First World War led directly to a British Protectorate in Egypt on account of British perceptions of its strategic importance in the Middle East. The problem was simple: through German influence on the government of Turkey, the Committee of Union and Progress had entered the war on the German side, threatening Britain's whole position in the Middle East.

The politics of this is too complex to be discussed here; it is sufficient to note that the Young Turk Revolution of 1908 had turned into a nationalist one with a strong Western orientation and was by 1914 a serious military threat to Britain. To prosecute the war Britain requisitioned supplies in Egypt. The Egyptian Labour Corps recruited peasants from Upper Egypt for service in the Gallipoli campaign. Stores and animals were requisitioned and these actions together alienated peasants and the war itself strengthened nationalist resolve to press for independence.

By the time of the Versailles Peace Conference Egyptians felt they had entirely legitimate claims for independence, especially since the

British and French were prepared to concede independence to Arab provinces of the Ottoman Empire which had served in the campaigns against the Turks. British intransigence and sheer political incompetence in dealing with the Egyptian delegation (the *Wafd*) sparked the disturbances of 1919 which persisted with bloodshed and repression for almost two years. The arrest of Saad Zaghlul brought students onto the streets and in the first few weeks over one thousand Egyptians were killed and property extensively damaged.

The final settlement, following extensive negotiations, was the constitution of 1923 giving Egypt a limited independence, a constitutional government but a system which retained the Khedive and effective British control over the country's defence. The constitutional settlement gave Egyptian landowners effective control of government but within an overall framework of economic and military relations which kept Egypt in a dependent state.

If the events of 1919 did, in fact, constitute a revolution as some have argued, albeit a revolution of the Pashas to secure their own political interests, it is remarkable to note how little some features of the society had changed. British perceptions of Egypt's problems, in particular, remained entrenched in the view that the disturbances were the result of a fanaticism. Lias, the British headmaster of Alexandria College told the Milner Commission of Enquiry into the unrest that he believed the problem stemmed from a fear on the Egyptian's part that the British had a deliberate policy of retarding their education. (Lias, 1920, p. 3). He felt that a course in English history should be offered 'to give the boys a clearer historical horizon than they have now, and in political affairs a due sense of proportion' (Lias, 1920, p. 3). He even advocated more time should be spent on sport, cricket in particular, since 'it teaches unselfishness and good fellowship' and for the cleverer boys Latin was to be recommended, 'the language to which civilisation in Europe owes so much'. Improvements in education, he felt, would convince Egyptians that their interests and those of Britain were identical.

Even more bizarre advice was given to the Milner Commission by the representatives of the non-official British community in Egypt Hooker of the Government Salt Monopoly thought that school discipline would be repaired if sound public school traditions were implanted in government schools: 'I am of the opinion that masters during school hours should wear cap and gowns and that on Fridays and certain holidays, their hoods' (Hooker, 1920, p. 23). And Kingsford of the Chamber of Commerce diagnosed the problem of student unrest as a problem of discipline in the home and school:

> The result has been to produce a large number of semi-educated youths, imbued with a sense of their own capacity, and a dangerous veneer of civilisation, whose ambition is to enter the overcrowded professions of the Government Service, Law and Medicine. These openings are limited to a small proportion, and the remainder, mostly unsuitably trained for agricultural, industrial or commercial pursuits, swell the ranks of the déclasses. (Kingsford, 1920, p. 33)

Such attitudes lay behind the day to day contact of Egyptians and British residents and officials, and it should not be forgotten that some of these Egyptians, often those with closest contact with the British, shared precisely the same views, at least until 1919. In a sensitively written and revealing autobiography, Edward Atiyah, a Syrian educated at Alexandria College, gives a strong indication of this speaking of the English master, Reed, with whom he identified strongly:

> Mr Reed was a Conservative. He did not believe in revolutions. I felt ashamed of myself for having admired the French Revolution. He believed in slow progress, and aristocracy, and expediency and Burke. He disapproved of Democracy and the Rights of Man and demagogues, and the Press and the Cinema. So I believed in slow progress and aristocracy and expediency and Burke. (Atiyah, 1946, p. 60)

And the young man accepted wholly Reed's view that the disturbances were provoked by demagogues, that Saad Zaghul was one of them and that the best people in Egypt wished a continuation of British rule.

Even Atiyah changed his views, however when, returning to the Middle East from being an undergraduate at Oxford, he could not tolerate any longer British superciliousness as he experienced it as a young teacher at Gordon's College, Khartoum. His subsequent career in the Sudan Civil Service corresponded with a growth in an Arab nationalism with which he identified strongly and which itself was given greater impetus through war.

Men like Atiyah were, of course, only a very small minority in Egypt; for others of his generation, particularly among the educated, nationalist politics were a passionate preoccupation and were to remain so. The First World war had, however, transformed the international political and ideological framework within which those aspirations could be worked through and realised; by 1919 the constraints on Egypt's development and the opportunities open to it were different. The Ottoman Empire no longer existed; the Russian Revolution of 1917 had caused a severe breach in the world development of capitalism; the major European powers were exhausted by the war. In the Middle East, where the most backward of the Arab provinces of the Ottoman Empire had achieve their independence, a problem emerged which was to have decisive and serious implications for the subsequent development of all the Arab states: the problem of Palestine and of the Jewish presence there which had been recognised by the Balfour Declaration of 1917 and which was accepted by Britain as part of its mandate for the region confirmed by League of Nations in 1923.

5 Education and the Nation State in Republican Turkey

The First World War ended in the total collapse of the Ottoman Empire. The Armistice which was signed on 30 October 1918 was followed by the occupation of large parts of the empire by the Allies. A British naval force arrived in Istanbul early in November. By this time, British forces occupied parts of the Arabian peninsula and southern Anatolia. British forces were followed by French and Italian troops and, in May 1919, under the cover of Allied warships an invasion force from Greece landed in Izmir (Smyrna). The treaty of Sèvres which followed in August 1920 amounted to a total dismemberment of the empire. Among its provisions eastern Anatolia was to be an independent Armenian state; south eastern Anatolia an independent Kurdish state. Thrace and Western Anatolia were to be ruled by the Greeks. Turkish rule to be confined to a small arid area in central Anatolia.

Opposed to the Sultan's co-operation with the Allies Mustafa Kemal, perhaps the only Turkish general to come through the war with any credit, volunteered to go to the east of the country to supervise the disarmament of Turkish troops. On 19 May he landed at Samsun on the Black Sea coast and from then on took up the leadership of the nationalist fight against the Allies and the government in Istanbul. What followed, between then up to the founding of the Turkish Republic in September 1923 was a war of independence the outcome of which was international recognition of Turkey in the treaty of Lausanne.

The success of the Turkish nationalists in overturning the terms of the Sèvres treaty was only in part a consequence, albeit a major one, of their ability to unite disparate interests in Anatolia from peasants to merchants and landowners behind their political cause. That they did this and gained such depth of support at the same time as they demanded almost sacrificial loyalty in desperately poor and bloody conditions, is testimony to their political skill. The independence war itself was a major achievement.

The final outcome of it, however, has to be seen against the unwillingness and inability of the Western Allies to conceive of further conflict in the Middle East. Turkey emerged therefore into a framework of international relations in which its eastern boundaries were acknowledged by the fledgling Soviet Union and its position on the Dardanelles acknowledged by the Western allies on account of their inability to do much about it. What they could see, however, was the logic of having a strong state other than Russia control the Bosphorous and Dardanelles. Such a position was entirely consistent with French and British strategy for the whole eastern Mediterranean. Both powers sought a politically favourable stability to protect their interests in Palestine and, in the case of the British, their routes to the oil fields of Persia and the canal route to India.

Geopolitical circumstances gave Mustafa Kemal his opportunity to develop a nation state in Turkey. How he defined that opportunity is something to be explained against the constraints he faced and against the idea of modernisation with which he and his supporters framed their views of the new state's future.

The obstacles to state development were formidable. The treaty of Lausanne required the repayment of Ottoman debts and Turkey's freedom to control tariff regulations was restricted. The capitulations through which foreign powers had eaten their way into Ottoman economic life were rescinded but to gain control of assets owned previously by foreigners the government had to pay compensation. Against a historic backdrop of underdeveloped industry and subsistence agriculture, these were conditions which severely restricted the economic resources of the new government.

The commercial life of the Ottoman Empire had always been in the hands of minorities – Greeks, Armenians, Jews – and in the early days of the Republic was in considerable disarray, for as a solution to the political problems of the new state Mustafa Kemal had forced an exchange of populations which rid Turkey of its Greek population. This was simultaneously a loss and a gain; it was a loss of commercial skills and contacts; but it opened up opportunities in business to Turks who had never before had anything to do with commerce.

To the Kemalists, however, a far more serious and urgent problem once the Republic had been proclaimed and the Sultan deposed was the cultural one of creating from among an overwhelmingly rural, Muslim population, and one lacking any distinctly national consciousness, a society and a political system which was secular and modernising but, above all, Turkish. The revolution which Mustafa

Kemal and his supporters in the army carried through was not one built on a revolt of worker and peasants. Nor was it, as Şerif Mardin (1971, p. 202) pointed out, 'the instrument of a discontented *bourgeoisie*'. Rather it was a revolution against the cultural and symbolic order of the Ottoman regime and in particular its religious framework. The well-known reforms of the period – the abolition of the caliphate, the imposition of a new civil code, the law abolishing the wearing of Islamic head-dress (the *fez*) and, of course, the development of a national and secular education system following the abolition of the religious schools (*madrasas*) and the latinisation of the alphabet – all have to be seen in this light. They are part of a programme of modernising consciousness, a programme carried out by a military based elite in conditions and in a manner which could have given them little confidence in the probability of success.

The cultural revolution which occurred in Turkey cannot be grasped without understanding something of Mustafa Kemal himself. His own career, from a relatively poor family background in Salonica through a military education to the highest ranks of the Ottoman army and a distinguished military career, was in itself remarkable. Primarily a soldier he was none the less much influenced by the intellectual currents of his generation. He learned French and German. He was much interested in the writings of the sociologist Ziya Gökalp and knew the work of Comte and Durkheim. These influences he translated into a secular nationalism and an ethic of service to the nation as the ultimate goal of moral conduct. Like the French philosophers he had read he continually insisted on science as the real guide to how people should act and nations develop. In these respects Kemal can be seen as heir to many ideas of the Turkish reform movements of the late nineteenth century. Without his leadership qualities and tactical genius, however, Turkish history would almost certainly have been different; as it was he was able to mobilise meagre resources to build a modern state.

The obstacles were, however, severe and were not entirely overcome. Turkey was a society of villages. Geographically isolated from one another and from the influence of cities, the villages were poor and although predominantly Muslim there were, too, clear differences between the Sunnis and the Shiites. Village religion was a folk Islam; it was fatalistic and deeply superstitious but there was a strong identification with the sultan-caliph. Village life centred on kinship and work on the land. One writer has summed up the Turkish village as 'an enormously stable, tradition-bound and highly conservative community, one exceedingly resistant to change at any level' (Robinson, 1963, p. 58).

The provincial towns were also deeply traditional in outlook and social structure. The small town 'middle class' of religious leaders, craftsmen and landowners were later to oppose Mustafa Kemal on religious grounds. Several writers have stressed that the political economy of Kemalism centred on making Turkey fit for the development of capitalism as the only way of defending its national integrity (Keyder, 1979. Kazancígil, 1981). But as the Turkish historian Feroz Ahmad (1981, p. 152) has underlined, this involved reforms carried out for the bourgeoisie in spite of itself. Mustafa Kemal told the Russian ambassador Aralov: 'In Turkey there are no classes . . . there is no working class as there is no developed industry. As for our bourgeoisie, it is necesary to raise it to the level of a bourgeoisie' (quoted in Ahmad, 1981, p. 157). In the early days of the republic, Kemal relied on the support of provincial notables, urban merchants and intellectuals and, of course, the military but the state he created was in a real sense independent of these groups.

Education was fundamental to the creation of the new state. It can be usefully thought of as having developed in two phases. The first, until the late 1930s was one of slow growth and political and administrative consolidation. During the second period from the early 1930s to the late 1940s there was a time of considerable experimentation with new concepts of education and strategies of rural development. The whole period encompasses the full emergence of Turkey as a modern nation state with a coherent national identity. At the same time, however, new patterns of social and political differentiation emerged which, against a background of a world economic crisis and of the uneven development of the Turkish economy, produced divisions which, in the period after the Second World War, severely tested the political and ideological foundations of the state itself. The Turkish example in this respect is one of the limitations of purely national strategies of development.

THE FIRST PERIOD

The specifically educational actions of the Republican regime cannot be separated from the broader cultural, legal and religious changes it brought about. These are well enough known only to be noted here. The Sultanate had been abolished in November 1922.

The republic had been proclaimed on 29 October 1923. In March 1924 the caliphate was abolished. All education was made a monopoly of the state and the *madrasas* closed. In April 1924 religious courts were abolished and this was followed in 1925 by action against the religious orders (*tarikats*). In 1926 the Swiss Civil Code was adopted as the legal framework of the new state and in 1928, in moves closely directed by Mustafa Kemal himself, Turkish script was latinised. In his speech on 9 August 1928 Atatürk welcomed the change saying: 'We must free ourselves from these incomprehensible signs, that for centuries have held our minds in an iron vice... You must learn the new Turkish letters quickly ... Regard it as a patriotic and national duty' (quoted in Lewis, 1961, p. 278).

The alphabet reform was, as Bernard Lewis said, like slamming a door on the past and opening up a future leading Turkey to the civilisation of the West. Arabic and arabic script was, after all, the language of the Koran and the script had been common throughout the Ottoman Empire. The symbolic break with the past was therefore a profound one.

More difficult was the task of building up institutions to reinforce the new state and secure commitment to it. This was only in part although, of course, a large one of the paucity of resources. Başgöz and Wilson (1968) noted that, in addition to the lack of teachers those who did work had themselves developed during the empire and retained something of the older way of thinking. In the early days of the republic radical educational ideas affirming the need to link education to the needs of villagers working on the land, met with some resistance and considerable administrative inertia.

Some of the ideas, however, still have a radical ring to them. Ismail Hakkı Baltacioğlu, for example, urged the development of an education linking theory and practice. He wrote, for example, that:

> If one wishes to form democratic citizens, schools must be set up which are organised for students to take part in the democratic process. If it is desired to have people who know how to raise chickens, then the schools must be equipped with a hen-coop with real hens in it and the pupils must be allowed to feed and raise them. (Quoted in Başgöz and Wilson, 1968, p. 62)

This was a powerful reaction to the scholasticism of the Ottoman notion of what proper education was.

The receptivity of the new government to modern and radical ideas is illustrated in the invitation which was given to Professor John Dewey to visit Turkey in 1924 to advise the government in education policy. He recommended better teaching training, mobile libraries and the development of schools as community centres.

In 1926 another foreign adviser, Dr Kuhne from Germany, visited Turkey on the invitation of the government and made recommendations about the expansion of vocational schools and emphasised the need for art and craft schools to reflect the problems of their own localities in the skills they taught. The Belgian educator, Omar Buyse, followed in 1927 to make further studies and recommendations about vocational education. In 1933, as further evidence of an educational openness, a group of United States experts arrived in Turkey in a team led by Walter Kemerrer. Their task was to make economic recommendations but they examined education too, and urged a strengthening of elementary education to equip students more effectively to utilise existing educational resources more effectively.

These foreign reports did not result in agreed plans for Turkey and some of their recommendations were totally impracticable, reflecting ignorance of the society and its traditions. Buyse had recommended that girls should be taught to make hats and mourning veils, not realising that these had no place in Turkish culture. Kuhne had recommended abolishing boarding schools to save money but this was, as Başgöz and Wilson note, the only way in which poor village children could hope for secondary education.

Turkish educators during this period were much more concerned with the secularisation policies. The Law of Unification of Instruction passed in 1924 abolished all religious instruction in state schools. Through the College of Theology the state took control over religious education by setting up a number of *imam* and *hatip* (prayer leader and preacher) schools, although these were closed down again by 1931.

What the Ministry of Education lacked, however, until well into the 1930s, was an effective mechanism to translate its wishes into local action. The problem, in essence, was this: education was controlled locally by boards of education and for much of the early period of the republic those who controlled those boards, i.e. local government officials – *valis* and *kaymakams*, who were themselves local notables and landlords – were often unwilling to do much about education. This amounted to a lack of local support. Even after the foundation of the Republican People's Party in 1923 (named at that time, the People's Party), the government had no direct control over these notables. One reason for this was that the People's Party was itself very much influenced by the involvement of these same notables.

Against this background the response of several Ministers of Education was to seek greater central controls over the provinces and this is the source of Turkey's very centralised system of education. This centralisation was paralleled in other departments of state and was prompted also by the Kurdish revolt of 1925 in some of the eastern and south-eastern provinces. The state reacted by attempting to crush the revolt, executing its leaders and supressing the dervish orders to which they belonged. It was at that time that Kemal enforced another symbolic change, the prohibition on wearing the *fez*, to underline the secular nature of the state. It was as a result of this emergency that Kemal curtailed his experiment in multi-party democracy by banning the Progressive Republic Party which he had allowed to form just a few months earlier, an act which consolidated the Republican People's Party as the only party in Turkey. It was, however, a party without a strong mandate at the local level.

THE SECOND PERIOD

Progress at all levels in educational development was very poor during the first full decade of the republic. Statistics issued in 1927 showed that the literacy rate in Turkish cities was only about 30 per cent and in small villages not much higher than 5 per cent. In many villages there were no schools and even in those villages where schools had been established few further opportunities for education existed.

Such deficiencies were in many ways threatening to the state itself since they amounted to a very fragile base on which to construct an entirely new national consciousness. But for the first two decades of the republic the more urgent problems were concerned with national security and economic affairs. It was to some extent therefore inevitable that the much longer-term programme of building up educational institutions did not receive the effective attention it needed.

During the 1930s and 1940s, however, significant developments took place, especially in respect of education in rural areas. Education expanded at all levels in the society and higher education was expanded and reformed (see Chapter 11) and attempts were made to improve technical education. Başgöz and Wilson (1968) correctly write of this period as one during which an 'educational vitality' emerged in Turkish society.

Before the details are examined, however, it is essential to frame this particular period of time in a way which highlights the constraints the educational planners had to cope with. The administrative inertia, local political opposition, especially in the rural areas, and limited resources both of money and personnel have already been indicated. These were real physical constraints on what could be achieved. But they also sustained an intellectual inertia which made it difficult for successive education ministers to transform prevailing concepts of education. The notion of a *lise* education as a precursor to the university had developed in Ottoman Turkey; nothing in the republican period challenged this elitist idea (see Kazamias, 1966). In the rural areas, moreover, peasants remained attached to their religion and suspicious of secular education and of any kind of education for their daughters.

There were, in addition, severe *external* constraints on what the new state could achieve which reflected its position in the international economy and the consequences of the economic crisis of the inter-war years. The economic policy of the republican regime during the first decade of its life had been non-interventionist, built on the hope that private enterprise would develop the economy.

By the early 1930s this strategy had in effect collapsed since it faced, among other obstacles, an international economic crisis affecting Turkish exports and trade balances (Keyder, 1981). In 1934 the new economic policy of *étatism* was introduced which involved the state taking a firm control over the economy and a planning framework of five-year plans. The aim was to stimulate industrialisation. Some success was achieved in this but it was at the expense of agriculture and this incurred a much longer term social and political cost – the emergence of an oppositional base to the republican leadership formed by the peasantry and those merchants who had done quite well in the early days of the regime when trade policy was less restrictive.

Some writers (e.g. Keyder, 1979) have suggested that this *étatist* period presupposed a repressive state apparatus. Laws were passed banning strikes and the labour law of 1936 made trade unions illegal. The Keyder thesis, in fact, is that it was only through repression that the state remained intact and that repression was cloaked in an ideological shroud of nationalism and secularism. It was this economic and political and ideological framework which strengthened the link between bureaucracy and the emerging industrial bourgeoisie which had emerged as the successful economic force in the society.

This reading of Atatürk's achievements put the cultural revolution he brought about in a new light. It would be too simple, however, to read off the cultural and ideological changes from the economic ones. In the educational field certainly, there were changes deliberately aimed to improve the lot of people in the villages and which were inspired by educational ideals and a strong commitment to strengthen the state and the welfare of the people as a whole.

There are three main issues to be highlighted to convey what mattered in the period of 'educational vitality'. They concern adult education, teacher training and the village institutes. In 1929 a National Schools Law was passed aimed at wiping out illiteracy. The law aimed to set up reading rooms or classrooms in every village and required all citizens between the ages of fifteen and forty-five to attend. They were staffed by teachers from elementary and secondary schools. It is claimed that in the first year of this law over half a million people were taught to read but such schools never became widely established and after 1932 their role was taken up by the policy of setting up People's Houses.

These can be understood as heirs to the system of Turkish Hearth Clubs which had grown up during the Young Turk period of the empire and which had been so important in propagating the ideas of Turkish nationalism. These were replaced in 1932 by the People's Houses; agencies designed to strengthen the political position of the Republican People's Party and the principles of republicanism, nationalism and securalism. The vehicle for doing this was an educational one which used drama, literature and the arts as its aids. They organised folklore research in the villages and published bulletins to report their findings as part of an attempt to root Turkish nationalism in the traditions of Anatolia. The houses stimulated an interest in writing and in the setting up of printing presses and one of their results was to encourage people to use simple and direct Turkish expressions. The archives of these institutions are thought by some to represent a major source for the historical and sociological study of the republican period and represent something of a turning point in

Turkish intellectual life (Karpat, 1974). In Szyliowicz's (1973, p. 217) view they disseminated 'new symbols and loyalties' throughout Turkish society.

This particular interpretation is not a one which is universally accepted. Başgöz and Wilson regard them as having failed to do very much for village development and were never a substitute for basic economic and social reforms. 'The People's House', they write, 'had been principally designed to fill the gap betwen the educated elite at the top of Turkish society and the large uneducated masses below . . . Unfortunately, the Houses became centres for bureaucrats and those who already had an education' (Başgöz and Wilson, 1968, p. 157). And in a very personal but damning comment Başgöz notes that between 1941 and 1946 he was an active member of the Ankara People's House 'but never encounterd a member of the working class there'.

An earlier but no less important development in the Republic's education strategy concerned teacher training and the development of programmes to link education much more closely to the village economy. In 1933 the Village Affairs Commission was formed under the leadership of the Minister of Education, Resit Galip. It aimed to 'create a new type of village teacher' to take the place of the village *hodja* and transform the material conditions of village life itself. The man whose ideas gave clearest definition to the task of achieving this was the educator, Ismail Hakkı Tonguç, a teacher in the Gazi Teacher's School, recruited to the Directorate of Education. His view was that teachers had to become educators able to understand the real problems of villagers and be of practical help to them. Influenced partly by John Dewey and other Western writers it was Tonguç's view that:

> Instead of trying to gather encyclopedic type of information of the teachers of the old school, the teachers of the new work school will be organisers: life, the society and work itself will be the means of instruction. Only after this will the schools be institutions which have the power to create a new and modern nation. (Quoted in Stone, 1970, p. 222)

In the plan for the training of rural teachers which he masterminded these ideas were translated into practice. Between 1936 and 1947, when they were closed down, the teachers courses (*eğitmen* courses) produced over 10,000 instructors almost all of whom subsequently went to work in villages which had no teachers (Stone, 1970, p. 224).

The basic scheme was to train those rural youth who had recently finished their national military service and who had attained non-commissioned officer rank. Such people were to be selected by their own villages for teacher training. The link with the army is of itself interesting because the army had its two literacy programmes and was for many conscripts their first school. The army, in fact, developed into a major educational institution in its own right promoting those who achieved literacy to officer rank and giving them responsibility for the training of new recruits.

Once selected the youths were given a one-year intensive course in village revitalisation. Financed jointly by the Ministry of Education and Ministry of Agriculture, these courses were designed to solve another problem, that of the failure of agricultural school graduates to return to the villages. Under the supervision of the Inspector for Elementary Schools these courses were mounted in specially provided settings on real farms and taught by a teacher and an agricultural expert. Başgöz and Wilson quote from some of the weekly reports of these courses to the Ministry and underline the enthusiasm with which students received their instruction. Two extracts illustrate the combination of theory and practice, learning and life:

> One of the students has malaria. Salih, the vetenarian took a sample of his blood and showed the malaria microbe under a microscope to other students. It was quite an experience to see these students peering through a microscope for the first time. One of them cried: If anyone had sworn by God and told me such things as microbes existed, I'd never have believed him. But now I can see with my own eyes, and wriggling their tails like tadpoles, too. . .
>
> Old Aunt Hatice spoke of her war experiences in such moving terms that some of the students wept. The next day, during the drawing lesson, the students were asked to reproduce some of the rug designs they had seen in her village. (Quoted in Basgöz and Wilson, (1968, p. 146)

These teacher educators were expected, on returning to their own villages to help in the construction of schools, teach adults in the evening and improve local agricultural practices. How successful the programme was is something impossible to assess because its goals cannot be easily measured. The hidebound traditionalism of village life, its suspicion of outsiders and hostility to secular education was vividly portrayed by one village teacher, Mahmut Makal, in his *A Village in Anatolia* (1954) and the theme of traditionalism is a persistent one in all subsequent accounts of Turkish village life (see, e.g. Pierce, 1964; Magnarella, 1974; Stirling, 1965; Roper, 1981; Ozankaya, 1973). But the courses clearly did meet an important need and as late as 1964 Vexliard and Aytaç were able to report that 2500 of teachers trained in this way were still working in the villages. As the programme of normal teacher training improved and increased its output of graduates the village teacher programme was merged with the new programme for village institutes, a major experiment in educational innovation.

Set up in 1940 following a decision of the National Conference on Education they were designed to provide a five-year training course for those who had already completed elementary education. The plan was to use the village institutes (*köy enstitüleri*) as centres for rural development. The teachers who would staff them were to involve themselves directly in rural development projects stimulating local handicraft, setting up co-operatives and improving agricultural techniques. They were drawn from the best graduates of rural primary schools and those who took the course were obligated to spend twenty years of their working life in the villages.

By 1948 there were twenty-one institutes in Turkey employing nearly seven hundred teachers. Many of the institutes had been built by the teachers themselves working with villagers. During their period of operation between 1940 and 1950 they trained about 2500 students per year.

The ideas behind the institutes were those of Tonguç. Frank Stone (1970) has summarised them as follows:

> Tonguç envisioned alleviating the gross inequalities which divided the urban Turkish population from the villagers in a four step programme. Rural development would be stressed until all of the normal needs for food, clothing, shelter and work equipment could be met locally. Then, an evolution in the economic, commercial and legal aspects of village life aimed at making these more productive and appropriate to the agrarian environment would be encouraged. The goal would be to elevate the villages to the point where they would abandon regressive customs . . . every effort would be made to disseminate the democratic principles of the Republic among the villagers in such a way that these would become their own. (Stone, 1970, p. 229)

Something close to ten thousand rural educators were trained under this programme. Their contribution to rural development is yet to be fully evaluated. There is little doubt that they generated very high levels of commitment from their students and that these students played a significant role in raising the overall politically awareness of peasants. Frank Stone (1970) has noted that there were always more applicants for them than they could accommodate.

Other writers, however, have stressed that there was considerable opposition to the Institutes by villagers. Keyder (1979, p. 14), for instance, has written: '"Village Institutes", designed to carry the revolution to the rural masses, were confronted with severe opposition from the local population. The gap between the ruling elite and the masses was at no time more clearly visible.' One facet of this resistance could well have been the peasant view that education should lead to employment outside the village and carry high official status. It is clear, too, that an experiment as imaginative as this required resources and co-ordination of a kind which a poor society could not produce. Above all else the agricultural economy required a much greater input of resources to give credence to the idea that an agriculturally focused education was worthwhile.

Finally, considering the demise of the programme, it is clear that it required much more than political support than it had been given or had been able to generate. By 1950 the programme of village institutes was ended under accusations that they were hostile to religion and that they inspired communism among their students. A more realistic charge was that they were too closely linked to the Republican People's Party. This was the claim made against them by the Democrat Party in the period of multi-party politics after 1946. It was the Democrats who closed them down by merging them into normal teacher training programmes.

The village institutes were therefore one of the victims of political struggle in Turkey. Why this was the case is something to be understood against the political and ideological weaknesses of the Republican People's Party, the patterns of social and economic differentiation of Turkish society and, finally, the changing geopolitical importance of Turkey in the period of the Cold War. These issues affected much more than education. The complex changes which each one signifies created new constraints and opportunities for social and political action in Turkey which different political groups could exploit in areas such as agriculture, trade and foreign policy and, of course, urban and rural development policies.

TURKISH SOCIETY AFTER THE SECOND WORLD WAR

Atatürk died on 10 November 1938. Among Turks who identify with what he stood for there is a widespread view that he died too soon. Until the elections of 1946 Turkey was still a one-party state in the Atatürkist mould led by his deputy and friend, Ismet Inönü. Bernard Lewis has noted that Atatürk was an autocratic man 'dominating and imperious in temperament', a political heir to the Young Turks, especially the nationalist, positivist and Western-oriented wing, and that the republic he created was a dictatorship (Lewis, 1961, p. 290). But Lewis qualifies this: 'His was a dictatorship without the uneasy over-the-shoulder glance, the terror of the door bell, the dark menace of the concentration camp.' It was a dictatorship, Lewis argues, of an old elite of men able to carry through their revolution 'by a kind of paternalistic guidance, without resort to the whole monstrous apparatus of demagogy and repression familiar in the European dictatorships and their imitations elsewhere' (Lewis, 1961, p. 291).

Atatürk's power rested ultimately in control of the army but was also dependent on the support of the bureaucracy. The social changes which his own revolution had brought about, however, served to fashion new interest groups in the society especially among businessmen and peasants, the former interested in more freedom for private enterprise, the latter concerned about secular changes in society and falling living standards as a consequence of the effects of the Second World War on the Turkish economy.

These were groupings to which the Democrat Party was able to appeal in its successful election campaign in 1950. But the conditions for that success have to be traced, too, in the post-war political alignment of Turkey with the Western powers after the war. Turkey had traded a great deal with Germany during the war but as it came to its end such trading was stopped and Turkey actually declared war on Germany in February 1945 as a precondition to joining the United Nations. By the end of the decade Turkey had received substantial assistance under the United States Marshall Aid programme thus freeing state resources for non-military investment (Robinson, 1963, p. 140). Under the Truman doctrine that communism should be held in check on a global scale Turkey's role was to maintain NATO's south-eastern flank. Involvement of Turkish troops in the Korean war emphasised these Western ties and gave greater legitimacy to the freeing of the Turkish economy and the growth of multi-party politics which the United States has regarded as a precondition to the successful fight against communism and a precondition of United States aid (Ambrose, 1971). These economic policies strengthened the position of the Democrat Party and the Western orientation of the Turkish state. They also accelerated social changes like rural-urban migration which, among other things, consolidated the power of rural magnates who benefited most from growing investments in agriculture and the urban construction companies who were able to cash in on a steady supply of cheap labour from the villages. This 'peasantisation of the city' had profound consequences, too, for Turkish social structures bringing with it new patterns of social and political differentiation (Karpat, 1976).

Keyder (1974) has suggested that the emergence of multi-party politics was a shift from one pattern of capitalist modernisation to another, a move from elite rule to class rule in which the bourgeoisie of Turkey emancipated itself from the rule of the Republican People's Party. Consistent with this interpretation were the changes in the law which allowed trades unions to organise and which opened up the countryside to the influences of the modern economy (Lewis, 1961). It was still, however, a peripheral form of capitalism which benefited greatly from the world boom following the Korean War but which could not attract foreign capital investment and which began to suffer badly from debt, foreign exchange shortages and inflation. These were to lead later to severe political crises and to military coups (see Chapters 8 and 11).

The social changes of this early post-war period were of a kind which favoured conservative rather than innovative policies in education and which did not challenge in any way the connection between education and elite recruitment (Kazamias, 1966). The *lise* remained the classic route to higher education and the failure of the republican regime to modernise the countryside left its mark in severe inequalities between urban and rural areas in the educational life chances they offered.

Nevertheless, judged by the conditions which had prevailed in the early days of the republic the development of education had been remarkable. The percentage of the population literate increased from about 10 per cent in 1927 to 30 per cent in 1950 and 40 per cent in 1955 (Robinson, 1963, p. 155). During the same period the numbers enrolled in primary education quadrupled; those in first-cycle secondary education increased sixfold. Second-cycle secondary education increased eightfold and the numbers in higher education increased during this period from 3918 to over 36,000 (see appendix 4 of Szyliowicz, 1973, p. 464).

Despite such expansion there was in 1956 in a population of nearly 25 million people only 7586 engineers and 910 architects (Robinson, 1963, p. 155). Many of the problems to which the republic's educational innovators like Tonguç had addressed themselves - low levels of education in villages, high wastage rates and poor vocational education - remained and the educational system legitimated newly emerging patterns of social inequality. Başgöz and Wilson (1968, p. 192) were surely right in their final assessment of the reforms Atatürk inspired:

> The school alone could not produce a new social order; neither alone could the adoption of republican political practices or the development of industries or changes in agriculture. It was only as they were inter-related that the goals of the revolution were attainable.

It was in this area of co-ordination that the 'revolution from above' faltered. The logic of its own development and the international circumstances which were part of it explain this failure. The window of opportunity which opened for Atatürk in the 1920s closed slowly to open again after the Second World War but then only for a while and by that time Kemalists had lost much of the initiative that Atatürk's revolution had given them.

6 Revolution and Modernisation in Egypt

Egypt's position after the First World War was very different to that of Turkey. The war had not changed the structure of power in the society and Britain maintained a firm military grip on the country. Economically Egypt was in a much better position than Turkey; its industry and agriculture were much more highly developed. This does not mean, of course, that Egyptian industry was in a position to develop independently. Quite the contrary; there was a massive foreign investment in Egypt; the country's trade was dominated by foreigners and much of the land was mortgaged to European financial institutions. These are some of the classic contours of dependency.

On the other hand, and again in contrast to Turkey, Egyptian society possessed a cultural unity and a much stronger and widely diffused sense of a national identity. This, of course, was both an advantage and a disadvantage; the advantage was that calls for national independence could strike resonant chords. The disadvantage was that cultural forms, the *mentalités*, of a sharply divided society with an overwhelming peasant population, were routinely reproduced and not seriously challenged. This meant that prevailing notions of what independence and development might mean were conceived in very narrow terms, and in terms which kept Egypt under direct British control until the 1950s. Egypt was, however, a fast changing society in which the conditions for effective political action on the part of different and changing social groups were themselves changing rapidly. The changes within which Egypt was inextricably caught up – changes in the fortunes of Britain itself, the development of a distinctively Arab nationalism and other profound changes in the world of Islam such as the Turkish abolition of the caliphate, and, later, of political and ideological developments in Europe and the Soviet Union – entered Egyptian political life to give direction to the ways in which different groups in Egyptian society articulated their understanding of the society and their own interests within it.

In this and the following chapter the intention is to show that the structure of Egyptian education as we know it today, together with the values it represents and the role it plays in the society, is something which must be understood historically in the light of the class divisions of Egyptian society and these have developed as an integral part of Egypt's status as an underdeveloped society. The analytical thread which holds the historical narrative together is that Egypt's education system embodies the poverty of the society, the different educational claims of different social classes, and that it responds directly to the ideological cross-currents of political struggle in the country; that the balance of opportunities it affords different groups in Egypt and the role it plays in relation to the economy are a facet of the distribution of wealth and of power throughout the society.

Finally, to emphasise the theme running centrally throughout the argument of the book as a whole, the structure of Egyptian society must be conceived of in relation to the wider international structures of domination and dependency as well as revolutionary upheaval against those structures, which have been so central in the whole history of the Middle East and which are such a cental part of the geopolitics of the region today.

The present chapter covers three phases in Egypt's history, the inter-war period, the period from the Second World War to the *coup d'état* of 1952 and the Nasserist period. In describing each phase the aim is to clarify the relationships between changes in society and changes in education in such a way that the constraints on what was possible in the country's educational development can be set against what different groups demanded from it.

THE INTER-WAR PERIOD

Samir Amin (1978, p. 37) has described Egypt for much of the inter-war period as a 'client state' of Britain. It was a society in which powerful groups among the Egyptian bourgeoisie were prepared in their own interests to co-operate with the British. It has been said often that Egyptian politics during this period became a three-sided contest between the Palace, the British and the *Wafd* (see, e.g. Richmond, 1977). Against a background of foreign involvement in the country's finances, high taxation as part of the management of the country's debt and growing social inequalities in the society, the standard of life of the *fellaheen* was a desperately poor one. Jacques Berque (1972, p. 421) has argued that there is a real sense in which the *fellah* was paying the costs of half a century of 'khedivial sumptousness' and were becoming totally alienated from the economic system of the society.

It was a society in which government was an activity distant from the mass of the people, in which there were profound ideological differences among the leading groups in the society and in which populist nationalism vied with Islamic reformism and as the major concern of petit bourgeois groups in state employment, small business and the professions. Such differences affected education directly; they governed what was provided, the demands people made of it and the kinds of conflicts which occurred over how it should develop. Above all, however, they ensured that young people, students in particular, would play a central role in the political life of the society.

At the apex of Egyptian society were large landowners and the largest of them were prominent in the political leadership of the *Wafd*. They brought to their understanding of politics in Egypt a strong sense of their own social importance as leaders of the people who worked the land they owned and they sought to maintain that leadership position.

Alongside the landowners there was an emerging Egyptian industrial bourgeoisie the leading members of which, men like Talat Harb, founder of the Egyptian bank, had their own roots in the ownership of land. Talat Harb was, as Robert Tignor (1982, p. 43) has stressed 'an unabasahed Egyptian nationalist'. But his economic strategy for the country was a capitalist one, he did not support land reforms and he ardently supported the rights of private property.

The general educational orientation of these groups, and one reinforced by Egyptian intellectuals like Taha Husayn (or Hussein) and Ahmad Lutfi al-Sayyid and Husain Haikal (sometimes transliterated as Haykal) was a Western one with strong ostensible liberal elements as part of it. A persistent nationalist criticism of the British was that the educational development of the country had been retarded. It was to be expected, therefore, that after 1923 educational provision in Egypt would be expanded. This was indeed the case. In 1925 a law was passed making education at elementary level compulsory in an effort to wipe out illiteracy. By 1930 the percentage of the state budget for education had risen to nearly 11 per cent from a figure of only 4 per cent in 1920.

Expansion took place, too, in secondary and higher education. Indeed, secondary education enrolments grew at a faster rate than elementary enrolments (Szyliowicz, 1973, p. 187). The University of Cairo was set up in 1925 and the numbers of graduates from institutions of higher learning increased from 1061 in 1928 to 2017 in 1932–3 (Lutfi al-Sayyid-Marsot, 1977, p. 202). The fact that the economy could not absorb this output of secondary school graduates and those from the university and other institutes must be noted for it added to the bitterness of the educated unemployed and played no small part in the student politics of the inter-war period.

More important for this analysis, however, is what animated that expansion of education. Close inspection reveals a double educational thrust; one part of it was concerned with the development of educational opportunities. The other was concerned to so educate the mass of the Egyptian people that the social fabric of the society would be preserved once the British had gone. This ambivalence reflects clearly the contradictory features of the position of the dominant groups in Egyptian society particularly those associated with the right wing of the *Wafd* and those others who were identified with Liberal Constitutionalist Party such as Lutfi al-Sayyid who was rector of the Egyptian University until 1928 and who became Minister of Education in the early 1930s. Among these men there was a very conservative approach to democracy, a suspicion that the Egyptian people were not yet properly educated to a responsible role in politics.

Charles Smith (1980) has argued that men like Haykal, President of the Liberal Constitutionalist Party, defended democracy but were averse to mass participation in politics and favoured a form of government in which an educated leadership was dominant. In Haykal's case, the necessity of having a political leadership in the hands of the educated elite was founded on his understanding of the writings of the French positivist, Comte, and the evolutionary thought of Herbert Spencer. Smith argues that such men felt alienated from the masses they sought to lead; that they possessed a strong sense of intellectual superiority and believed the masses to be essentially irrational.

During his period as Minister of Education in 1938–39 Haykal attempted to further the development of primary education among the peasantry. Smith interprets his concern, however, as one of trying to prevent the political instability which urban migration and increased landlessness had engendered in the countryside. Haykal was fearful, too, of the unrest he saw being nurtured by the demands of the emerging labour unions, the Muslim Brothers and groups like Young Egypt which all pressed for economic reforms.

A similar case has been made out for the views of the Egyptian scholar Ahmad Amin by William Shepard (1980). Amin was influenced in his youth by the work of Muhammad Abduh and later became a colleague of Taha Hussein in the Egyptian University. Throughout his writings, claims Shepard, there is a concern for democracy and an enlightened body of public opinion which presupposed an educated population. But such a public opinion did not exist in Egypt so the task of national leadership was to produce it. What emerges, then, is a technocractic model of government and little understanding of how the governed might participate in the process of government.

Even in the writings of Taha Hussein there are hints of the attitude that the mass of the Egyptian people are not to be trusted with too much political power. Taha Hussein's concern for the values of western scholarship and education are well known. He saw Egypt's civilisation as being essentially European since it, too, drew on the classical civilisations of Greece and Rome and he was a severe critic of traditional education in Egypt. Hussein became by the early 1950s Egypt's most important man of letters, a man who had held senior positions in the Egyptian University and who was also Minister of Education of a *Wafd* government. Like his friend Amin, it could be said of him that he was one of those who were the teachers of the present day generation of Egyptian leaders (Shepard, 1980).

Yet there is still an ambivalent note in his writings about the education of the Egyptian people. In his short treatise *The Future of Culture in Egypt* (1954) Taha Hussein set out his views on education. They cannot be easily summarised and the book is hardly a work in educational philosophy. It does, however, stress the importance of education for democracy and the personal development of individuals and it does celebrate the achievements of Western scholarship and the values which he took to lie behind it. He did consider that the state had a central role to play in education in Egypt and one of the reasons for this concerned the inadequacy, as he saw it, of the Egyptian family:

> Educators in some advanced countries concentrate on mental discipline because they feel they can rely on the family to provide the necessary physical and moral preparation. However, two generations will have to pass before the Egyptian family can be

> reasonably expected to play this role. (Hussein, 1954, p. 29)

He was an advocate of secondary education, too; and it should not be confined just to secondary school pupils. It should cover, too, vocational education and extension studies for those who have to work. He writes of such provision:

> By intelligently and methodologically training the minds and bodies of the younger generation the state will produce a citizenry that will not be content with the meanest form of living, but that will desire to know how to obtain the better things of life. Such Egyptians will understand the meaning of country and their obligations to it . . . They will be, in short, a responsible youth. (Hussein 1954, p. 33)

The argument is developed to claim that if the state neglects its duties here then it will have violated the democratic rights of the people so that 'they might become so resentful as to endanger the peace and the social system through a revolution of unpredictable magnitude, a revolution which, if we are able to see how it would begin, we are unable to see how it would end' (Hussein, 1954, p. 34).

There is no hint in this work that the state might not always act in the interests of its citizens or of the nation itself; there is no suggestion that the form of the Egyptian state might itself be an obstacle to the realisation of democratic rights. In Hussein's view the state is the guarantor of those rights, a view about and an attitude towards the state which was and still is extensively held among Egyptian nationalists.

But there were other ideological cross-currents during the inter-war period and afterwards which conceived of Egyptian independence in quite different ways. The most important of these were part of an Islamic movement, the Muslim Brotherhood, and injected into Egyptian politics a strong religious orientation which was away from that of those Western influences which were a major part of the nationalist movement. Here was a different framework within which to construct a political identity.

Sheikh Hassan al-Banna founded the movement in 1929 in Ismailia and the movement gathered strength during the 1930s to become, in the period after the Second World War a powerful political force in Egypt. The aim of the movement was to purify Islam and build a political order firmly on the precepts of the Koran. Its supporters were drawn largely from petit bourgeois groups in Egyptian society, minor officials, clerical workers, skilled artisans and small business men. Gilsenan (1982) has charactised this group as one unable to break through to the social heights of the Egyptian bourgeoisie and that social realm dominated culturally by English and French and one which was threatened from below by the prospect of becoming proletarianised.

They gained a great deal of support among young people both in the university and in schools but also in villages where people who had been adversely affected by urban migration and rural poverty could identify with a group which seemed to promise improvements by spiritual redemption. They were able in this way to root their politics in the religious values of rural dwellers. But they sought to provide practical help, too: they set up mosques and schools and encouraged local industries and networks of collective help and by the 1940s became a significant political force in Egypt and one which found support among some of the junior officers in the army.

The army, too, was experiencing change. Of particular importance after 1936 were changes in the military academy, the training school for officers. The 1936 Treaty of Alliance with Britain allowed for an expansion in Egyptian forces. The new recruits to the academy came from what Lutfi al-Sayyid Marsot (1977, p. 203) calls 'the middle income brackets, urban and rural, and formed the growing middle class of professionals, bureaucrats and intellectuals.' One of the academy's most famous graduates in 1938 was Gamal Abdul Nasser. Seven other members of what became the leadership of the Free Officers in 1952 entered the academy with him, including Anwar Sadat.

Nasser himself was later to write that 'in countries like Egypt the army is a force of education' (quoted Stephens, 1971, 41). He believed it to be the only truly national force capable of wresting independence from the British while being able simultaneously to avoid the class conflict which Egypt's social revolution would bring with it. It was the context in which men like Nasser and Sadat could sharpen a self-image as true nationalists with an obligation to provide leadership to the toiling masses of Egypt. They saw themselves as being essentially different to the 'society' of Cairo and the corruption of the court and its compromise with the British. The experience of fighting in the Arab-Israeli conflict of 1948 was later to strengthen the view that the Army had a national political role to play in rescuing Egypt. But this takes the account too far ahead too quickly; the point for the moment is that young, highly politicised officers found the opportunity to develop their political ideas and contacts and to become a potent force in Egyptian politics.

Throughout the inter-war period the Egyptian economy experienced directly the effects of recession in the international economy. During the 1930s, for instance, to protect Egyptian industry tariffs were raised with the effect of driving up the price of basic necessities for the poor of Egypt's countryside and rapidly growing urban areas.

It was here, at the base of Egyptian society that the overall poverty of the country was most acutely felt although the city and the countryside constituted two quite different ideological matrices. In the period up to the Second World War a large proportion of Egypt's growing working class was organised into unions and some small sections of the Egyptian labour movement turned to socialist and communist ideas. by 1930 there were over 15 000 workers organised into unions and the major political parties, particularly the *Wafd* sought to work closely with them and to control them, particularly the leftist elements among them. It remains the case, however, that industrial workers, even as late as the early 1930s constituted only about 10 per cent of the urban population.

A militant working class inspired by leftist ideas was a force which emerged after the Second World War in Egypt; for the period before the war, as Jacques Berque (1972, p. 499) has pointed out, the deprived groups of town and country were deprived 'by the very excess of their wretchedness, of active social expression' the Marxist intellectuals who sought to provide some sort of leadership 'were recruited at the time almost exclusively from among foreigners or minority groups'. They applied, Berque (1972, p. 501) insists 'to an all-too-copious reality formulae derived from elsewhere'.

At the base of this society was, of course, the peasantry, the 'foundation of Egyptian society' and 'still in bondage to the Nile' (Berque, 1972, p. 484). It was a differentiated group reflecting changes in the commmercialisation of agriculture, the regrouping of land-holdings, rural population increases (from about nine million in 1907 to nearly fourteen million in 1947), urban migration, growing landlessness and a steady deterioration in material conditions.

Land competition was fierce and so too was competition for employment. An United States observer, Wendell Cleland noted in 1938 that the 'sinister trio' of poverty, ignorance and disease were pervasive in the Egyptian countryside (see Berque, 1972, p. 487). Peasant society retained its tribal loyalties and patriarchal bonds and, as

Berque (1972, p. 485) has stressed: 'The wretched fellah, while a proletarian in his indigence, remained a peasant in his archaism and in his loyalties.' Peasant life was lived within the cultural frameworks of village and of religion. One observer of village life in Silwa in Aswan province noted in the early 1950s that: 'For the villagers, the world is classified into believers and non-believers, on the basis of the Muslim faith, and they are hardly aware of concepts like race or class' (Ammar, 1954, p. 73). Religion pervaded every feature of their lives and local religious leaders were held in very high regard.

Peasants in this village retained a deep respect for religious education. But as a measure of the way changes in Egyptian society as a whole had penetrated to the countryside, it was also clear that villagers expected state-provided schools to offer them opportunities for government employment. They showed great reluctance to support the state elementary school for it offered no further opportunity for primary and then secondary education.

The point to stress is this: while peasant life retained many of its traditional features it is wholly misleading to regard it as unchanging. But how peasants reacted to change and what political values they would give support to is not something to be read off from their economic position alone. Cultural traditions, social obligations and religious outlook have to be considered, too; they each contribute to very different conditions for social action among the diverse groups which made up Egyptian society.

THE SECOND WORLD WAR AND THE *COUP D'ÉTAT* OF 1952

The framework of social relations sketched out above is the backcloth against which the turbulent politics of inter-war Egypt must be read. Strikes, student demonstrations, the suppression of opposition by the government, the development of diverse ideological groupings of militants some of which were radically Muslim in orientation, are all facets of Egyptian society and its emerging social divisions, economic circumstances and political order.

The Second World War injected a whole series of new dynamics into Egyptian society. Robert Tignor (1982, p. 27) has written that 'The war had a decisive and radicalising impact on Egypt. It generated vast social changes and dislocations in Egyptian society.' Inflation depressed the incomes of the poor while war contracts and the absence of foreign competition favoured local business. The overall effect was to sharpen up the class divisions of Egyptian society. Black markets, profiteering and inflation, together with the presence of thousands of foreign troops which, at times during the early part of the war looked as if they would be defeated by the Axis powers, all contributed to a strengthening of nationalist opinion. As the war progressed there was a growth, too, in Arab nationalism to provide yet another framework in which Egyptians could conceive the meaning of independence.

The ending of the war brought with it dislocating consequences; unemployment increased as those engaged on war-related work were laid off. Inflation increased and so did industrial unrest among workers; there were student demonstrations in support of British evacuation and the whole field of political opportunities in Egypt opened up within which to press Egyptian claims in a new post-war world. For the constraints and opportunities on Egypt's development had been changed fundamentally by the war. After the war British strategy in the Middle East had to cope with two new elements, the weakness of the British economy and the development of Cold War politics. Both made it inconceivable that Egypt could be occupied as before the war. The Labour government of Attlee in Britain signalled the evacuation of Britain and Egyptian political life became turbulent as different groups staked their claims for the future.

The complex politics of this period cannot be discussed here; it is sufficient to note that the public sphere of politics became a battle ground for competing interest groups. Young people and students in particular were caught up in the struggles; student-worker committees formed and so did cultural associations and publishing houses. Vatikiotis (1969, p. 359) notes that 'What was interesting about these new groups was that they combined a programme of national liberation (i.e. evacuation of British forces from Egypt) with "liberation of the exploited masses from a capitalist minority".' Egyptian writers like Mahfuz in his famous book, *Midhaq Alley*, turned their attention to depictions of the life of the poor and helped fuel an interest in socialism and communism among the many leftist groups which formed after the war. The response of Egyptian governments, however, was repression and action against the leftist groups (Vatikiotis, 1969, p. 362).

The thread which ostensibly runs through the main issues in Egyptian politics in the post-war years is that of securing a settlement with Britain. Events outside of Egypt were critical, however, particularly the ending of the British Mandate in Palestine in 1948 and the Arab-Israeli war in which the Arab armies were defeated. The army officers in Egypt who had participated in that humiliating defeat were strengthened in their growing resolve that they should act against ineffective and corrupt governments. The end of the story is familiar. Following the failure of negotiations with the British as well as at the United Nations, political disturbances in Egypt prompted British moves to control the situation militarily. The political crisis which followed was brought to a new point when Colonel Nasser's free officers took over the army headquarters at Abassia on 23 July 1952.

NASSER'S EGYPT AND STRATEGIES OF MODERNISATION

The takeover of power by free officers ended the monarchy; it led eventually to the dissolution of the existing political parties and the replacement of the old political elite by military officers, many of whom had a technological background, to the commanding positions of Egyptian political life. For reasons connected with world political changes, including the development of the hydrogen bomb which reduced the need for massive military presence in the Middle East – a presence which, in any case, a Britain straitened by post-war austerities could barely afford – the free officers were able to negotiate a British withdrawal from the country. In this respect Nasser's government had realised the historical ambitions of Egyptian nationalism.

Egypt remained, nevertheless, a desperately poor, markedly inegalitarian society and the military officers who controlled the government had no clear perception of how Egyptian development should be organised. Many of the difficulties which Egyptian people have had to face since the revolution reflect this.

Three complex moments of change interacting dynamically together explain the pattern of development of the Egyptian revolution. First, there is the revolution itself. As Tignor (1982) has pointed out, the regime had its own dynamic. Secondly, the structural logic of Egyptian society must be understood. Class inequalities, poverty, rising population, rural-urban migration all play their part alongside and through diverse cultural and ideological and religious divisions which constituted the frameworks through which different groups articulated their political goals. Thirdly, Egypt's relationships with the Arab world, the great powers of West and East and the regional conflicts of the Middle East itself, particularly in Palestine, represent another set of rapidly changing constraints on what the Free Officers regime could achieve.

One way in which these issues can be clarified and the educational strategies which have developed in Egypt is suggested by Saad Ibrahim's (1982) characterisation of the different phases of the revolution during the twenty-five year period to the mid-1970s. In a paper concerned with changing opportunities for social mobility Ibrahim identifies five stages in Egypt's revolution. The first is the hesitation phase between 1952 and 1956, a period of consolidation where the only significant initiatives bearing on the class structure of the society were land reforms to weaken the old aristocracy and favour the small farmer.

The ideological rationale of the new regime was not, at least initially, very clear and the Free Officers could not be described as a cohesive ideological group. Their interests, it has been suggested, at least in the first phase of the revolution up to 1956, were pragmatic Dessouki, 1982). They were, however, against privilege and were keen on principles of fairness and of equal opportunities. They abolished the aristocratic titles of *pasha, bey* and *effendi* and they committed themselves to expansion at all levels in the education system.

The consciousness phase followed between 1956 and 1960 Nationalisation of foreign assets, particularly the Suez Canal, and programmes of central economic planning developed during this period. It was during this period that Nasser staked his claims for leadership of the Arab world, in which the United States refused aid for the High Dam at Aswan prompting Egypt to turn to the Soviet Union for help. In Saad Ibrahim's view the less well-to-do strata especially in urban areas gained during this period.

The socialist transformation phase followed between 1960 and 1966. This brought with it a massive expansion in the public sector and in particular in education as the state demanded more trained personnel for industry and the civil service. Ibrahim notes that these policies of expansion resulted in substantial changes in opportunities in Egyptian society. But it is also during this phase that the Nasser regime settled into that of a bureaucratic and managerial oligarchy exercising very tight control of Egyptian society.

Gilsenan (1982) has suggested that during this phase, i.e. prior to the 1967 war, a new kind of hierarchy consolidated itself. He argues that the failure to develop a genuine political movement to mobilise the Egyptian masses during this period led to the state being widely seen as something which acted on society despite the fact that by this time Nasser himself had become a major symbol of national unity. Nevertheless, the ideological themes which were important were those of socialism despite the fact that Nasser cracked down on communists and leftist sympathisers in Egypt.

The period between 1965 and 1970 is described by Ibrahim as the stagnation phase. The Arab-Israeli war of 1967 was critical here; the loss of the Sinai oil fields, canal revenues and massive destruction of the Suez Canal cities all combined with declining investment to compound the problems of an already overstretched and fragile economy. In the aftermath of the war Nasser's prestige fell; there were strikes and demonstrations and among the educated groups in Egyptian society there emerged evidence of a strong sense of resentment against what they understood as the 'army class' and its old boy network (Stephens, 1971, p. 534). In November 1968 there were student demonstrations against the government which deteriorated into riots in Alexandria and the government retaliated with arrests and further suppression.

In 1970 Nasser died opening up, with Sadat as President, the phase which Ibrahim calls the socialist restreat phase. Sadat was able by the end of 1973 to consolidate his position, building on what in Egypt was seen as the successful counter-attack on Israel during the October war. There followed a new policy to encourage private capital investment and stronger links with the West. This policy of *Infitah* – the Open Door Policy – signalled the reversal of socialist-type policies.

There is growing evidence to show that social inequalities in Egyptian society intensified from this period. 'There are indications', wrote Ibrahim (1982, p. 382) 'that some elements of the pre-revolutionary upper and upper middle class are resurfacing. Upward social mobility is mainly accomplished through (1) private sector activities or (2) migration to oil-rich Arab countries. Strata with fixed income seem to have suffer the most in this phase.' The overall period is one in which the strong links with the Soviet Union were broken off; Egypt came tacitly to accept the regional political supremacy of the oil rich Arab states and United States influence, both military and technical, increased substantially. Sadat's co-operation with President Carter's Camp David agreements on peaceful co-operation with Israel isolated Egypt from the rest of the Arab world and catalysed an Islamic opposition to the Sadat regime.

This is, of course, a highly schematic summary of a complex

period. What would stand out in a more detailed account of it is this: that changes in politics and policies cannot be explained by reducing them to the consequences of Egypt's external dependency or even to the constraints of the country's poverty. Both matter; but what is also clear is that the regime itself in seeking to solve the problems of the society imposed on Egypt by its own revolution generated a whole series of new problems which it then sought to solve (see Trimberger, 1978; Waterbury, 1983). In trying to solve them it created new problems, examples of which include policies such as those of subsidising basic foods or maintaining political ambitions to the military leadership of the Arab world. Both forced the regime into external borrowing and severe budgetary problems.

The whole field of education policy illustrated the degree to which state policies have to be seen in the light of the character of the regime itself and not just against features of the country's dependent status *vis-à-vis* the developed world. Such dependency, as well as the resource constraints of a poor society are also critical in shaping education policies and structures, but not necessarily decisive. The irony in the Egyptian case is that a regime which justified itself in revolutionary terms developed a system of education which functions in a most unrevolutionary way; that failures in educational planning, economic mismanagement and an overall political failure to mobilise the mass of the Egyptian people behind the overt values of the state itself, compounded the problems of an already inadequate system of education. Reform of education was very high among the priorities of the Free Officers. In this sense they were the heirs among the tradition of Egyptian nationalism which had criticised the British for denying education to Egyptians. The educational system became a key instrument for the dissemination of the regime's basic ideology, particularly during the period after 1960 when President Nasser created a Committee on National Education.

The officers of the revolution faced, however, many obstacles. Mahmud Faksh (1980, p. 43) has noted that they 'inherited a nation deeply split over modernist and traditionalist orientations, an unreformed Azhar, and a religious class which was desperately trying to defend its crumbling position while refusing to participate in the modernisation of Egyptian life and thought'. Nevertheless in the course of ten years they made some substantial changes in education and credibly extended the range of educational opportunity in Egypt.

Key elements of their educational revolution include (1) the rationalisation of educational provision and the removal of fees (2), the expansion of education at all levels in the system and (3) the inclusion of an Arab nationalist orientation into the curricula of both school and university courses and the use of schools as agencies of political socialisation.

The outlines of the educational system which the new regime created can be only broadly sketched here. An education law in 1953 brought together the primary and elementary schools with the aim of improving transfers into secondary education. All fees were abolished. In the early years of the revolution educational planning was initiated to define such goals as the universalisation of primary education within ten years. The government committed itself to the eradication of illiteracy which was a particularly serious problem among women. The female illiteracy rate in 1952 was close to 90 per cent. And only about 26 per cent of girls who could have been in primary school were actually enrolled (Howard-Merriam, 1979).

In the field of secondary education there was reorganisation defining two phases, a four-year preparatory phase (up till the age of about sixteen) followed by a three-year secondary phase. The private schools of Egypt were brought under the jurisdiction of the Ministry of Education and in the technical education field some attempt was made to inject more technical education into the general curricula of the schools. Waterbury (1983, p. 219) has argued that these politics 'elicited an enthusiastic social response and endorsement unequaled by *any* of the regime's other major goals'. Unfortunately, as will be seen more clearly in the following chapter, the early educational aspirations have not, in fact, been realised.

The most obvious success of the Nasser regime in the education field was its expansion of the system. In 1952, 1.5 million children were enrolled in primary schools; by 1969 this figure had increased to 3.6 million (see Waterbury, 1983, p. 222). Secondary school enrolments during the same period increased from 181 789 to 293 991. In the technical schools the numbers went up from 5200 to 35 000. Spending on education went up from £23 million in 1952 (less than 3 per cent of GDP) to £130 million in 1970–71 (approximately 4.1 per cent of GDP) (Abdel-Fadil, 1982, p. 352). Abdel-Fadil writes:

> It is easy to see that the numbers of enrolments at all levels of education has risen tremendously. Nonetheless, it is equally easy to deduce that the process of educational expansion was highly *skewed* in favour of secondary and higher educational levels. This

> makes the history of educational expansion during the period under review (1962–1977) a history of *unbalanced growth.* (Abdel-Fadil, 1982, p. 353)

Insufficient attention to the planning of physical resources and the heavy weight of poverty have meant that a very high proportion of Egyptian primary schools were for much of this period, and continue to be, very overcrowded and have to operate on a shift basis. School drop-out rates have remained high. The consequence has been, as the next chapter will show, that the expansion of education did not significently transform the relative educational life chances of the mass of the Egyptian people.

Education had to expand, apart from anything else, on account of the increase in the Egyptian population from about 20 million in 1951 to over 30 million in 1970. The rate of growth in the school-age population has continued to be greater than the rate of growth of school places. Similarly, the rate of growth of new jobs in the economy has been insufficient to keep pace with the supply of labour to the economy both of those who are educated and those who are not (Korayem, 1984).

It is indeed fortunate, though in the longer term perhaps very unfortunate, that Egypt has been able in the 1970s to export labour to the oil states of the Middle East. The educational ramifications of this aspect of Egypt's dependency on employment opportunities abroad as a solution of its steadily growing problems of unemployment at home, are complex in the extreme and will be discussed in the next chapter.

The Nasser regime probably had its greatest success in the education field in the realms of political socialisation, in the way it instilled into young Egyptians a powerful sense of national pride. Increasingly that pride became focused on President Nasser himself who began to appear after his success in 1956 as the personal embodiment of the Egyptian revolution earning the gratitude and admiration of the people. One observer of village schools noted in 1967 that, despite denials by school teachers, political indoctrination was extensive in school. The observer wrote:

> Usually when entering the classroom, the teacher would ask the students to stand. Rising to their feet they would shout 'Nasser' or 'freedom' or pehaps 'independence', and when asked to sit down they again would shout, usually a word symbolising some aspect of their regime's ideology . . . A song popular among elementary

students was 'Nasser, all of us love you, we will remain by your side, Nasser, leader of all, oh Nasser.' (Quoted by Hopwood, 1982, p. 137)

Mahmud Faksh (1980) has indicated in his own case what it was like to be a school student in Egypt during this period:

> Textbooks are full of stories about the glory of medieval Islamic heroes and the great Arab nationalist struggle against colonialism and other political and socio-economic injustices that culminated in the 1952 revolution. Many pages are given over to Quranic passages and sayings of the prophet on ethics. This overt and general pattern of socialisation might on frequent occasions take the form of celebrating Port Said Day (the evacuation of British and French troops in 1956) or Palestine Refugee Day, or any other nationalistic event.
>
> Based on my own experience with this kind of socialisation I underwent in my primary, preparatory and secondary school years, it would be safe to assume that such ceaseless efforts to bring about an identification with the regime have been somewhat successful. My classmates and I developed a strong sense of identification and pride with Arabism, anticonolialism and nationalist leaders of Nasser's calibre. (Faksh, 1980, p. 52).

If this is indeed correct then the regime was remarkably successful in building support for itself. The question remains, though, what kind of regime was it? Faksh (1980, p. 50) describes it as a 'military technocratic' one which is 'administrative-oligrachic' in nature and Writers on the left have analysed it as one dominated by the military whose senior officers have formed the nucleus of a new ruling class, a state bourgeoisie (see Hussein, 1973).

However the political character of the regime is typified, the extent to which it was able to impose itself on Egyptian society should not be overestimated. It is true that when Nasser died in 1970 the crowds who followed his funeral experienced a deep sense of loss, of being in a mystical way *abandoned* (see Hussein, 1971). But in the course of the 1970s ideological fracture lines opened up in which Islamic movements increased their support and in which the Sadat regime could put the State's ideological course fully into reverse. To contain Nasserite and Marxist groups Sadat, it is claimed, encouraged the Muslim Brotherhood and other Islamic associations (Waterbury, 1983). His economic reforms were to open up the Egyptian economy to foreign capital investment and throughout the 1970s Sadat allied Egypt firmly with the United States. The shifting ideological sands of Egyptian politics and the growing problems of the economy combine with the volatile politics to the Middle East as a whole to render Egypt's political stability a precarious one. Sadat was assassinated by a Muslim fanatic. His successor, Hosni Mubarak has precious little room for political manoeuvre. Without United States support his regime could well collapse.

The reorientation of Egyptian economic strategies, the export of Egyptian labour throughout the oil-rich Middle East, the dependency on United States military and food aid, the growing social inequalities of the society – all are facets of changing dependency relationships. In the following Chapter and in Chapter 10 which deals with higher education in Egypt, some of the educational ramifications of these changes will be discussed.

7 Education in Egypt: Constraints and Opportunities

Egypt is a poor society seeking ways to develop to give a better standard of life to its growing population. Since the 1952 revolution it has become something of an axiom that the country must develop its human resources to the full if development itself is to be a possibility. For this reason education is seen as playing a vital role in the future development of the society as well as being a basic human right. Its role is conceived of both in terms of the training of human resources and of fostering national integration (NCFER, 1980. Hyde, 1978). It remains true, however, as Egyptian authorities will readily admit, that the system of education in Egypt displays many weaknesses and must change to fulfil the aims required of it by the constitution and to meet the needs of the society and the economy with greater effectiveness.

A growing recognition that the expansion of education at all levels in the system during the 1960s and 1970s had outstripped growth in the economy resulting, for example, in the phenomena of graduate unemployment and falling standards in schools, prompted the government in 1979 to submit a working paper on reform of education to the People's Assembly and the National Council on Education to mobilise support (in the manner of Egyptian politics) for a sweeping programme of educational reform and innovation (Ministry of Education, 1979). This working paper was subsequently revised into a document containing detailed proposals for implementing reforms (NCFER, 1980). The stated policies for development and innovation include: expanding education, improving its quality, eradicating illiteracy, improving technical education, developing comprehensive education which aims to combine theoretical study with practical work and developing the practice of what is referred to as basic education.

These working papers represent the guidelines of educational policy in Egypt, and their central thrust is to forge closer links between education and the needs of the economy, balancing the output of the system with what the economy can absorb. Of particular significance in this respect are the proposals to try to improve the quality and quantity of technical education, an area which, by common agreement between the Egyptian government and the several international aid organisations that work in close co-operation with it, is very deficient.

It is too early to assess the significance of these developments or their effectiveness, but this much is clear; Egypt is poised to try to shift the emphasis in its pattern of educational growth. Just as the economic reforms of 1974 following President Sadat's *October Working Paper* (which urged the opening up – *Infitah* – of the Egyptian economy to foreign capital investment) had such far-reaching consequences for the economy and the society itself, so the proposed education changes threaten to bring about important changes in the life chances of different groups in Egyptian society.

Whether the government will be successful in its policies is not a matter of the quality of its rhetoric, however, but of the way in which different groups in society respond to and judge the reforms themselves. That, as it is hoped will be shown, is a matter of expectations, attitudes and the distribution of power in society.

THE FORMAL SYSTEM

In Egypt today some seven million boys and girls are enrolled in about 13 000 schools and twelve rapidly expanding universities. About 10 per cent of the 19–22 age group, approximately 450 000 people, are enrolled in the universities (Ministry of Education, 1981). The Ministry of Education describes the education budget as amounting to eighteen per cent of the total national budget although this is lower than most other Arab states (Ministry of Education, 1981, p. 22).

Up until 1980–81 the system of education consisted formally of six years of compulsory primary education followed by three years of preparatory school and then three years of secondary school. Secondary education was divided into two types, general and technical. Post-secondary education includes universities and higher institutes covering teacher training and further vocational education. The system is represented in Figure 7.1. It is a centralised system. Long-term planning is the responsibility of the National Council for Education, Scientific Research and Technology which is directly

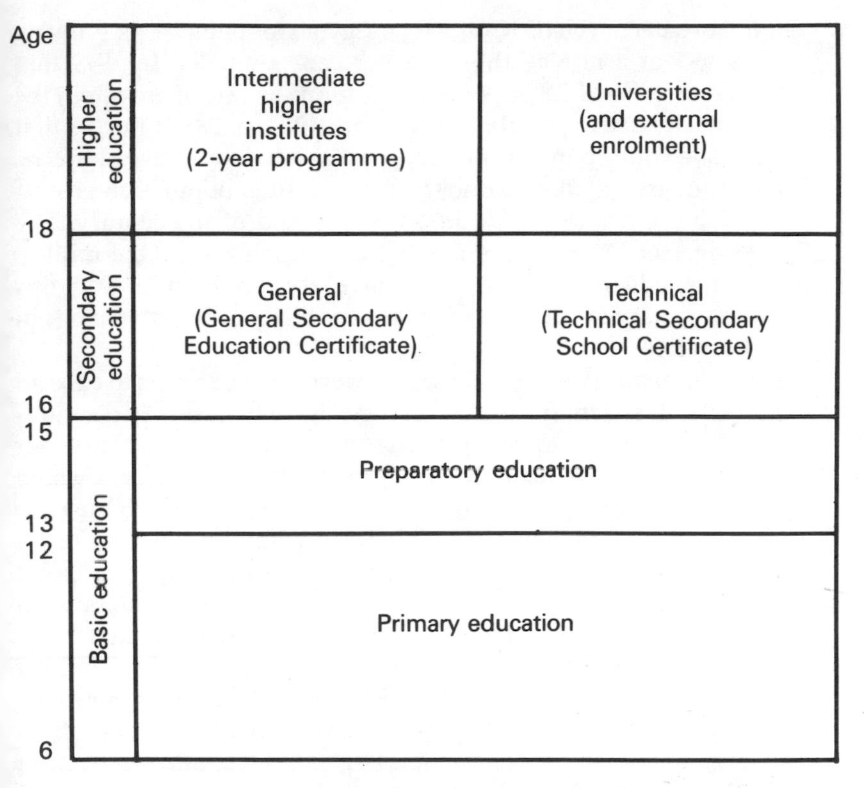

Figure 7.1 The Egyptian education system 1981

responsible to the President. Detailed administrative control rests with the Ministry of Education which makes decisions about staff appointments, resource allocation, curricula and assessment (Hyde, 1978). Other ministries are involved in education through the training they provide for their employees but, as I shall indicate, this part of the system has many problems. There have been administrative changes recently to try to decentralise the system of control to the local governorates and, within them, to smaller educational zones, but such changes have not gone very far.

In comparison with other Arab states Egypt is a country with a very large population and although the proportion of that population under the age of seventeen is in line with the other Arab states, the numbers of children in that group is very high. From the total population of about forty million nearly twelve million are under the age of seventeen. (UNESCO, 1981). Egypt's population is growing rapidly too, at a rate of about 2.2 per cent annually. In 1979 that growth rate reached 2.9 per cent, faster than the rate of growth in the economically active population (UNDP, 1981, p. 38). It means that Egypt has a young population: 31.6 per cent is below the age of twelve. If the crude fertility rate cannot be reduced then population growth will reach sixty to seventy million by the end of the century. The figures, in fact, amount to a demographic nightmare. One million people are added to the population every ten months and this threatens to wipe out any growth in the economy or improvements in social services.

Population pressure together with government attempts to expand the education system from 1952 onwards have bequeathed a serious problem of numbers on schools and universities. In 1951 just over one million pupils were enrolled in primary schools, a figure which increased fourfold by 1981 (Ministry of Education, 1981). One consequence of this is that number of places in schools has not kept pace with the rate of increase in the number of pupils so that in over half of the primary schools children are taught on a two shift system (Ministry of Education, 1979). Nor has it been possible to match the growth in pupil numbers with the supply of suitably qualified teachers. Almost one-fifth of primary school teachers are untrained. This figure rises to almost one-third in the case of preparatory school teachers and one-quarter of teachers in general secondary education (Ministry of Education, 1981).

In higher education the numbers problem assures different guises, some of which will be discussed in more detail later. They include critical shortages of staff, overcrowded lecture halls, very inefficient methods of teaching and learning and a generally low level of research. This latter problems serves, of course, to reinforce Egypt's reliance on research and development in science and technology from abroad thus emphasising the country's technological dependency. But perhaps of even greater significance is the way in which the rationing effects of examinations have had a distorting effect on the way students are distributed across subjects. Many students find themselves pursuing higher education in courses for which they have little interest.

Such problems will test severely the resources and the imagination of any government. But it cannot be stressed too heavily that numbers alone is not the problem. Large numbers of pupils needing education is a symptom of something else; of the failure, born of dependency, of the state itself to mobilise the resources of the country to achieve development. There are many countries with a larger population than Egypt which do not face the same kinds of educational problems. The numbers problem does add to the underlying structural weaknesses of the economy and to the difficulties which Egypt's educational planners face. The tragedy is, of course, that some of these problems are intractable. Without a profound change in dominant conceptions of what development must mean then there is little scope for any fundamental change in education. The basic reason is this: the structure and functioning of education is a consequence of the way in which different groups in society, possessing different amounts of power, have pressed their claims on educational resources to meet their own expectations. In this sense the real demand for education in Egypt, or any other society, does not follow directly the size of the population in the younger age groups. It reflects, rather, the significance which different groups attach to education and the choices they make about how they will use educational resources. To understand such expectations they have to be located in time against the experience and development of different social groups. The differences which exist, for example, between the educational aspirations of peasants and middle-class people from cities are rooted in the fact that the former have been denied education and the latter have achieved their social status because of it. Education therefore carries quite different meanings for both groups and they value it in different ways.

This point can be well illustrated by three issues which are symptomatic of the general crisis of Egyptian education. The first concerns the problem of drop-out rates. The second is the question of the meaning attached to secondary and higher education. The third concerns the question of technical education and its perceived inadequacies in the Egyptian case.

These interconnected issues reflect, as will be illustrated, the structure of class inequalities in Egyptian society. Egypt's educational system resembles that of many other Third World societies. Educational life chances are unequally distributed along lines of social class and sex and there are marked differences in opportunities between urban and rural areas.

The theoretical challenge presented to those who wish to explain this is to relate such patterns of distribution of educational life chances to the model of development which the state is pursuing against the resource constraints and the claims of different social groups on those resources which the state inherited from the past.

DROP-OUT RATES

The rate at which different age groups effectively terminate their educational careers is a good measure of the perceived utility of education. At the same time it is a figure which indicates the extent to which potentially valuable human capital is being wasted in a society. Finally, it is a figure which has to be read against the background of the general level of educational attainment in a society and the most important measure of that is the percentage of a population which is literate.

In Egypt the proportion of the population which is illiterate is decreasing, if slowly. In 1902, 90 per cent of the population was illiterate – some seven million people. By 1960 the proportion was reduced to 75 per cent, or twelve and a half million people. By the time of the last census, 1976, the figure had dropped to 56.5 per cent of fifteen million people (report of the Joint Egyptian–American Team, 1979, p. 78). The apparent paradox, therefore, is that while the proportion of illiterates over the age of ten years is decreasing their numbers are actually increasing.

The Egyptian government is aware of this problem and understands too, the connection between combatting illiteracy and improving the capacity of schools to retain pupils. The government recognises in addition that:

> illiteracy is not confined to the absence of reading and writing skills – a narrow concept still lingering in the minds of many people – but rather extends to a broader and comprehensive sense, namely, social and cultural unawareness, professional insensibility, and political and national unconsciousness. (Ministry of Education, 1980, p. 79).

The government is attempting to respond to this by improving the absorption ratio of the primary schools and providing various types of non-formal literacy training for adults. Government departments which employ a large number of illiterates are expected to set up literacy programmes. So, too, are trades unions and in the villages the government is seeking to develop a network of one class schools as agencies for community development.

The government also has given a lot of support for many years to a UNESCO-sponsored literacy training centre for the whole Arab world at Sirs-el-Layyan in the Delta. This institution, boycotted by the other Arab states following President Sadat's trip to Jerusalem, aims to link the training of literacy cadres to community development projects in villages (ASFEC, 1978; 1981). The framework within which it works, however, is one with a strong service delivery orientation aimed at improving the quality of literacy training, reducing the number of illiterates, improving the efficiency of schools and through these efforts, improving the quality of technical education throughout the Arab world and fostering a coherent Arab identity (ASFEC, 1981). Such a programme can be contrasted with an approach to illiteracy which is concerned with the development of a political consciousness among the poor and it part of a larger strategy of the political transformation of society (see, e.g. Friere, 1970; 1972; Galtung, 1981). The work of Friere, for example, is not taught at the Sir-el-Layyan centre because it is thought to be too left wing for the Arab world.

There is none the less, a clear connection in Egyptian education policy between fighting illiteracy and improving the capacity of schools to hold on to pupils and the hope here is that better educated pupils will become better workers and technicians and contribute to economic development. For these reasons the drop-out problem is perceived as being a very serious one, something which the government feels must be overcome if the basic education programme to which they attach so much importance is to have any hope of success. One of the ironies of the situation, however, is that if they were successful in overcoming the drop-out problem then, given the present level of resources applied to education, the system itself would not be able to cope with the numbers (Swanson *et al.*, 1981).

The problem is this: non-enrolment rates are estimated to be as high as 30 per cent of the eligible population and for some groups, for example, rural women, the figure might be as high as 60 per cent. Furthermore, it is yet another irony of Egyptian education that the drop-out rates for schools in urban areas is increasing while it is decreasing in rural areas. One study estimates that in 1974/5 for the age cohorts in school grades three to six, the proportion of drop-outs was 13.1 per cent in urban areas and 24.2 per cent in rural areas. By

1976/77 the figures were, respectively, 20.6 per cent and 22.4 per cent. Swanson, *et al.* (1981, p. 18) note:

> The uptrend in urban areas is disturbing and suggests that in these areas economic and social incentives to leave school may be increasing while, at the same time, schools are being forced to serve a rapidly increasing population.

To my knowledge there are no studies available which directly treat the problem of drop-out rates in terms of the social class backgrounds of pupils, but there is no doubt that there is a social class gradient to it. Children from middle-class backgrounds remain in school. For middle-class parents, the opportunity costs of not doing so are high indeed and they are prepared to spend a lot of money on private education or extra tuition to ensure their children gain access to university and find secure employment, which the state guarantees to all university graduates.

In contrast, drop-out rates in rural areas and among the urban poor are high. There is no simple, single-factor explanation of this. A study by the Egyptian National Centre for Educational Research grouped the explanatory factors into three main groups: economic factors, social factors and educational factors (Saad, 1980). Economic factors include the need in some families for the earnings of children and the high incidental costs, particularly for families with many children, of sending their children to school. The joint Egyptian and American team investigating basic education in the country makes a similar point but puts it into an historical frame (Joint Egyptian–American Team, 1979). Referring to the period of the 1950s and 1960s the authors note:

> A number of factors prevented the children from working class or peasant family backgrounds from receiving more than elementary levels of education. Parents found it expensive to send children to free schools. It required special dress, school supplies, tutorial fees, sacrificing the child's labour potential and a number of other costs that are perceived as significant only by people with very low incomes (Joint Egyptian–American Team, 1979, p. 49)

The social factors associated with high drop-out rates include the early marriage of girls in rural areas and a lack of awareness of what benefits might come from education. This is not to say, of course, that the rural poor do not value learning. There is some evidence, for instance, that in the very early stages of primary schooling children from rural areas have a lower drop-out rate than comparable groups in urban areas and the reason is connected with the importance of learning as a part of Islam. The Joint Egyptian–American team (1979, p. 43) noted, for example, that 'Children in villages still often give as a reason they want to be literate, that they want to understand Islam better.'

Among the poor in urban areas the most important calculation concerns the earning opportunities available to children. Andrea Rugh (1981) believes that this would explain a rather paradoxical result in her data on 228 households in the Bulaq district of Cairo, a poor quarter near the city centre. She noted that among some of the better-off families there was significant lowering in the participation rate of children. The major reason for this, she says, 'is that a number of these families either own small businesses or have contacts who can provide opportunities to learn well-paying skills (Rugh, 1981, p. 50).

Closer still to the patterns of family life, particularly among the poor, one writer has distinguished between 'aspiring' and 'divided' families – a distinction based upon whether the family's income is spent jointly on family requirements or determined almost entirely by the man – and claims to have found that in divided families mothers make a great effort to educate their children. In such cases mothers regard the possibility of a successful son or a well-married daughter as an insurance against the penuries of old age and a possibility of upwards social mobility, while fathers are likely to feel threatened by the success of a child for any success would merely reflect badly on the father's own failure. In aspiring families a significant proportion of the joint income of the family is allocated to education (Wikan, 1976).

Among some of the educational factors which Saad (1980, p. 73) associates with high drop-out rates are inefficient teaching, poor buildings and a poor distribution of schools.) A further Ministry of Education study in six schools in two villages in Sharqia and Dagahlia referred to by the Joint Egyptian–American team confirmed these observations:

> Teachers (over 70 per cent) do not live in an area near the school so they are often absent; school buildings and resources are not adequate: two shift crowded schools do not allow for activities that make schools attractive; the absence of an appropriate educational environment. (1979: 78).

Closer inspection of the relationship between background and drop-out rates thus reveals a need to conceive of this relationship dynamically as a series of choices families must make given their perceptions about what is valuable to the future lives of their children. It is hardly surprising that such perceptions will reflect directly the economic realities which parents face, and it is perhaps this which explains the apparent and recent increase in drop-out rates as more children seek relatively well-paid unskilled employment rather than plan for a career based on further schooling and technical training.

The overall outcome of such patterns of drop-out is that only between 32 per cent and 40 per cent of the age group are in preparatory and secondary education. Those who leave school, paradoxically, do not deteriorate in terms of their educational skills. Swanson *et al.* (1981, p. 20) cast a different light on the consequences of dropping out: 'The problem, in short, is not that the drop-out's skills are eroded once he or she leaves, but rather that the drop-out leaves school with little or no skill in reading, writing, or arithmetic.' For those who drop-out yet can read and write, it seems likely that the skills they have acquired will not develop further since literacy and numeracy are basic skills which improve with practice.

For the Egyptian government this is considered a serious problem because it means that the capacity of a significant number of people to receive further technical training is low. Illiteracy represents therefore one of the many brakes on economic and social development in Egypt (Ministry of Education, 1979). Necessarily, it is a phenomenon closely connected with the way in which secondary schools function for it determines the size of the group from which such schools can recruit their pupils.

THE SOCIAL MEANING OF SECONDARY AND FURTHER EDUCATION

Within the traditions of Islam, the man of learning has always had an honoured status in society and the Koran itself enjoins the faithful to seek knowledge. The educated man has always, therefore, been held in high regard. In modern Egyptian society education is still prized very highly, but not just in religious terms; it is valued for the status it can bring. The roots of this valuation extend deeply backwards into the modern history of Egypt.

The connection between educational certification and state employment has always been a strong one in Egypt. It was a connection which the Nasser regime strengthened as it sought to increase Egypt's output of trained personnel and to employ them in state enterprises. The state itself was instrumental in fuelling widespread popular expectations that education should lead to prestigious employment in the army, the professions, particularly medicine and engineering, and the civil service.

Two further points need to be stressed in this context. Despite the fact that state employment is not lucrative the demand for education which will lead to safe positions in the bureaucracy remains high. In fact, it is probably the case that the demand for education in Egypt far outstrips the capacity of the economy or the education system ever to meet it. A Joint Egyptian–American research team looking into the problems of basic education in Egypt noted, for example:

> Parental aspirations are naturally high for their children, especially in the early stages of education before the child's capabilities have been tested. Groups of elementary school parents in various parts of Egypt reported most frequently that they wanted their children to become doctors and engineers, both high status careers requiring high scholarship attainment.
> (Joint Egyptian–American Team, 1979, p. 6)

Because of this parents often react conservatively to any proposals to change education. Such expectations represent political constraints on what the government can hope to achieve in its reforms of school and university education in Egypt.

A second issue, and a further limit on the possibilities of real change, involves migration. Education is valued in Egypt not simply because it can lead, and has led since 1964, to guaranteed employment in the state bureaucracies. It is something that can lead to much better earning opportunities abroad, which has some very important implications for the way in which patterns of demand for education should be explained. One central feature of an underdeveloped society is its inability to create real and lasting employment opportunities. It is not necessarily the case, however, that expectations about work and employment in a society will be focused on just what that society, itself can offer. The Egyptian case points to the need to widen our conception of the labour market in which people feel they will seek work.

Since the early 1960s and in response to growing problems of graduate unemployment, the Egyptian government has had an active policy of encouraging labour migration abroad, particularly to the oil rich (but labour hungry) economies of the Gulf and Libya. The earnings of expatriate workers represents a substantial contribution to Egypt's foreign exchange earnings (Messiha, 1980). Official estimates put the number of Egyptians working abroad at 600 000, i.e. approximately 5 per cent of the labour force. Saudi Arabia and Libya are the most important recipients of Egyptian labour. A sample survey of 34 614 migrants conducted in 1975 showed 38.58 per cent to be working in Libya and 30.6 per cent in Saudi Arabia (Birks and Sinclair, 1978, p. 61). Furthermore, the survey revealed that a very high proportion of the migrants were very highly trained. Approximately two-thirds of them possessed secondary education certificates or higher qualification and only about 6 per cent of them were without any qualifications. A quarter of them had passed technical education certificates, a figure which can be regarded as serious for the Egyptian economy given its desperate shortage of skilled and technically trained workers. In the short run, however, it may be that external migration is positively beneficial in that it absorbs unemployment and earns foreign exchange.

Labour migration is a facet of Egypt's changing relationship to the international economy and is something which feeds back into the structure of educational opportunity and patterns of social differentiation, particularly in the countryside. The mechanism is one which drains male labour from the countryside leaving women and children to cultivate the land. This might explain why children in rural areas are much more likely than their urban counterparts to drop-out from school early.

Two facets of this deserve more attention. One concerns the effects of *Infitah* and labour migration on patterns of social inequality Nicholas Hopkins (1981), for instance, has suggested that both policies adversely affect the rural poor who ultimately bear the costs of them. *Infitah* fuels consumer imports with adverse consequences for the balance of payments and the accompanying policies of farm mechanisation tend to improve the position of richer peasants as against poorer ones.

The second issue concerns the educational life chances of women. Women in Egypt have undoubtedly benefited from the expansion of educational opportunities that took place after 1952 and have been able to capitalise on a revolutionary rhetoric which since the revolution has claimed an equal place for women in Egyptian society. Nevertheless, the enrolment of eligible females in primary schools is not much more than 50 per cent compared to 80 per cent in the case of boys (Waterbury, 1983, p. 220) and there is a marked difference in the opportunities of urban and rural women. In many rural areas the education of girls, for reasons which would have to be traced back to the male-dominated cultural traditions of the society, is not taken seriously. The problem of restricted opportunities for women is, of course, related to their class position (Howard-Merriam, 1979). Middle-class women in urban areas have established themselves in the student body and have made headway in the professions. Their rural counterparts have been much less successful, although the evidence is that if women avoid dropping-out in the very early stages of their education they have a good chance of following through to higher levels of educational attainment than boys from the same background.

It is government policy to improve further the educational life chances of women, especially in the rural areas, since there is evidence that there is a strong correlation between womens' education and fertility. Those with the least education have the most children. Those with better education have fewer children, understand health care and hygiene better and provide better role models for their own children (Joint Egyptian–American Team, 1979, p. 46).

It remains true, though, that the lives of women are still circumscribed by traditional constraints in which the men of the family exert a powerful control over them and in the period since 1974 there is growing evidence of a reassertion of Islamic values among women, particularly the educated. More young people have taken to wearing the *hegab*, the garment which covers the hair but not the face. Most political commentators on Egypt attribute this to a stirring of opposition to the secularising and Westernising tendencies of the Sadat–Mubarak period. At the same time, however, distinctly feminist ideas have attracted a great deal of attention for some groups of Egyptian women (see El Saadawi, 1980). The only safe generalisation to be made is by comparison with Egyptian men; women still have poorer educational life chances and for women in rural areas life is an arduous round of hard agricultural and domestic labour. None of this is attributable to Islam; a fuller examination of the status of Egyptian women (and women elsewhere in the Middle East) would relate the discrimination they experience to class differentiation, patriarchy and to strategies of dependent modernisation which limit their economic and political participation (see Beck and Keddie, 1978).

TECHNICAL EDUCATION IN EGYPT

It has been Egyptian policy to expand the number of students enrolled in technical training. By 1978–9 the numbers admitted to technical education exceeded those of general secondary education, the ratio being 57 per cent to 43 per cent, and the aim of government policy is to increase the ratio to 60:40 (Ministry of Education, 1979). Technical education takes place in two broad types of school, the three-year technical school for skilled workers and the five-year school for technicians. In addition, government departments run training schools and centres of their own. The Ministry of Reconstruction, for example, has a training organisation which operates sixty-two different training centres and the Ministry of Education operates in the fields of commercial and technical training through the higher institutes (Ward, 1979). Clearly, too, the universities are involved in technical training in that they prepare specialists in science and engineering and medicine and make their contribution to the formation of Egypt's stock of training technical and scientific human resources.

The system of technical training must be seen from three points of view. First, there is the question of its effectiveness. How well does it prepare people? Does it meet the demand for labour which exists in the economy? Secondly, what role is technical education playing against the background of changes in the international division of labour in the Middle East? In effect, what role is emerging for the Egyptian economy in the context of changes in the economies of the Middle East as a whole? The issue at stake is whether Egypt is being prepared as a labour reserve economy for the oil states and whether the technical training which is taking place is in the long-term interests of Egypt or the shorter-term interests of the foreign firms which have invested in Egypt in the past few years and might do so on a greater scale in the future if the right kinds of labour conditions existed. This, essentially, is a question of the model of development which the Egyptian government is pursuing.

Finally, the system has to be examined in respect of its contribution to reducing the dependence of the country on foreign expertise and on imported science and technology. Is the system geared to furthering the development in Egypt of an autonomous research and development system which will contribute to industrial growth and development?

On the question of effectiveness there seems to be unanimous agreement that the system is very poor. During the current educational plan the government is seeking to increase its expenditure on technical training. The aim, as described in the World Bank (1980) report is to achieve 'a major expansion in the supply of suitably trained industrial construction and agricultural managers; commercial, agricultural and industrial technicians; better trained farmers; and skilled and semi-skilled workers.' This report calculated that despite the expansion in the system envisaged there will still be serious shortfalls in certain areas. This is indicated in Table 7.1. What this table shows is a considerable shortfall in skilled workers in construction and other skilled trades but an over production of people trained for commerce. The distribution of students across the three main types of secondary technical school, in 1979, for example, is shown in Table 7.2.

There is a tragic irony here, agriculture is the mainstay of the Egyptian economy providing employment for about 50 per cent of the labour force. Its contribution to the gross national product is approximately 30 per cent and agricultural exports account for nearly fifty per cent of all exports (UNDP, 1981). Despite this, agricultural enrolments in secondary technical schools are very small. The reason for this is not difficult to find. Philip Foster (1965) pointed out some time ago that vocational education will always be the poor sister of mainstream academic education so long as its graduates faced employment carrying poor remuneration and lower status than their counterparts who seek and find work in urban centres and particularly in state bureaucracies and in the modern sector. Egypt is no exception to this. Expectations about employment and earnings have come to be fixed on work in urban areas in the modern sector of the economy. It is this which has fuelled both the massive urban migration which Egyptian cities have had to cope with and also the migration of Egyptian workers to other Arab states.

The quality of technical education is another issue. It has been criticised for the way in which it tends to separate theoretical and practical training and reinforces a demarcation between classrooms and workshops (Ward, 1979) and it is widely acknowledged to be poorly equipped and housed (World Bank, 1980). A team for the

Table 7.1 Estimated human resource requirements and shortfalls, 1976–87

	Annual output	Shortfall 1987
Technicians		
Industrial	13 500	5 600
Commercial	11 400	+ 200
Skilled and semi-skilled	29 700	11 400
Construction	71 700	2 700

Source: Adapted from Staff Appraisal Report: Third Education Project, *Arab Republic of Egypt*, Report no. 3096–EGT, p. 6 (World Bank, 1980).

Table 7.2 Enrolment in technical secondary schools in Egypt (by sex and type of school), 1978/9

	Total number	% female	% male	% total
Commercial secondary schools	312 000	53	47	63
Agricultural secondary schools	50 000	10	90	10
Industrial secondary schools	131 000	11	89	27

Source: Adapted from Ministry of Education, National Centre for Educational Research. *Working Paper on Developing and Innovating Education in Egypt*, 1979, p. 27.

International Labour Office found that class sizes in technical schools were much too high for effective teaching to take place and since technical schools have to recruit their teachers from the graduates of the five-year technical schools, the quality of the instructors themselves leaves much to be desired (Hansen and Radwan, 1982).

Such men have simply not had sufficient experience of industry to be effective instructors. The implication is that Egypt remains dependent in critical areas on the importation of foreign personnel. Paul Shaw (1981, p. 637) refers to one case in 1978 which illustrates this dramatically; to ensure the completion of construction contracts, German and Swiss crane drivers had to be imported commanding salaries thirty times greater than those of their Egyptian counterparts.

Improved technical education is seen by many of the aid agencies as a step towards solving such problems. The World Bank (1980) has loaned Egypt over 100 million dollars to establish skill training centres and in its current requests to UNDP the Egyptian government has requested over four million dollars worth of aid to train technical teachers.

A parallel strategy to shift the balance of Egyptian education towards a more practical and technical curriculum is the government's basic education policy. It, too, is in receipt of United States aid although on a small scale. By 1982, the United States had undertaken to finance 6000 classrooms providing them with basic educational kits including things like maps, carpentry equipment, simple scientific aids (Brown, 1982). The rationale, worked out by the Joint Egyptian-American team on basic education is that 'Those not wishing or able to continue their education should be prepared to be good citizens, should have good general education, and be prepared to enter the job market with some saleable skills, (Joint Egyptian–American Team, 1979, p. 5). The aim is to overcome the academic bias in Egyptian education but it is a recognition, too, of the fact that a very large number of children do not go on beyond the preparatory stage so that what is offered to them has to prepare them for a productive working life. The schools selected for the basic education programme are in rural areas and sited where possible to serve the most deprived and poor communities (Ministry of Education, 1979). Despite the gloss put on this policy that it should enable children to proceed further in education it is clear that it is intended primarily for the poor. Whether the policy will work is another matter. There is no historical precedent in Egypt to be confident that it will; even in rural areas expectations for an academic education are high and politically significant. Without a fundamental change in the structure of opportunity for a better standard of life in rural Egypt the basic education programme, with its strong emphasis on work-related relevant curricula, is almost certain to be limited in its achievements.

CONCLUSION

Egypt is a society in which education matters. The state is clearly concerned to mobilise its educational resources to support its policies for economic growth and development and there is clearly a high demand for a formal and modern education from all groups in Egyptian society. These two things cannot easily be reconciled and neither can be seen apart from the changing economic and political alignments of the Middle East. The direction in which Egypt has developed under Sadat and Mubarak, i.e. a pro-Western one with strong United States ties and with economic policies designed to liberalise the economy and reduce subsidies, is one which is generating severe social inequalities in Egyptian society. David Rockefeller of the Chase Manhattan Bank may have been correct in his assessment in 1974 that 'Egypt has come to realise that socialism and extreme Arab nationalism . . . have not helped the lot of the 37 million people they have in Egypt' (quoted Abdel-Khalek, 1981, p. 407). But it is by no means clear that, in the light of what has happened since, that Rockefeller's conclusions about what should be done to help them would be accepted. What he said was that 'if President Sadat wants to help them, he has got to look for private enterprise and assistance . . . I have discussed this to a considerable extent with some of the Israeli leaders, and they agree with us' (quoted Abdel-Khalek, 1981, p. 407). During the period since these observations were made Egypt has received massive injections of United States aid, but the expected foreign investment to create jobs has not materialised as expected. The country's economic problems have been exacerbated by the boycotts it suffered by the Arab states critical of the Camp David accords.

Unable to overcome some of the country's massive economic problems and unable to legitimate its actions within a coherent and supported ideological framework, it is hardly surprising that divisions have opened up in Egyptian society and political life and that, in some of the ways sketched out above, they have entered the educational system directly. The analytical point to stress is this; there is no practical solution to problems of the educational system outside a solution to the changing structures of Egypt's status as a dependent society.

8 Education and Society in Modern Turkey

Education is a subtle and sensitive indicator of the political and ideological differences of any modern society. These differences are traceable through the development of education, its funding and control and, of course, the values incorporated into what is taught. The structure of educational opportunities which a society sustains is both a reflection and determinant of much wider patterns of social inequality and cultural diversity which exist within it. In many societies these linkages between education and social structures are not obvious. In Turkey, however, during the 1970s, they were all too clear, for the violence which erupted throughout the society bringing it close to the point of civil war was particularly acute in the education system. The social inequalities and ideological polarities of the society have always been precisely outlined in its system of education.

The government of General Kenan Evren following the military coup of September 1980 has put a stop during the past four years to the killings which were taking place in schools and universities and on the streets of Turkish towns. But the root causes of that violence stretch deeply back into the fabric of Turkish society itself. It is the aim of this chapter to show how the logic of Turkey's underdevelopment explains much of the structure and functioning of education in that society. The problems of education to be discussed, however, cannot simply be read off from economic and social consequences of underdevelopment. They have instead to be set against and traced carefully through social and cultural patterns of the society, to its political divisions and how different political groupings have seen fit to act. Finally, they have to be seen in the light of how Turkish domestic policies have been influenced and constrained by the political and economic role the country plays on the European periphery and how role has changed.

THE EDUCATIONAL SYSTEM

The educational system of modern Turkey is a highly centralised one organised by the Ministry of Education in Ankara. It is largely a public system of education in that private schools cater for only about 2 per cent of pupils in middle schools and less than 4 per cent in the prestigious secondary schools, the lise (Oğuzkan, 1981). It is a system which caters for nearly six million pupils at primary school level, two million at junior high schools, half a million in high schools, a further half million in vocational and technical schools and about 300 000 students in higher education (Statistical Yearbook

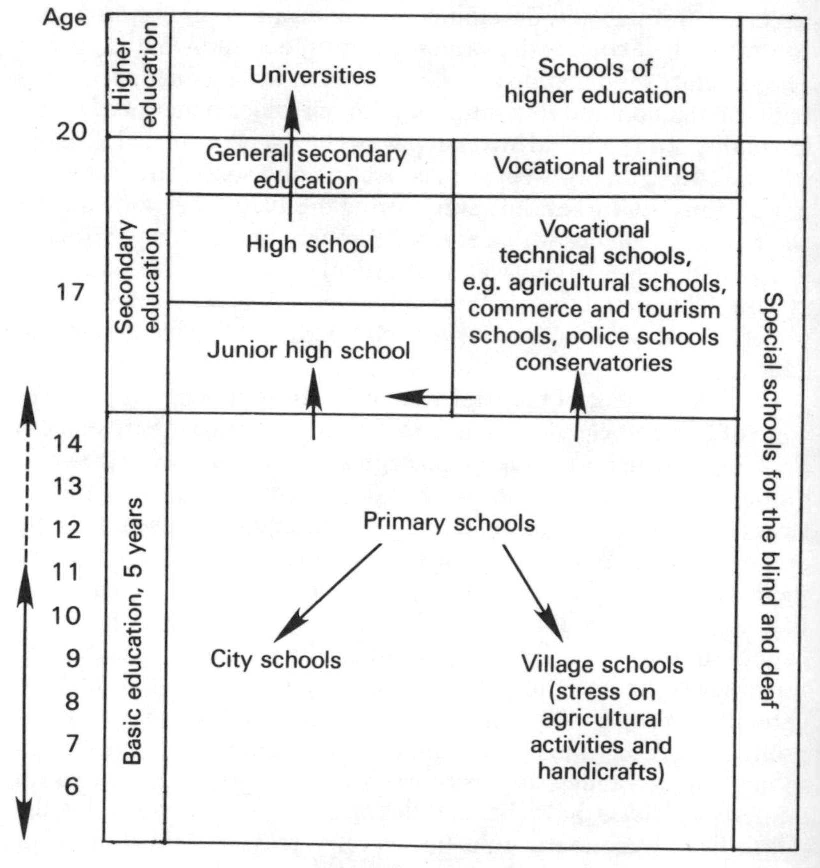

Figure 8.1 The Turkish education system 1981

of Turkey, 1981, p. 102). The structure of the system is represented in Figure 8.1. The rate of growth of enrolments in the various educational institutions since the period after the Second World War is shown in Table 8.1. What the table indicates is very rapid expan-

Table 8.1 Enrolment in different schools and higher education in Turkey

	Primary	Junior high	Lise	Vocational & technical	University & others
1950	100 (1 591 000)	100 (65 000)	100 (21 000)	100 (56 000)	100 (25 000)
1955	117.3	172.3	166.6	116.0	112
1960	158.0	392.3	295.2	175.0	216
1965	236.8	544.6	466.6	291.0	336
1970	303.6	1078.4	1023.8	387.5	588
1975	338.1	1455.3	1614.2	558.2	1048
1980	353.3 (5 622 000)	1813.8 (1 180 000)	2533.3 (532 000)	919.6 (515 000)	1080 (270 000)

Note: Figures in brackets = total numbers.
Source: Adapted from Table 89, *Statistical Yearbook of Turkey* (Ankara: State Institute of Statistics, 1981).

sion in Turkish education particulary in the number of enrolments in the academic secondary schools. What will be indicated a little later, however, is that despite the rapidity of growth in education, Turkish society itself has, in a real sense, changed much faster than the educational system could ever hope to cope with.

Additionally, since Turkish education is heavily centralised and operates rather rigidly in terms of its bureaucratic procedures, it is a set of institutions which are inherently resistant to change. Change is, however, countenanced and under discussion. During the 1970s two National Councils of Education were convened to consider ways of changing secondary education and some of the views expressed by them were formulated into legal changes in 1973 specifying more clearly than before the principles and organisations of different educational institutions and these legal changes have been incorporated into recent development plans for the economy as a whole.

A well-known Turkish educator and member of the National Education Council, Turhan Oğuzkan (1981) has listed some of the problems which are felt, at least officially, to beset Turkish education.

> The established school system has been under criticism . . . Some of the outstanding areas of concern include lack of opportunity for large segments of population beyond the five year primary school; implementation of uniform curricula regardless of individual or local needs; inadequate articulation between school offerings and the work life; little professional help for vocational choice and career planning; excessive enrolments in academic lycees, and mounting pressure for entrance to the universities and to other institutions of higher learning. (Oğuzkan, 1981, p. 80)

The catalogue of problems could be extended. There is, for example, still a high level of illiteracy in Turkey, about 38 per cent for men and 52 per cent for women. Among the younger age groups it is, of course, much lower at about 18 per cent for those aged between eleven years and twenty-one years (National Census, 1976; see also Hale, 1978). This has implications not only for the way people can or have participated in formal education but also for the ability of the government to mobilise peasants and workers to adopt new methods of production and for the ability of people to participate effectively in politics. Further problems include the quality of teachers and their commitment to working in rural areas and styles of learning in Turkish education with their heavy emphasis on memory and memorisation.

The problems which the system faced in the 1970s have not been solved; their worst manifestations have been controlled but the system of education is still in a state of crisis and one made even more serious by the economic problems of Turkey, problems of inflation and high energy costs, of foreign debt and a poor balance of payments position. It is a crisis which is not eased by the demographic fact that, like many underdeveloped countries, Turkey has a very young population; approximately 40 per cent of the population is under the age of fifteen years and nearly a full third are under the age of twelve, the legal minimum age for leaving school (Hale, 1978).

The military government has taken a firm grip on the system, particularly the universities where the new Higher Education Council has effected and is currently carrying through a veritable purge of academic staff and is opening up new universities to cope with the massive demand which exists for higher education (see Chapter 11). Policy is less clear at the secondary and primary levels. The 10th National Education Conference laid stress on the need to expand basic education in Turkey and integrate the primary and middle schools under one concept of basic education. There are plans to improve on technical and vocational education and to develop strategies of non-formal education and reduce illiteracy. It is impossible at this stage, however, to be clear about what precisely is happening since both the society and the educational system have been in considerable turmoil.

What is clear, though, is that the new government is determined to strengthen what it takes to be the principles of Atatürk at every level in the system. At a press conference in June 1982 the Prime Minister put it this way: The aim of national education was

> To educate our children and youth in primary, secondary and higher educational institutions with all the benefits of contemporary science and in full realisation of [the fact] that Atatürk's nationalism is the basic philosophy of our national educational policy. (*Daily News*, 28 June, 1982, p. 5)

As a small step towards this end the Prime Minister announced increases in the salaries of teachers to improve their status and strengthen their support for the broad principles of the educational philosophy.

Whether the government will have any success with these policies is impossible to tell. Much depends upon how the different claims of different social groups in Turkish society are actually resolved and in how imaginatively educational policies can adjust to tackle the serious problems of the system.

Four issues illustrate well the magnitude of this task. A discussion of them not only reveals what underdevelopment means in the Turkish case but simultaneously the political and economic and cultural constraints which must be overcome and accommodated if education in Turkey is to play a much more positive role in the development of the country. The issues are: (1) inequality, (2) urban and rural differences in educational provision and attainment, (3) the relationship between the educational system and the labour market and finally (4) the issue of political socialisation and the curriculum.

SOCIAL INEQUALITY IN TURKISH EDUCATION

In previous chapters the structure of social inequality in both Ottoman Turkey of the nineteenth century and republican Turkey has been described. In essence the discussion showed that, in contrast to Western capitalist society, the Ottoman Empire was a social formation which lacked a strong entrepreneurial bourgeousie which possessed political power. During the course of the second half of the nineteenth century reforms encouraged the growth of a bureaucratic class distinct from the Sultan and religious leaders whose power and status depended largely on their education.

During the republic period this class, together with the military had come to constitute a 'guardian bureaucracy' dominating the political system and projecting the Kemalist ideology of secularism, populism and *étatism.* Economic underdevelopment and the exchange of populations left republican Turkey with a large population of peasants, a small industrial working class and an almost insignificant class of industrialists or capitalists.

After the Second World War, however, structural changes in the economy together with political changes in electoral law allowing the formation of political parties, led to the development of new social groups distinct in their outlook and ambitions from the Kemalist elites who dominated the political system. These included industrialists, large farmers, merchants who supported the Democratic Party. The growth of the liberal professions and white-collar workers gave definition to a small but new middle class and economic growth and urban migration fuelled the growth of an urban proletariat. The social, historical and politico-economic processes behind these shifts are the themes of a different study, but it is vital to appreciate such changes since it is against this background that data about social inequality in educational opportunity must be interpreted.

It is not sufficient to think of the relative life chances of different social groups as being contingent upon the social or cultural characteristics of different groups themselves. It is important, too, to examine the relationship between different groups to see in what way struggles in 'cultural markets', e.g. for status, honour and, in this case, for education, both reflect and shape the class chances of different groups of people (see Collins, 1977). Patterns of social stratification always reflect the structure of economic life of a society although the relationship is never direct and the subtleties of social hierarchies can never be read off from descriptions of the occupational division of labour.

In Turkey the largest field of employment is in the agricultural sector of the economy. Agriculture contributes about 20 per cent of the gross national product (manufacturing 16 per cent, commerce 13 per cent) but accounts for about 62 per cent of the labour force. In this respect Turkey's economy displays a dualism, a contrast between the agricultural and industrial sector, which is untypical of the more developed economies of Western Europe (Dervis and Robinson, 1980).

The differences between these two major sectors of the economy explains much of the social inequality of Turkish society where, on the whole, people employed in industry and living in urban areas are better off than those in agriculture, particularly in the East and South East of the country. A recent study of income distribution in Turkey based at Hacettepe university in Ankara and based on a State Planning Organisation population survey classified the Turkish population into eleven socioeconomic groups (Dervis and Robinson, 1980).

These groups, however, can be recombined into a smaller number of distinctive social categories. In the urban areas they distinguish the capitalist urban elite, government employees, the urban working classes and the urban traditional sector. Each group occupies a different position with respect to the market for income in Turkey. Capitalists derive their income from the ownership of property and shares while government employees and urban workers are dependent almost entirely on wages and salaries for their incomes. The 1973 data on income distribution indicates a high degree of income inequality with some interesting differences among urban white-collar groups. Independent professionals earn considerably more than government employees. Dervis and Robinson (1980, p. 102) speculate that the relatively low mean income of this latter group might explain 'the relatively left-of-center orientation of the urban middle class'. It might also be the case that this structure of income distribution is what lies behind the very high (and unmet) demand from such groups for university places in Turkey.

Among the rural groups in this survey a distinction is drawn between farmers and rural labourers, the latter forming a very small part of the farm population. Dervis and Robinson (1980, p. 105) note that 'Turkish agriculture is characterised more by small farmers and small cultivators than by large masses of totally landless labour. Of course there are are also very large landowners – capitalist and market oriented in some regions, still feudal in other regions.' These divisions matter since they lie behind the migration of people from rural to urban areas to seek a better life and they explain much of the particular cultural and religious attitudes towards education in the Turkish countryside and through these, the urban-rural, male-female patterns of differentiation in education.

Industrialisation and urbanisation have accelerated and there has been a massive migration from the countryside into the cities. Turkish cities have been 'peasantised' (Mardin, 1978; Karpat, 1976) and the growth of shanty town areas (*gecekondu*) on the periphery of the major cities is a major feature of urban social structure in Turkey with profound implications for many aspects of social planning.

How best to provide shanty towns with amenities such as piped water, transport, electricity and sewers is a serious problem in Turkey. The same difficulties arise about schools and health care and law enforcement. (Karpat, 1976). But the point for the moment is that the categories of workers described earlier will include people who live in *gecekondu* areas as well as those who have for generations been city dwellers. Similarly, it will include people whose social and cultural roots, religious orientation and, for the purposes of this chapter, attitudes about education are still firmly part of a rural past.

Surveying the structure of educational opportunity in Turkey in 1966, Kazamias used the metaphor of the 'minaret pattern' to describe it (Kazamias, 1966). This was a reference to the way in which the proportion of the population enrolled in school at the different levels of education declines dramatically at the higher levels of the system. This pattern still persists and can be seen in Table 8.2, which draws together the results of the studies by Kazamias (1966) and Hale (1978). The table does not indicate directly the relationship between social class and educational opportunity but it does show how the higher levels of education cater for only a relatively small proportion of the population in the relevant age group. Table 8.3 illustrates the strong link between education and occupation, a further way of looking at social inequality.

Another way of reading such data is to see it as measuring wastage in education. Something like 50 per cent of primary-school graduates leave the system altogether and do not proceed into middle school.

Table 8.2 Minaret pattern of enrolment (percentage of age group by school type)

	1961–62	1975–76	
		Upper limit	Lower limit
Primary school	54	98.8	82.6
Academic middle school	14.7	30.8	22.6
Vocational middle school	2.3	1.3	1.0
Academic high school	4.8	10.8	8.1
Normal school or vocational	3.0	10.2	7.6
Higher education	1.0	7.8	6.4

Source: Adapted from Kazamias (1966) and Hale (1978).

Once people are in the system they tend to complete the secondary school course but over 60 per cent of secondary school graduates leave the system. Turhan Oğuzkan (1981, p. 87) has summarised the problem this way:

> Among the several possible reasons behind these two important breaks in the student flow in the Turkish educational system, the most common reason for low entrance to middle school seems to be the lack of access to school facilities in many places, especially in rural areas, while the break at higher educational level is due mainly to the lack of capacity for greater student intake on the part of higher educational institutions.

Such data point to a field of interlocked influences shaping the careers of Turkish pupils; children in urban areas have better life chances than those in rural areas. Children of the urban administrative and professional elites have educational life chances far superior to those of people from a worker or peasant background (Kazamias, 1966; Özgediz, 1980). In addition, something not highlighted so far, the educational life chances of males are much greater than those of females (see Abadan-Unat, 1981). This is a reflection of both

Table 8.3 Occupation at completed education, Turkey 1980

	%				
Occupational group	Primary school	Junior high school	Vocational high school	Lise	Higher education
Scientific, Technical and related workers	12.5	4.3	33.3	55.2	41.1
Administrative and managerial workers	29.5	8.9	6.4	10.8	37.4
Clerical and sales workers	43.7	12.7	6.5	9.4	6.8
Agricultural workers including forestry and fishing	42.2	1.6	0.2	0.6	0.07
Production and related workers including transport	70.7	6.5	2.2	2.2	0.3

Note: Figures are percentages of numbers in each group who have at 1980 completed the given level of education.

Source: Adapted from Table 9, *Social and Economic Characteristics of Population 1% Sample Results* (Ankara: State Institute of Statistics, 1980).

traditional values concerning the position of women in Turkish society and of the division of labour itself. Özbay (1978) has noted, for instance, that the great majority of women active in the labour force work on the land. In/urban areas approximately 10 per cent of uneducated women are in active employment compared to 28 per cent among educated women.

Relevant to the discussion of social inequality but not directly measurable by data on educational and occupational life chances is the question of the cultural meanings attached to education and the kinds of social values and ways of thinking incorporated into the curriculum (formal and 'hidden') of Turkish schools. In a society which has changed as rapidly as Turkey and in which the opportunities for employment of one generation are markedly different from those available to older generations, it is hardly surprising that discontinuities emerge between generations, classes and regions of the country in attitudes and outlook (Mardin, 1978).

In the Ottoman period the division between the educated and uneducated was clear; it was reinforced by the division of labour and the political system and it was overlaid by differences of culture, language, religion and life style. Between the political elite and the peasantry of a far-flung empire there were few intermediary groups. Republican Turkey therefore faced the problem of building up a national consciousness from the peripheral consciousness of peasants, i.e. people whose social and political outlook was part of a traditional world view in which the values of social equity, science and even nation held little sway. It was a society in which the social distance between office holder and peasant was vast.

Spectacular social mobility – was Şerif Mardin (1969) once called the 'Aladdin's Lamp Effect' – was possible in this society as previous chapters have explained, but neither the *Tanzimat* reforms of the nineteenth century or the cultural revolution of the early republican period erased the subtly woven ties between the cultural traditions of the elite and Turkish education in a way which would have overcome the cultural divisions of Turkish society. Elite culture in Turkey remains distinct from folk cultural traditions; 'elitism', argued Mardin (1969) remains 'the prevailing world view of the educated.' In their language, secularism, fashion and life style, the educated of Turkish society, particularly those with a higher education, are sharply distinguishable from their compatriots in the rural areas and in the lower socioeconomic groups of the cities. Such differentiation implies ascending levels of cultural and social exclusivity in the society and the very limited data on social mobility in Turkey confirms high levels of occupational self recruitment among the liberal professions and, at the other end of the social scale, farmers (Aral, 1980).

URBAN-RURAL DIFFERENCES

The social inequalities of Turkish education are a reflection, too, of the spatial inequalities of the society particularly the differences which exist between the urban centres and the rural villages of

Anatolia. Cities and villages give the appearance of being in two different worlds though economically they are, of course, completely integrated. In discussing the rural areas it is vital to remember the Ottoman neglect of them and the limited achievements of the pre-war republican regime in modernising them. Indeed, it was only during the multi-party era after the Second World War that the rural areas experienced the pressures of rapid modernisation. Competition for peasant votes, the development of the transport network, agricultural mechanisation and a population increase which prompted urban migration were among the key catalysts of rural change.

As late as 1970, 60 per cent of the population still lived in localities classified as villages (Weiker, 1981) and most villages were by this time provided with schools, health-care facilities and transport. Difficulties still remain, however, in each of these areas and many villages have problems with basic facilities, such as water supply. Nevertheless, as Weiker (1981, p. 54) has emphasised 'Turkish villagers are now to a significant degree materially integrated into the mainstream of the nation.' This integration has been a source of profound social change.

Modernisation of the countryside both economically and culturally had been a major goal of republican Turkey, but one which met with many difficulties both of resources and political support. After the Second World War an increase in cash cropping and agricultural mechanisation brought many changes to village life, particularly new forms of rural social stratification. Deniz Kandiyoti (1975, p. 201) summed some of the changes up in this way: 'There was a general shift in land tenure and share-cropping practices leading to an increase of seasonal wage labour, to underemployment due to mechanisation and consequent rural-urban migration.' The implications of urbanisation will be discussed shortly. The point to be stressed here concerns rural differentiation and variation within rural Turkey for rural areas have been affected in different ways by these changes.

In a survey carried out by the Institute of Population Studies at Hacettepe University, Özbay (1978) identified four different types of rural social structure in Turkey, each with different implications for labour force participation, education and the position of women. First, there are areas of large enterprises, mechanisation and the employment of wage workers. Secondly, there are the areas with very small land holdings and finally, areas of landless wage labourers. Özbay's main point was to show that, where family labour was required, particularly that of women, then educational opportunities of women were restricted. The implication is that they are better off in the more modernised villages but this must be qualified; such opportunities can often only be grasped through migration to the towns and cities. The root problem is the inadequate provision of schools in rural areas. The Hacettepe survey of thirty villages revealed, for example, that 46 per cent of the population over the age of twelve was illiterate and that 63 per cent had not graduated from the primary school. The survey revealed inadequate facilities and poor teaching:

> Primary school teachers in Turkey receive 11–12 years of education including five years of primary education. By European standards this is the lowest number of years for the training of teachers. Also Turkish teachers are the youngest in the continent, they become teachers at the age of 17 or 18 . . . teachers in the villages are younger and more inexperienced both in teaching and in public relations than the city teachers. (Özbay and Balemir, 1978, p. 40)

Further studies from the larger research project point to a high demand for education in Turkish villages but one which varies considerably according to family income, land-holding and school facilities. The general theme of the study (based on a survey of 1470 men and 1254 women in twenty-three villages) was that the higher the level of educational services, the higher the level of attainment which was achieved. Nevertheless, attainments were generally poor. Only 17 per cent of the boys went on to further education and only 3 per cent of the women. The author of this study noted that 'The boys enjoy the priority of being sent to school at the cost of the girls' (Balemir, 1981, p. 56).

This is not just a facet of how gender roles are perceived. It is also connected with the village economy and debt levels. Where debt repayments are high through usury or through people extracting high bride prices, then communal contributions to educational facilities tend to be low.

The conclusion reached in this research about the position of women is entirely consistent with other work on villages. Joyce Roper's (1974) study of Nar, for instance, a village in Anatolia, provides vivid illustration of the tenacity of traditional attitudes as these bear on the educational life chances of women. She observed, for instance, that from the time of the announcement of an engagement, a girl is expected to veil herself in the street. Roper notes that women in Nar work hard in the fields and are intensely proud when they give birth to sons. Although there were some women from Nar who had reached higher education – one woman studied biology at university, another became assistant head of the village school, another studied at a craft school – there were yet others for whom there remained terrible obstacles. The father of one girl, on hearing from the school secretary that his daughter had been talking to a boy, threatened her with a gun and the termination of her schooling. For him it was a matter of protecting the honour of the family.

The persistence of such traditions rooted in semi-feudal villages and peasant religion has other implications for education. For this peripheral social structure inhibits the full spread of modern ideas throughout the country. One researcher reporting the results of research into four villages in both central and eastern Anatolia noted that:

> The school and its teacher are not a natural and integrated part of the village community. School's activities do not cover the whole community. Though in recent years peasants appreciate more the value of literacy . . . they send their children – their daughters in particular – to school primarily because it is a legal obligation. (Ozankaya, 1973, p. 621)

Ozankaya noted further that peasants were more prepared to pay money for their children to attend Koran classes and were unwilling to help finance government schools. Many villagers believed that schools teach 'infidelity and immorality' and that those in particular who attend higher learning institutions 'become sheer atheists and communists' (Ozankaya, 1973, p. 623).

Something of this response is perhaps explained by the kind of contact villagers may have had with the teachers sent to teach their children. Practically all teachers beyond the primary school level in rural areas are outsiders, graduates from universities and teacher colleges in the large cities. In his study of Susurluk, a Western Anatolian small town, Paul Magnarella observed in 1969 that secondary school teachers often feel very hostile to the views of the villagers. He quoted the views of the local president of TÖS, the Turkish teachers union that, 'Religious leaders have been the brake on Turkey's progress. Religion has been used to exploit the people materially and mentally' (Magnarella, 1974, p. 153). He noted further that in their social life teachers in this small town remained aloof from the townspeople, although this was not the case with primary school teachers, the group who are less well trained and who are more likely to come from the province in which they work.

Magnarella's inquiries led him to conclude that townspeople did value modern education and that they had high aspirations for their children hoping they would attain a university degree. But they hope that education will reflect, too, religious and moral traditions and be within the ethical framework of Islam. For this reason many townspeople regarded teachers as 'itinerant invaders with offensive ideologies' (Magnarella, 1974, p. 159). Interestingly, however, Magnarella reports that they compare the modern teachers unfavourably with those from the republican era who participated much more fully in the life of the community.

Religion remains a very potent force in Turkish society, particularly in the villages and religious ritual continues to play an important role in the lives of villagers and small townspeople. What that religion is, however, is not something which can be deduced from the formally codified principles of classical Islam. Özer Ozankaya (1973) noted that in the villages he studied folk Islam was full of superstitious beliefs. Peasants believed in praying for rain, in the evil eye, in having a *hodja* pray to help a person recover his health and in such things as the irreligiosity of hanging pictures on the wall or of translating the Koran into Turkish.

People from such a background have not been fully integrated into the dominant political framework of secular Turkey. It is hardly surprising, therefore, that there has been in recent years a considerable growth in Koran courses in Turkey and in religious secondary schools (*imam-hatip* schools) to satisfy traditional expectations that the young should learn the ways of Islam and that the mosques should find their supply of trained prayer leaders (Scott, 1971). There are now 200 000 students enrolled in *imam-hatip* schools and there has been a great increase in enrolments since the 1980 *coup* (DPT, 1982).

Such developments have been encouraged by politicians, particularly those on the right who sought the support of peasants and rural merchants against the urban supporters of the Republican People's Party. During the 1970s when Turkish politics polarised the National Salvation Party gained great influence in the Ministry of Education. The price it extracted for supporting the government of Demirel was control of education. Textbooks were rewritten to strengthen religious values, socialist teachers were transferred. The Republican People's Party saw this as a return to pre-Kemalist dark age in which the masses were to be kept in a state of ignorance (Fişek, 1977).

The ostensibly surprising growth of *imam-hatip* schools since the military coup of 1980 is perhaps best explained as a tactical concession by the army to religious interests hoping thereby to secure their support for the regime and to keep religious education under official control and surveillance. The alternative would have been to see the potential growth of clandestine religious education among outlawed religious movements like the Nurculuk or Süleymancis. By condoning religious education the Turkish government can exert greater control over it.

Migration brought the problems of the rural areas right into the heart of the urban centres. The population of the major cities of Turkey more than tripled their size in the twenty years from 1960 to 1980, spawning the growth on the periphery of Turkish cities of shanty towns (*gecekondu*). This was more than just a geographic shift in the population; it implied, too, profound cultural dislocations (Karpat, 1976) and it brought with it seedbed conditions for political extremism. The majority in the *gecekondu*, having come from more traditional rural areas had voted during the early 1970s for the conservative Justice Party but later turned to the Republican People's Party. During this period radical student groups, both on the left and the right, were active in these areas and both found ready recruits. This takes the account too far forward, however. The point for the moment is that rural migration generated new kinds of social divisions, not just in the rural areas but in urban areas as well. They were divisions which directly affected the functioning of Turkish schools, pitching them directly into the sphere of political conflict.

YOUNG PEOPLE AND EMPLOYMENT

Migration from rural areas adds to the already severe problems of demographic pressure, particularly in the cities, on educational resources and also to the problems of human resources planning in the economy. Turkish education has to expand just to be able to stand still and the pattern of growth in enrolments has not been in the technical and vocational areas which the government feels is needed for the sake of the economy. Indeed, it is almost ironic that there are now more *imam-hatip* schools in Turkey than vocational and technical schools (Mehmet, 1981).

The inadequacy of vocational and technical education is a long-standing problem. Kazamias (1966) noted in the mid-1960s that despite an active government policy to expand it stemming from as far back as the 1930s, such education has still undeveloped and was much less prestigious than other forms of secondary education. The problems, as Kazamias saw it, was that the earnings of technical workers were too low. This was something which explains also the growth in interests among Turkish workers in migration to Europe where, during the 1960s and early 1970s a labour shortage existed.

In 1961 Turkey took part in the Mediterranean Regional Project, an educational planning project of the OECD. Research during this project showed Turkish vocational education and the training to be insufficient to meet the needs of the economy for technically trained personnel (OECD, 1965). The first five-year plan introduced by the military government and the second plan which followed both sought to improve this. But by 1972 a review of the plans pointed to high levels of unemployment among the graduates of technical schools, poor quality in the training they received and poor co-ordination between the schools and industry (Szyliowicz, 1973, p. 357). The most recent plans are to increase the numbers of vocational schools, although it is expensive to do so, and strengthen their ties with industry. The DPT, the planning organisation of the government has already opened technical *lises* for girls to work alongside some firms in the ready-to-wear leather section of the clothing industry (DPT, 1982, p. 314).

In the short run, however, there can be few grounds for optimism since young people and their parents calculate the value of vocational and technical education to be inferior both in financial rewards and social status to the academic *lise*. For the social groups which might have been expected to supply more entrants to these schools, the urban working class, people from the countryside who have migrated to the towns, i.e. those who might value a practical training, there was no real need during the 1960s to do so. A significant number of them were able to migrate abroad. By the mid-1970s upwards of one and a half million workers left to work abroad attracted by high salaries in Western Europe and the possibility of saving large capital sums for future investment in Turkey (Hale, 1978).

Among the migrants the younger age groups predominated and as the 1960s drew to a close the proportion of those migrating who were skilled increased to almost 75 per cent of the total. Migration served as a safety valve for rising levels of unemployment in the Turkish economy and the foreign exchange earnings of migrants play an important role in supplying Turkey with foreign exchange with which to pay for imports.

The long-term consequences of this migration on the attitudes of migrants and their families, on social differentiation in Turkish society itself and on the Turkish economy are properly the themes of a different study. Two points, however, need emphasis: first, the migration was not the major cause of labour shortages in the Turkish economy itself (it accounted for perhaps about one-third of such shortages); secondly, it is clear that migrants have been better educated than the national average for Turkey and the loss of their skills was a gain to Western Europe and an important factor among many others explaining the chronic state of the Turkish economy in the 1970s.

Throughout the 1970s Turkey suffered a high level of unemployment at about 13 per cent of the labour force (Hale, 1978). Estimates for 1983 have put the figures between 15 and 20 per cent (Mehmet, 1981). What proportion of this can be attributed to the unemployability of workers on account of their having inadequate skills is impossible to tell. Similarly, it is only possible to guess how far a sense of hopelessness and lack of real opportunities for employment fuelled the political and social unrest among young people in the late 1970s. All that is clear is that human resource planning in Turkey has faltered badly on the rocks of economic failure, cultural expectations for an academic education and the vulnerability of the Turkish economy to world economic forces which have exposed its weaknesses with such dire political consequences.

POLITICAL SOCIALISATION IN EDUCATION

It is something of a sociological truism that schools in any society function as agents of cultural transmission and social control. In this way, while pursuing their distinctive educational goals, they serve to reproduce the social relations of a society. It is because of this that education also reproduces the contradicitions and divisions which exist in a society in its prevailing attitudes, values and ways of thinking. In the period since the Second World War the social and ideological strains of Turkish society which had been muted during the republican period became much more visible and particularly so in education.

Atatürk defined a vital role for young people in building Turkish society. No educational theorist, he none the less grasped clearly that Turkish independence and the development of a modern political culture depended on building a firm foundation for education. The roots of these ideas are traceable, through the writings of Ziya Gökalp to the work of Emile Durkheim with its stress on education as a moral force in society. Başgöz and Wilson (1968, p. 192) summed up the importance of Atatürk himself in this way:

> Twenty five years after his death, almost every school building in Turkey has a little shrine built around a figure of him. The walls of classrooms, assembly halls and stadiums are all decorated with selected Atatürk sentences. He came to be regarded by many educators as the special patron saint of education.

What Atatürkist symbolism emphasises is the national character of education, its secular foundation and its scientific basis.

The national question was particularly vital; through the language reforms and education republican Turkey sought to root a new national identity in the routine practice of its schools. In the early days of the republic the battle for a distinctive Turkish identity was critical to fend off the force of Kurdish and Armenian nationalism and to transcend the ethnic divisions. More than this, schools had to bolster a national identity among people whose sense of their Turkish identity was fixed in their religion. Atatürk's aim was to build a Turkish identity freed from a religious frame. Courses on the history of the Turkish revolution and history books which emphasised the bizarre idea that Turkey was the centre of all the major civilisations of the world, were central to this objective.

Başgöz and Wilson wisely noted, however, that there is a sense in which Turkey was born thirty years too soon for without parallel changes in agriculture and the economic development of a new society, change in education alone cannot be expected to produce a new social order. Economic difficulties have left Turkey for much of the post-war period with a large agricultural sector, the base upon which traditional mentalities still stand.

Şerif Mardin (1978) has detected in Turkish culture what he calls 'core authoritarianism' which is the product of socialisation patterns in traditional family life. But it also has a political and cultural dimension which, through the internalisation of hero images drawn from the past, links the great and folk traditions of classical Ottoman culture. Mardin notes that heroic imagery surrounding the founding fathers of the republic is important in Turkish primary education.

But as Turkish society polarised during the 1950s and 1960s under the weight of growing inequalities and rapid urbanisation, the emerging factions of both left and right acquired their own epic heroes. The poet, Nazim Hikmet, became an important symbol for the student left and the right could take comfort in crudely patriotic sentiments of the sort expressed in the ideas that 'one Turk is worth the whole world' (Mardin, 1978, p. 242). Those migrants from the villages upset by the city could take comfort in symbols evoking their religion and this was something which right-wing parties, such as the National Action Party, could exploit. During the late 1970s, for example, the Atatürk *Lise* in Ankara was a stronghold of the National Action Party. Gangs of students would stop passers-by and check if they knew the nine principles of the NAP. If they refused to answer or could not reply they would be beaten up. Parents who sought to withdraw their children from the school would be victimised. In some parts of Turkey it was dangerous to be involved in education particularly if a teacher was thought to have left-wing sympathies. Murder, torture and beatings were frequent occurrences as the youth of different political factions fought it out.

These problems were solved by the military coup of 1980 although a strengthening of political control, e.g. through banning teachers from being involved in politics, is of itself no solution to the problems in the society which fuelled the violence and ideological polarisation. Schools in Turkey could not perform their central ideological role of consolidating Kemalist philosophy.

Quite apart from the rigidities of a centrally controlled curriculum and the absence of effective methods of political education, the facts of demographic pressure and the changing social composition of the student body in consequence of rural migration, conspired to split Turkish education ideologically and to render schools ineffective as instruments to fashion a secular and national consciousness. It must not be forgotten that the embattled generation is still in the educational system.

The national question remains a central one for the Turkish state and for the geopolitical role it plays in the Middle East. Since the 1980 coup much has been done to strengthen private enterprise and encourage foreign investment and the export trade. But strenuous efforts have been made, too, to bring education under control in a way which bolsters Kemalism and Turkish nationalism. The new constitution, for instance, makes it illegal for any language other than Turkish to be the main language of education. This is clearly to prevent Kurdish nationalism from striking firm linguistic roots, but it is something which affects other minority groups, too. The Churches' Working Party on Christian minorities in Turkey, for example, expressed concern in 1982 about these policies. Mention was made in particular of the Syriani, a group in south east Turkey which uses and teaches Aramaic, the language of Jesus Christ, who were being persecuted by Kurds. Since the military coup of 1980 all religious minorities have greater physical protection but the new laws on language teaching and religious education present a new kind of threat. The military regime in Turkey will simply not tolerate forms of instruction or thinking which are not strictly Kemalist or which they cannot directly control.

CONCLUSION

The need to modernise Turkish educational institutions has been a constant theme of Turkish politics since the founding of the republic. There is no doubt that there have been substantial strides forward against a background of serious resource constraints and the persistence of traditional attitudes and values, particularly in the villages. In comparison with what the World Bank calls 'middle income countries', Turkey achieves high levels of primary school enrolments and slightly above average levels of secondary school enrolments. Assessments of achievements are always, however, dependent on standpoint. Measured against the state of education of the country in the early days of the republic there have been changes so profound they can only be described as revolutionary. The record in the period after the Second World War is, however, mixed and if Turkey is compared to the societies of Western Europe, which it seeks to emulate, then clear deficiencies in education are revealed. The most appropriate comparison, however, is one which measures achievements against goals. In this way Turkey's system of primary, secondary and vocational education displays many disappointing features. It revolves, as has been shown, around the issues of inequality and economic relevance. Most worrying to the present regime, however, is the failure of the system to become the main scaffold on which an integrated national consciousness and political morality can be built.

The violence and terror of the 1970s was a facet of this, but it was by no means its cause.

As the analysis set out in this chapter shows, education cannot bear the weight of a cultural revolution by itself for social and cultural changes can overtake it; change in education is inseparable from political change and conflict. Turkish education has been at the centre of the conflicting claims and expectations of different social classes as these groups themselves acquired a distinctive sense of their interests and identity in post-war Turkey. What those expectations were is something to be uncovered against the pattern of development of Turkish society and its state form. This is a purpose of tracing the contours of Turkey's underdevelopment and of describing how a changing international framework set the constraints within which Turkish development could evolve.

9 Higher Education, Technical Change and Dependency

Higher education plays a central role in any modern society as a supplier of qualified personnel to industry, government and the professions. In this respect it combines what has become an important social function, that of satisfying demands for social mobility, with the economic one of selecting and training people for economic roles and of carrying out scientific and technical research. In modern Western societies higher education is the major source of ideas and of scientific and technical personnel for the research and development centres of both industry and the state which are so integral to their economies. In Britain, for example, universities contributed about 60 per cent of all basic (as opposed to applied or developmental) research and development (Herman, 1984).

The largest proportion of research and development (R and D) budget throughout the Western world is met by industry and in France, Britain and the United States a large proportion of the overall budget is spent on defence. What is more, in both the United States and Britain, R and D is concentrated in large firms. In Britain 40 per cent of all R and D is accounted for by five companies: Shell, Unilever, ICI, Plessey and Lucas (Herman, 1984). There is close co-operation between industrial research and research in higher education and most Western governments, for economic and strategic reasons, seek to strengthen those links. This was not always the case. As has been shown in an earlier chapter (Chapter 3) throughout most of the nineteenth century, and particularly in Britain, universities were much more closely involved with the training of traditional professional groups – lawyers, clerics – and men of letters who could later be recruited to the civil service or to business, both at home and abroad. The contribution of universities in Britain to the growth of industrial society was negligible.

Eric Ashby (1966, p. 466) attributed this fact in the case of British to the structure of British society itself. 'The very stratification of English society', he wrote, 'helped to keep science isolated from its applications; it was admitted that the study of science for its useful applications might be appropriate for the labouring classes, but managers were not attracted to the study of science except as an agreeable occupation for their leisure.' On the continent of Europe similar conditions prevailed; the universities of Germany and France throughout the nineteenth century were not centres in which applied scientific and technical research took place. Such work was done instead in technical institutes (in Germany in the Technische Hochschulen, in France in the École Polytechnique and in Britain in institutes like Owen's College). Later in the nineteenth century universities did come to assimilate applied science and technology and in Britain did so, at least in the provincial universities, with a strongly utilitarian bias but certainly not in a way which challenged fundamentally the dominant model of the university which has reflected the older values of an aristocratic-gentry culture modified by the individualism of an increasingly self-confident bourgeoisie.

It was the members of this latter group who saw in a university education the opportunity to acquire those gentlemanly marks of respectability and fine taste associated with the life styles of an older aristocratic elite and who pressd their provincial demands for the development of new universities to compensate their inability to penetrate with ease the traditional universities of Oxford and Cambridge.

Throughout the twentieth century, and particularly in the period since the Second World War, universities in the developed Western societies have had to cope with different demands which have given them both distinctive yet diverse institutional forms and a central role in economic and political life. In the British case, Eric Ashby (1966, p. 474) has noted 'It has required more than sixty years of pamphleteerring and propaganda, reinforced by the anxieties of two world wars and the fear of foreign competition, to persuade British Parliaments to take full financial responsibility for teaching and research in higher technology.'

To account fully for how these changes came about would involve explaining how governments perceived their strategic military and economic needs. It would also be necessary to discuss how science and technology themselves really have to be thought of in terms of the groups of people whose research interests and political influence define what themes and issues have been important and which deserve financial support. Science, as it has often been pointed out, is also a community (Merton, 1957). Irrespective, therefore, of what governments insist are the problems requiring research the scientific community itself, from the nineteenth century onwards, has been able to define research priorities.

It would be important to consider, too, the whole question of the social and political accountability of science, technology and higher education, to ask, in effect, what justifications have typically been given to allocate resources in science in the particular ways in which they have been allocated. Finally, though not exhaustively, it would be important to ask questions about which people in different societies or which social groups, have given universities and technical institutes their particular character and ambience, their particular career structure and what principles explain how the access of people to these institutions, either as teachers, researchers or students, is regulated.

These are all questions pertaining to what Max Weber (1970, p. 129) called the 'external conditions' of science. It was Weber, in fact, who pointed to the importance of such conditions in giving shape to scientific careers themselves and to science itself as a social institution. He saw a parallel in the development of large, state-funded university institutions with what happens wherever capitalist enterprise comes into operation, namely, 'the separation of the worker from his means of production' (Weber, 1970, p. 131). Just as in the past when the artisan was deprived of his ownership of the means of production, changes in the external conditions of modern science threatened the same fate for university scientists. Weber is raising the theme here of the rationalisation and bureaucratisation of science itself.

Weber was writing at a time before the development of international organisations which increasingly in the modern world influence the distribution of scientific resources and establish priorities in scientific work. Such organisations include the International Atomic Energy Authority, The United National Educational, Scientific and Cultural Organisation (UNESCO), the Organisation for Economic Cooperation and Development (OECD), the World Health Organisation (WHO) and in addition to these intergovernmental organisations there are specific project oriented institutions like the European Organisation for Nuclear Research (CERN), which requires levels of funding beyond the ability of individual governments to provide. These are organisations with very close connections with higher education institutions in all their member states.

Internationalism and 'disciplinary communism', an expression coined by Merton to describe how scientists freely exchange the results of their research with one another, is both an important feature of the social organisation of scientific work and one of science's most important ideological claims, i.e. that science is open and accountable. But there are two facets of the whole organisation of science which need to be highlighted in this respect and which bear directly on questions about the scientific dependency of Third World countries and what universities in those countries might achieve. The issues are the degree to which scientific and technological research is open and accessible and the extent to which different groups in society, particularly through the educational system, can have any access to scientific knowledge in a way which would allow them to participate creatively and effectively in discussions about priorities in scientific research and expenditure. On both counts the 'external conditions' of science in modern Western society illustrate acutely some of the terrible dilemmas which Third World societies face.

Universities in Western society, though differing considerably from one another on account of national differences in policy and tradition, all make special claims to be independent, at least in their scholarly work, of sectional interests in society and to be open in principle to all those qualified and able to benefit from the teaching available to them. In fact, the pattern of their scholarly work is everywhere influenced by the kinds of resources made available to them and the principles which have regulated student access have always reflected the contours of social differentiation in society itself. Both aspects of the social organisation of learning and research in higher education define issues concerning the subtle and changing connections between knowledge and power in modern society.

How far sectional interests in society have come to define what takes place as scientific and technological research is something extremely difficult to assess. It is a commonplace to note, for example, that research linked to projects in private industry or with national ministries of defence is subject to many controls so that research results may not be made available freely to the international scientific community (Rose and Rose, 1969) and it would certainly be a naive assumption that the great growth of national expenditure on science and technology was fuelled by an organised concern for science and technology in themselves. Krishan Kumar (1978, p. 229) has noted, for instance, in a critical discussion of theories of post industrial society that

> An explanation for the rapid growth of knowledge institutions and the knowledge classes offers itself in the shape of Cold War politics. . . The science-based 'welfare' state can rapidly be classified as the science-based 'warfare' state, and with greater respect for the actual history of the last fifty years.

The grounds for this claim is a rejection of the view that science and technology become in some way neutral in a post-capitalist society which is itself no longer so clearly organised around the pursuit of profits. Kumar rejects the view that the search for knowledge in modern society is inspired by a general concern for welfare; indeed the opposite is true:

> There are familiar examples of the atomic bomb, other weapons of the biological and chemical kind, space exploration, and large scale capital-intensive technology with its propensity to pollute the environment and exhaust the earth's supply of fossil fuels. Then there is the ingenious and expensive gadgetry of the mass consumer industry, with its built-in principle of planned obsolescence and marginal technial improvements (the ceaseless concern of the R & D departments . . .) And finally one hardly needs to add that ninety-nine percent of the knowledge effort of the industrial societies is devoted to the problems of the developed world, considered as a self-contained entity, a 'post-industrial enclave'. (Kumar, 1978, p. 230)

Related to the question of what principles regulate the funding and direction of scientific research and, through these, the kinds of institutions which have developed in higher education each with their own structure and organisation, there is the problem of who gets access to the knowledge which is generated.

In Western societies (and, so it seems, in the Soviet Union and Eastern Europe) social class differences in educational attainment ensure that people from a working-class background are much less likely than those who are econimically and socially better off to reach higher education. The reasons for this well-documented fact reflect the historical development of higher education, its institutional forms and 'ethos' and the barriers these have created to limit the access of working-class people.

This is not to claim that these are intentional outcomes although such a case could be made out. It is rather that higher education is a resource among other, including investment capital, private property of all kinds and publically provided welfare goods, which is woven into a complex of constraints and opportunities which define at any point in time the class structure of a society. In Western societies throughout the nineteenth and twentieth centuries the logic of the relationships between social classes has pressed higher education to a particular functional form. Essential to the education of elites, higher education has come to reflect the social and political expectations of those social groups which have most effectively secured access to it and the form of higher education itself can be seen to reflect the social differences of Western societies themselves.

In the nineteenth and early twentieth centuries universities rather than technical institutes of various kinds were attended by students from bourgeois backgrounds. Working people had no part in universities and it was not until the end of the nineteenth century that science and technological studies found their place in British universities. Throughout the twentieth century universities have maintained a higher status over and above those institutions specialising in the training of technologists with discernible differences in the social backgrounds of those recruited to them.

Even a brief consideration of the external conditions of science and of university and higher education in modern industrial societies illustrates that both institutions must be seen in their social and political and economic contexts. Universities on what Sagasti (1980) has called 'the first civilisation', i.e. those countries in the modern world with a capacity to sustain independent research and development programmes and meet most of the conditions for modern scientific research to take place, are, in practice, subject to severe constraints. The work they do, the priorities in science and technology they reflect, must be seen in the context of the external conditions of the societies in which they function. This, of course, is an obvious point to make. But it does have rather profound implications for the character of higher education in Third World countries. For it is the work of researchers in the developed societies which established what counts as scientific knowledge among the international community of science and technology. It is this work which lies behind the international transfer of technology which has such profound and costly consequences for the economies of Third World societies. The model of what constitutes a proper scientific education is one which many Third World countries derive from the West and one which, from the mid-nineteenth century onwards, they have sought to emulate and experience by importing foreign academic personnel and by seeking to have their own students trained abroad. In a world economic order imbalanced in any case by the economic strength of the Western economies, scientific and technical knowledge and higher education itself, becomes a kind of commodity with its own special price which the poor cannot properly afford.

Knowledge is big business and to the extent that it is accessible through such things as books, conferences, libraries, computers and courses in higher education then, like any other commodity it can be given a price and be marketed in particular ways (Hall, 1980). Philip Altbach (1980) has pointed to the existence of what he calls 'the international knowledge system' to explain the role of Third World countries as consumers of the knowledge which the developed countries produce. Several factors, he argues, lie behind this inequality: the adoption of foreign models of what higher education should be, the use of western language to maintain access to the international language of science, the absence of world-wide publishing facilities in Third World countries and the persistence of an academic brain drain which encourages students from such countries to leave and study abroad.

In this context, Altbach notes, 'Foreign aid programmes, cultural exchange efforts and similar policies often have the result of continuing relationships of dependency.' What is more, though educational aid from the rich to the poor countries is only a small part of the total aid which is given there is no doubt that it is given, in part at least, to encourage commercial success in book exports, advertising, communications technology and all of this in the hope that commercial ties will underwrite political loyalties.

There is, for this study, one further aspect of the relationship between the developed societies and the dependent ones which must be stressed; it concerns the cultural consequences of technical dependency. Johan Galtung (1979, p. 277) has pointed out that

> technology is not merely a mode of production and therefore neutral; it carries within it a code of structures – economic, social, cultural and also cognitive . . . The economic code that inheres in western technology demands that industries be capital-intensive, research intensive, organisation-intensive and labour extensive. On the social plane the code created a 'centre' and a 'periphery', thus perpetuating a structure of inequality. In the cultural arena, it

> sees the West as entrusted by destiny with the mission of casting the rest of the world in its own mould. In the cognitive field, it sees man as the master of nature, the vertical and individualistic relations between human beings as *the* normal and natural, and history as a linear movement of progress. The transfer of western technology is thus a structural-cultural invasion.

Galtung does not stress the point but institutions of higher education are major carriers of the codes he describes and his later pleas for appropriate technologies for Third World contexts and much more careful assessments of technical needs have little chance of being realised unless the involvement of universities is properly understood. For the dependence of Third World universities on the West creates distortions in the curricula of secondary schools and in the aspirations of their students. The high social selectivity of secondary schools in dependent societies widens the already large gap between the educated and the uneducated and strengthens career aspirations among the educated towards 'big science', international respectability in the scientific community and an orientation to the technologies of the West rather than to those which would be more appropriate to the needs of their own society.

This brief account of some of the mechanisms of technological dependency is, of course, highly schematic. In what follows there is an illustration of the specific ramifications of such an approach in the cases of Egypt and Turkey. The specific case studies of each society indicates the importance of taking into account the historical specificity of each society's pattern of development and unique profile of resource constraints. They also point to the ways in which some groups in the two societies have come to understand these processes which reinforce dependency, how they impose alien cultural forms and how these are resisted.

10 Higher Education, Science and Technology and Dependency in Egypt

The state of scientific and technological research and of their development in Egypt must be seen against the pattern of the country's modernisation and of its system of higher education and training. In an earlier chapter the modernisation plans of Muhammad Ali were discussed. Egypt's reorientation away from Ottoman politics towards those of Europe stems from this period.

During the inter-war period of the twentieth century some expansion took place in higher education. Until 1909 when a private university was founded in Egypt higher education was organised into a small number of professional schools with those of medicine (1828) and engineering (1820) dating back to the time of Muhammad Ali. The others were set up later; the School of Law in 1867 and the Teacher Training Institute in 1880. In 1925 an Egyptian state university was set up in Cairo and incorporated the professional higher schools as its colleges. Universities opened in Alexandria in 1942, Ain Shams in 1950 and Assiut in 1957.

But the system of higher education to this point reflected several facets of the country's particular history, the form of its underdevelopment and its dependency of the West. In the first place, higher education was divided both on religious and social lines; the ancient university of Al-Azhar maintained its traditional position as a centre of Islamic learning. Although it retained traditional methods of teaching and had lost any intellectual vitality, it still recruited students from religious and peasant backgrounds and was a considerable source of recruitment of conservatively inclined political leaders. The University of Cairo, on the other hand, recruited its students from Egypt's upper classes, from rich landowning families and from high government officials.

Secondly, reflecting British policy that secondary and higher education should be strictly limited to produce no more graduates than government service could usefully employ, the early development of higher education was both held back by inadequate resources and distorted in its form by the requirements which the occupying power posed on it. The distortion affected directly the kinds of subjects which students demanded; there was, for example, a very high demand for legal studies, medicine, to a lesser extent engineering, and at the same time a very low demand for the poorly paid profession of teaching.

For those who were rich, exclusion from the professional schools did not mean exclusion from higher education; many were able to send their sons abroad for training in France and in Britain. Such shortages, however, ensured that access to higher education became an important demand of Egyptian nationalists and given the prominence of lawyers in higher education it is not surprising that such men occupied the leadership roles of the nationalist movement and that students were an active group within it.

Students, of course, still play an important role in Egyptian political life and this will be discussed a little later in this chapter. It is a role which relates to the importance of universities and of higher education as avenues to state employment. To understand what the connection is between students, universities and the state and how these connections have come to have such critical political importance, it is vital to grasp in the first instance what changes in Egyptian society and higher education were brought about by the Nasser regime.

NASSER AND HIGHER EDUCATION

The Nasser regime was one which sought the industrialisation of Egypt free of foreign domination but in a way centrally organised and controlled by the state. It was at once a bureaucratic regime and an authoritarian one, but it was also a technocratic one. Analyses of the composition of Egyptian political elites since the revolution have shown that the military has consolidated its political position as the dominant group in the state; that key posts have been staffed with technically trained military personnel and that although the largest group of cabinet personnel have been drawn from civilian backgrounds, they have been drawn mainly from people with a technical background of one sort or another (Faksh, 1976).

This development is reflected, too, in the changing educational backgrounds of top political leaders in the years since the revolution. Those trained in humanities and the law have declined in number relative to those with a scientific or technological training. The reasons for this shift, Faksh has suggested, lie in the regime's mistrust of the old and corrupt traditions of upper-class ministers and managing directors 'trained in law schools and deeply ingrained with French influences' and the need to staff the growing public sector of the economy with people both able and committed to developing industrialisation and modernisation plans.

It was an expansion facilitated from 1962 onwards by the abolition of all fees in education and by the state agreeing, in 1964, to guarantee all higher education graduates a job. But the expansion of higher education could not be coped with by the existing universities. In 1953 a system of external students was set up which allowed those secondary graduates who failed to gain a place in a university or other institutions to take their exams externally. From 1957 onwards a number of higher institutes were set up to cope with the growing demand which trained people in various professional fields.

The expansion of higher education during the early phases of the revolution was, in fact, remarkable but the pattern of expansion created subsequent problems of human resource supply and quality that remain stubborn. The basic problem is that the system of higher education has consistently produced more people than the economy could absorb and that growing numbers of students has led to a deterioration in the quality of education and training that they experience.

The expansion of higher education opportunities was, however, remarkable and is indicated in Table 10.1.

The distribution of students across subject areas and faculties was not consistent, however, with human resource requirements; it reflected rather the value placed on education by better-off people in Egypt as a measure of social status, access to state employment and for employment outside Egypt elsewhere in the Arab world. While it is true that, helped by government financial support, enrolments in science, engineering and agriculture all more than doubled in the decade from 1954 to 1964, there was a parallel increase in the numbers of students in colleges of law, commerce and arts, particularly among less qualified secondary school leavers (Szyliowicz, 1973, p. 286). The growth in student numbers across different faculties is shown in Table 10.2.

Such figures mean little, however, unless they can be set alongside

Table 10.1 Enrolment in higher education, Egypt 1952–82

Date	Universities	Higher and technical institutes
1952–3	51 681	5 285
1965–6	140 143	34 702
1970–1	177 955	35 300*
1975–6	558 527	6 935†
1980–1	559 292	14 209†
1981–2	594 597	16 768†

Notes: † Technical Institutes only.
* 1969–70.

Sources: Waterbury (1983, p. 222). *Statistical Yearbook 1983* (Cairo: Central Agency for Public Mobilisation and Statistics).

Table 10.2 Patterns of course enrolment, Egyptian universities, 1974–80

	1974/5		1979/80	
	No.	% total	No.	% total
Science	10 904	4.06	18 744	4.2
Medicine	27 309	10.1	37 680	8.5
Dentistry	3 347	1.2	3 989	0.9
Pharmacy	6 666	2.4	8 439	1.9
Engineering	26 001	9.6	51 854	11.8
Agriculture	30 734	11.4	34 775	7.9
Veterinary medicine	4 584	1.7	6 302	1.4
Arts	29 575	11.0	49 309	11.2
Law	31 098	11.5	54 599	12.4
Commerce	59 830	22.3	112 203	25.5
Other	38 232	14.2	60 915	13.8
Total	268 280	100	438 809	100

Source: Adapted from Arab Republic of Egypt report, *Education in Egypt* (Cairo: Ministry of Education, 1976 and 1981).

judgements about what the economy actually required and the quality of the education offered by the universities.

Finally, there are judgements of an essentially political kind to be made. They concern what contribution higher education really makes to national development goals. Of these, two are critical: national independence and the development of equal opportunities throughout Egyptian society.

Four issues give focus to these themes. They are: patterns of recruitment to higher education and the experience of being a student; the resources available for higher education, the output of the system; and, finally, the relationship of higher education to Egypt's scientific and technological development. In each of these areas there are severe weaknesses yet rich opportunities for change and further development. Egypt, after all, is richly endowed with natural resources to make important advances in agriculture, hydroelectric and solar energy production, petrochemicals, textiles, manufacturing of all kinds, shipping and, of course, tourism. Whether the opportunities which exist can be exploited depends only in part on the way the country's educational system functions. But that part is crucial and can only be played well if the right balance is found between economic policies and educational policies. Up to the present that balance has not been struck. The result is damaging to the economy and to education.

RECRUITMENT TO HIGHER EDUCATION AND THE STUDENT EXPERIENCE

There is a broad base to education in Egypt. There are two university students for every five secondary school pupils and thirteen primary students for every one university student. Post-revolution expansion in education has been dramatic both in scale and consequence (Birks and Sinclair, 1978). Saad Ibrahim (1982, p. 406) has described the expansion of educational opportunities in Egypt as follows: 'The expansion of education in Egypt after 1952 allowed new groups in society to send their children to school, enlarged the pool of literate population, and increased the size of those groups in the medium and higher education levels'.

Such growth has contributed to and in turn has been fuelled by a generally diffused growth in educational aspirations. Egyptian parents have high expectations for the education of their children, particularly their sons. The occupations of doctor, lawyer, engineer and army officer are held in high regard and this itself is part of a wider cultural shift in Egyptian society, the migration to cities which has accompanied population growth and economic development.

Such expectations generate a great deal of anxiety, however, and failure in education, at least for those who have access to it, can be a cause of considerable shame and distress and of parental pressure on young people to do well in secondary school. Saad Ibrahim told the author in private conversation that the period before the secondary examinations in Egypt is a 'state of emergency' for many families. The reason is that the allocation of students to places in universities is determined by a central office on the basis of examination scores. These are used to ration out places among applicants so that the high scoring students can gain access to the most prestigious courses. The result, of course, with considerable implications for students morale is that many students find themselves allocated to courses they do not wish to follow but with little opportunity (save, perhaps, corruptly) to do anything about it. The admission system is complex and modified by the Co-ordination Office for universities and institutes to allow in those students who are outstanding in sport and social service. It discriminates further in favour of the children of university staff, ex-ministry employees, war veterans from 1973, students from Sinai and other remote areas.

One study of the system based in the Universities of Zagazig and Ain Shams, underlined the frequent lack of fit between student interests and places offered by quoting from an article in *Al-Ahram*: 'If Picasso was born in our country we would offer him a place in the Faculty of Commerce' (quoted in Yussef Gamal Al-Din, 1979, p. 157). The same study underlined heavily how the demand for higher education in Egypt was high in anticipation of social status. Al-Din (1979, p. 205) notes: 'Egypt shares the same attitude as other developing countries in valuing people by their degrees not by their merits.'

Two questions need answers for the full significance of such rising expectations to be appreciated; what principles in practice govern access to higher education and how have patterns of access changed through time? Saad Ibrahim (1982), reviewing what little direct evidence on social mobility there is in Egypt has answered both questions unequivocally. He believes that opportunities for social mobility in Egypt have followed closely on the changes which have taken place in Egyptian society since the revolution, particularly in the system of social stratification.

On the basis of a review of official data and a survey of heads of households in Cairo in 1979 (a survey based on 322 people) and the results of two previous studies in 1962 and 1966, Ibrahim (1982, p. 431) concluded that

> Egypt's stratification system reached its maximum fluidity from the mid-1950s to the mid-1960s . . . Along with ambitious programs in education and industrialisation and with bold socialist policies of equalising opportunities, the Egyptian society witnessed more social mobility than in any single decade in this century. But from the late 1960s on, the class structure appears to have been hardening again. During the last fifteen years, upward mobility has increasingly become 'confined' to children of the middle and upper strata. For young members of the lower rungs, the system does not offer as many opportunities to move up. For them, such opportunities are to be found outside the Egyptian system. It may be a sheer accident of social history that, as Egypt no longer held as bright promise for its dispossessed children, other parts of the Arab world were openening doors of opportunity to them.

The general thrust of Ibrahim's argument is further confirmed by Moore's work on the engineering profession in Egypt. Moore has tried to show that the engineering profession in Egypt has failed, as an organised profession, to contribute creatively to the modernisation of the country. Part of this failure, although only part, is explicable in terms of the recruitment patterns into this prestige occupation. Moore has suggested that in Egypt, Nasser's democratising of higher education had the paradoxical and unintended effect of increasing the access of middle class and the bourgeois young people to the universities.

The rationale, of course, is that such an education led to state employment and to opportunities for status and wealth in the economic interface between state organisations and private industries, particularly in the civil engineering and construction industry sectors. 'Though Nasser had destroyed the old *haute bourgeoisie* as a cultural and economic force', writes Moore (1980, p. 130), 'the remnants of this class, supplemented by Nasser's new managerial bourgeoisie, were a hundred times more likely than other families to get their children into an engineering school'.

Moore does not explore all the mechanisms operating to produce such an outcome but they include the ability of middle-class people to purchase private educational tuition for their offspring and to send them to the better schools in the more congenial parts of Cairo and Alexandria. Such families are able to avoid the increasingly stressful conditions of the state secondary schools, to pay for private tuition for their children and generally enhance the educational life chances of their offspring through the home environment they can sustain and the influential contacts they can manipulate.

The Egyptian revolution during the Nasser period was committed, at least ideologically, to improve the status of the rural poor and to open up opportunities for women in Egyptian society. The state's development plans, the expansion of state employment and the drafting of men into the army all facilitated the entry of women into the economy and into higher education. Since 1952 when there were hardly any women at all in universities there has been a steady increase in their numbers. Women now account for almost one-quarter of all professional and administrative employees in Egypt and in some professions, particularly medicine and allied occupations, there has been a marked increase in the numbers of women (Howard-Merriam, 1979).

The position of women in higher education and subsequent professional employment is still, however, contradictory. Traditional notions that their main role is in the home under the authority of husbands persist and there is obvious discrimination against them with respect to promotion (see, e.g. El Saadawi, 1980; Beck and Keddie, 1978). Such discrimination has a double edge. Moore's small survey of engineering students carried out in 1973 showed, for example, that nearly two-thirds of the women in engineering courses came from the urban bourgeoisie and the aristocracy. Male engineering students were not from such privileged backgrounds (Moore, 1980). What is more, Moore claims, the growth in numbers of women in engineering has had as one of its consequences the effect of lowering the status of the profession.

The revival of Islam in recent years throughout the Middle East has added to some of the problems educated women have to cope with. No quantitative measures can depict the subtle pre-occupations women must have about appropriate forms of dress while on campus or the care they must exercise in their contacts with fellow students, particularly the men. They have to cope with these things with care to avoid sanctions from their colleagues and their families and from religious students with whom they cannot avoid contact. They have to take care not to appear too independent, to be too clever or too ambitious; they have to balance circumspection and respectability with ambition. As a group they still have a long way to go before their opportunities become comparable to those of men.

The divisions within Egyptian society itself, particularly those between the rich and the poor and between men and women, have, not surprisingly, a direct effect on the structure of opportunities for higher education. Those same divisions, however, are reflected in the attitudes and behaviour of Egyptian students.

If the role of higher education in the development of Egyptian society is to be properly assessed then this aspect of the student's experience of it must be examined. The reason is this; students eventually become the people who play leading roles in industry and the state. How they conceive of themselves and their futures, particularly their relationship to and responsibility towards the poor, especially in rural areas, for whom modernisation and development is vital, is one of the keys to a country's ability to achieve development and has a direct bearing on what forms development might take. The tragedy in the Egyptian case is that those who are the best educated have been unable, and too many have been unwilling, to involve themselves creatively in the country's development. The Nasser regime encouraged students to see themselves as some sort of vanguard group in the society and the growth of state employment certainly fuelled aspirations for higher education. Unfortunately, as Malcolm Kerr (1965) pointed out, the early expansion of higher education under Nasser occurred in subjects for which there was no real need in the economy – subjects in the faculties of arts, law and commerce – and dire shortages of personnel existed in science, medicine and engineering. University graduates became, therefore, a disappointed group whose jobs did not match their expectations.

President Nasser was able, however, at least until 1968 to mobilise student support behind his policies. Malcolm Kerr (1965, p. 189) summed this up with a comment that, almost twenty years later seems incredible, although it was, of course, true:

> Student political activity is now a tame affair organised in support of the regime through various officially inspired channels such as the Arab Socialist Union, which is the sole and official party. Indeed, students and the younger intelligentsia as a whole are now perhaps among the most reliable enthusiasts of the regime, to which they look to provide them with opportunities for successful careers.

Kerr was prescient enough to realise that whether this support continued depended on the ability of the regime to deliver economic growth. The disaster of the 1967 war breached the walls of that support and student demonstrations against Nasser in 1968 had to be suppressed. In his attempts to consolidate his own power after the death of Nasser in 1970 Sadat clearly manipulated student policies by encouraging the Muslim Brotherhood (which Nasser has banned) to suppress Nasserist and leftist factions in the student body. Throughout the 1970s the activities of radical Islamic students became a threat to Sadat and a presidential decree in 1979 made such groups illegal on university campuses and banned the wearing of clothing or beards symbolising religious identity and support.

Student politics in Egypt have to be seen in the light of the employment opportunities available to university graduates and in relation to their experience of higher education itself, the quality of the instruction they receive and the kind of resouces made available to them. These will be discussed shortly. Students must also be considered, however, against the political stance of the government and, in the case of all societies in the Middle East, against the profound and ubiquitous presence of religion and of religious responses to modernisation.

It was one of the great achievements of Nasser to reform the ancient and prestigious university Al-Azhar (see Hyde, 1978). An important element in that reform, however, was Nasser's attempt to undermine the political power of religious leaders and particularly of the Muslim Brotherhood, a group perceived by the Free Officers in the 1950s as their main source of opposition. The Brotherhood was, in fact, behind an attempted coup and assassination against Nasser in 1954.

Against such a background where religion has such a high profile in politics it is inevitable that students would be closely involved and that they would be a divided group. Some have adopted extreme left-wing political positions, others have been drawn to fundamental Islamic attitudes and have felt deeply suspicious of the post-1952 regime in Egypt. One simple explanation of this is that the closure of religious courts and the development of a fully secular legal system meant that the graduates of Al-Azhar faced growing unemployment and those students from petit-bourgeois religious backgrounds in the state universities felt that some of their most important values were being undermined by a secular state. But this was precisely the group which, as Fischer (1982) has pointed out, benefited most from the expansion of universities.

Islam has been resurgent all over the Middle East in recent years (Jansen, 1979) and in Egypt also. It is a development connected, at least in the Egyptian case, the rapid urbanisation and blocked opportunities for occupational advancement. Studies of the social backgrounds of arrested Muslim brothers in recent years shows them to be drawn frequently from recent urban migrants holding salaried jobs but feeling their promotion chances, because of their lack of personal connections in the bureaucracies, to be blocked (Fischer, 1982).

A survey of members of one such fundamentalist group whose members were arrested and in prison confirmed this general description. The survey, carried out on prisoners by Saad Ibrahim (1980), showed that the members of the group belonged to a lower middle class stratum in Egyptian society with a predominantly rural background. A further study based on press reports of the Repentance and Holy Flight Group shows that its members have extensive contacts with Egyptian youth, particularly in the universities (El Safty, 1982). Safty has argued that such groups represent an extensive network of covert opposition to the regime, alienated from its ideology, particularly since 1974 when President Sadat's policies of *Infitah* or 'open door' began to encourage foreign trade and investment in Egypt in an attempt to recover from the economic mess which war, the energy crisis and the failures of Nasserism bequeathed to him.

Their alienation, however, lies deeper. It is rooted, too, in the ideological swings of the Nasser regime from nationalism through Pan-Arabism to socialism, and recently, pro-Americanism. Safty (1982, p. 12) has suggested that in the absence of a coherent ideological system many young people have become 'lost'. They have become bitter, too; bitter at military defeats in the 1967 war; bitter about the economic crisis; bitter about corruption and nepotism and bitter at growing inequalities in Egyptian society.

In this context the Islamic groups have been able to offer students in the universities a coherent analysis of their position and considerable welfare support in the form of help with accommodation, books and so forth. President Sadat was shot by a Muslim believing that his place in paradise was guaranteed for having destroyed someone who was destroying the faith.

The data is too thin and sketchy to speculate further on the importance of such groups in the political life of Egypt at the moment. But in so far as the Nasser regime and its successor has failed to mobilise the people of Egypt around a coherent ideology and reacts to the existence of political opposition through repression, it is likely that the only way many people will feel able to express their opposition to the regime is through a stronger identification with their traditional faith.

RESOURCES FOR HIGHER EDUCATION

Egyptian students are a vital human resource for the whole society, at least in principle. In practice, however, there are many obstacles preventing that resource being used effectively. One aspect of this concerns the quality of the education students typically receive. How they make use of their education will be discussed later.

The quality of the education offered by any university in any society is governed primarily by the amount and quality of resources, particularly human resources applied to it. Both of these bear directly on the nature of the learning experience students undergo. In Egypt, student numbers have increased dramatically and there has been greater political pressure on the Ministry of Education to upgrade some of the Higher Institutes into universities. Student pressure has therefore had two facets, the numerical one reflecting demographic pressures and patterns of graduate employment, and the cultural one that higher education should mean university education. There are twelve universities in Egypt. It has been estimated, however, that Egypt needs twenty-five universities by 1990 to provide for the demand for places and to allow for a balanced coverage of university places throughout the country (Yussef Gamal Al-Din, 1979, p. 98).

Student numbers across a number of faculties have expanded much faster than university resources, particularly of teaching staff, with the obvious consequence that teacher : student ratios have deteriorated. Lecture halls are crowded and teaching methods are unable to cope with the problems created by overwhelming numbers. This has been a long-standing problem, exacerbated by the fact that salaries for university teachers are low. The result is that qualified academic personnel have had many incentives to emigrate or to boost their current earnings in Egypt with additional employment such as private teaching.

Egyptian society places a high value on formal educational qualifications and this explains, from the time of the British occupation onwards, why the passing of formal examinations has been such a central part of education and why students typically orient their work to this end. It is a common complaint among Egyptian educators that students are too prepared simply to learn their lessons by heart and regurgitate the material in examinations. Some writers have suggested that this is also a reflection of distinctively Moslem traditions of learning and that it stifles imagination and creativity among students (Kerr, 1965).

It is a problem made worse in some faculties, particularly engineering and medicine, where textbooks and instructions are in the English language. The pressure is great on such students to purchase additional tuition from their teachers and since academic salaries are low many teachers are keen to earn the extra money. One can only speculate on the effects of this on the quality of university teaching and research and it is certainly the case that Egyptian academics are themselves very worried about the state of their universities.

HIGHER EDUCATION AND THE ECONOMY

The Egyptian government views the universities as institutions responsible for 'training the manpower needed for social and economic development plans, conducting scientific research in order to solve national problems, preparing cadres of teaching staff and giving expert advice in all that interests society as they are centres of ideological and cultural illumination,' (Ministry of Education, 1981, p. 38). In the same document (p. 29), however, there is formal recognition, too, that the government sees them as 'providing qualified manpower to meet the needs of the Arab world'. This is an acknowledgement of the importance of labour migration in the Egyptian economy, especially the migration of highly qualified personnel whose foreign earnings have become such an important source of foreign exchange earnings in Egypt and a major contribution to the country's balance of payments.

The migration of skilled and technically trained labour abroad is also a source of some new inequalities in Egyptian society as foreign earnings are many times higher than those within Egypt (Hansen) and Radwan, 1982). Up until 1973 the highest proportion of migrants were in the fields of teaching, medicine and other scientific and technical professions. This was the group which, constituting about 5 per cent of the total labour force, accounted for over one-third of the outflow of migrants in 1973. Since that date the numbers of production workers, unskilled workers and farmers has increased. It was estimated in 1976 that 60 per cent of the construction labour force had migrated from Egypt (Hansen and Radwan, 1982). In all countries of the Arabian Gulf more than half of the teachers employed are from Egypt. During the period 1970–75, 18 per cent of the university staff of Egypt was working abroad. This represents a considerable 'brain drain' from the Egyptian economy, although migrants' remittances have made an important contribution to easing the pressure on Egypt's foreign exchange position.

A particularly alarming aspect of the 'brain drain' is that a significant number of Egyptian university staff sent abroad for further training or research do not return. Of those sent abroad in 1976, 10 per cent did not return, but this included 58 per cent of the staff at Cairo university (Ayubi, 1983, p. 435). Of this group, claims Ayubi, there is every reason to think that the majority are in the sciences and that their migration is not temporary.

There is a growing official recognition that this exodus represents a loss to Egypt's scientific development. In 1981 a special government minister was appointed to encourage contact between those academic abroad and those who remain. From 1980 Egypt has co-operated with the United National Development Programme (UNDP) to finance the temporary return of Egyptian scientists to work with national research organisations.

Migration, however, is likely to have direct consequences on two areas of higher education policy; the demand for higher education and the pattern of graduate output. The Egyptian experience of migration points to an awful truth its education planners must face. Students intending to secure a higher education do so to improve their life chances for income and prestige but their calculation about how best to achieve this involves taking into account the possibility of working abroad. What students seek to study, therefore, depends only in part on what employment opportunities they calculate are available to them in Egypt. This makes rational planning of places on the basis of Egyptian human resource needs almost impossible yet the demand for places in higher education continues to increase. It means, too, that the Egyptian economy has to suffer critical shortages of highly trained personnel. This is particularly true in the technical fields critical to the country's ability to modernise its industry.

If the universities are included in the system of technical training then the lack of alignment between the output of the training system and the needs of the economy becomes even clearer. Egypt produces far more university graduates than it can productively employ and the pattern of university enrolment is skewed towards commercial, legal and non-science subjects.

Medicine and engineering remain in high demand but the quality of the training given there must be seriously questioned. Too often classes are too large for effective teaching and Egyptian students in all faculties face extra costs to buy private tuition from their professors. Medical education especially is inadequate. With large classes there is little scope for students to gain any practical experience in dissection or clinical practice. Medical textbooks are still in English and instruction is dependent primarily on the formal lecture or on distributed notes which students can purchase. The data discussed earlier indicate how rapidly higher education in universities has expanded. Hansen and Radwan (1982, p. 271), however, counselled:

> As far as university education is concerned, we feel that the establishment of new universities must be discontinued. We realise that there is a growing popular demand to increase the number of universities, but this should be strongly resisted. At present, universities are short of teaching staff and the quality of education therefore leaves much to be desired. University graduates have great difficulty in finding employment and had it not been for the guaranteed employment schemes large numbers of them would have been unemployed. This is an area where improvement of quality and reorientation should dominate over quantitative expansion and where admittance requirements should be tightened.

The conclusion has to be that the system of technical training in Egypt is deficient in several important respects. Egypt is not unique in this, of course, but these deficiencies are clearly not a simple outcome of bad planning and resource allocation, although this is certainly involved. They are also a reflection of deep-seated social expectations about education and employment which themselves reflect the particular development of the labour market in Egypt.

SCIENCE AND TECHNOLOGY

It is the policy of the Egyptian government 'to approach self-reliance in questions of science and technology' (United Nations Conference on Science and Technology for Development, 1978). In the paper which Egypt submitted to the United Nations several deficiencies in the nation's scientific resources were noted. These included the poor organisation if scientific resources and poor co-ordination among different departments of state, the shortage of scientific information and a shortage of scientific personnel. 'This shortcoming is evident in Egypt despite the fact that Egypt contains the largest techno-scientific manpower resource in the Arab world' (UN, 1978). The report concluded that Egypt had to find some way to stop its 'brain drain'.

In order to do this, however, important changes would have to take place in the 'external conditions' of science, to use Max Weber's phrase. In 1973, Szyliowicz was led to a very depressing portrayal of Egyptian science. Poor equipment, mediocre research staff, heavy teaching loads, poor salaries and the ever open door policy of migration all led to intellectual isolation and limited scientific achievement. Five years later, Georgie Hyde (1978) was able to report a growing official recognition of some of these problems and some improvement in the contribution of Egyptian scientists to the country's development problems, but argued, nevertheless, that the picture remained bleak. To put such comments in perspective it must be remembered that in comparison to many other Middle Eastern societies, Egypt has a very strong system of scientific and technological research. In a general review of science and technology in the Middle East, Ziauddin Sardar (1982, p. 129) said this of Egypt: There is a tradition of research and development work and the country has some of the most established and respected laboratories and scientific institutions in the Arab World. The National Research Centre is the largest research institution in the Middle East and Organisations like the Remote Sensing Centre are doing work of fundamental importance for the whole region.

Three problems stand out, however, when science and technology policies are closely inspected; the nature and quality of scientific education, the lack of co-ordination between development planning and scientific research and, finally, the dependence of technology on foreign firms. Each of these issues illustrates different facets of the dependency status of Egyptian science and of Egyptian society.

The problem of scientific education is that Western models of what this should be have been adopted without the same level of resources applied to it. Sardar (1982, p. 14) has identified the problem in this way, although not specifically in relation to Egypt.

> The continuous reliance on European and American universities for the training of their scientists has meant that universities in the Middle East have not had adequate opportunity and government

> support to develop research infrastructures and the skills and resources necessary for postgraduate teaching. As most of the teaching staff are educated abroad, the little research that is carried out tends to bear no relationship to local needs and requirements.

Sardar notes further that science courses are typically examination oriented, that there is an emphasis on premature specialisation and through a strong aversion to experimental work, an emphasis on rote learning, scientists are produced without any real understanding of what scientific research is or how it might be applied.

The problem of co-ordination is simply this; successive Egyptian governments have sought to define a policy for science and technology but none so far has managed to devise a system of science management which co-ordinates research with development plans across the whole spectrum of government departments. Furthermore, there is a lot of evidence to show that science policy has been manipulated for short-term political gains and that this detracts from there being clear overall goals to which the scientific community might effectively respond (see Zahlan, 1978, 1980, 1981).

Finally, there is the enormously vexed and complex question of technological dependency on foreign firms and aid organisations. Zahlan (1980, p. 176) has argued that it is this which, alongside the destitute state of the universities, which accounts for what he calls the 'present impoverishment of science and technology in the Arab world'.

In several fields of research this dependency is evident. They include solar energy research, nuclear power engineering, micro-electronics and desalinisation. Egypt, for example, has a developing nuclear power programme and accords for the supply of nuclear plant have been signed with the United States, France and West Germany (Sardar, 1982, p. 43) and Egypt's solar energy research programme relies on funds from the United States and West Germany. Almost all the research projects at Cairo's National Research Centre are funded by United States aid through AID and Sardar (1982, p. 68) has observed 'most AID projects in Egypt are big, conspicuous technology projects which involve American companies transferring technology'.

Technology transfer is a serious issue throughout the Arab world since it bears on questions of national sovereignty, military policy and, of course, though in a less directly measurable way but perhaps far more profoundly on the cultural and educational development of these societies. It is, indeed, one of the undercurrents of political life throughout the Middle East, that a growing number of people, particularly among the recently educated, are calling into question the validity of development models which all too often seem to conflict with the basic tenets of the faith and which imply too many compromises with the secular and capitalist forces of the West. These are issues which, as will be shown later, governments in the West should consider, for the problems of education and of science and technology highlighted here are not the outcome of something peculiar to Egypt alone; they are a part of how Egypt, as a poor society, has been brought into relationship with the developed economies of the world. They are, in short, a facet of dependency and they admit of no solution which does not face this fact.

11 Higher Education in Turkey

The system of higher education in Turkey displays many formal parallels with that of Egypt. Both societies have attempted to develop universities modelled on those of the West but in conditions which are entirely unfavourable for the success of such developments. Except in the case of a few institutions internationally recognised for their research and teaching the universities of Egypt and Turkey, though straining towards a Western ideal, fall far short of realising it. In the course of seeking such recognition they may well have contributed less effectively to the development of the two societies than had been hoped. The failure of higher education institutions in the two societies to meet the goals that have been set for them cannot only be attributed to weaknesses in the universities themselves, although these do matter; the failure is an aspect of the structures of underdevelopment of the societies in which they have grown.

The universities in both societies are overcrowded. Their output of students is not closely aligned with the needs of their national economies. There are great social inequalities in both societies which are reflected in patterns of admission to higher education; some groups, particularly among the poor and those from rural areas, especially women, are badly under-represented in the student body. Although the reasons behind the eruptions have been different in each case both in Egypt and Turkey, students have come to play a direct and often violent role in the political life of the society and the university campuses have become political battlegrounds for warring factions. That, at least in the Turkish case was until 1980 when the Turkish army, for the third time in post-war history, took over the running of the state.

Since 1980 universities in Turkey have faced a new set of problems. The problems of political unrest have been overcome, although for how long no one can tell, and the military regime has consolidated itself. Universities have been brought strictly to heel under the direct central control of a Higher Education Council (YÖK). They have been purged of staff thought to be politically unreliable and their former autonomy has been taken away from them. National curricula have been imposed and new institutions set up to cope with the large numbers of young people who seek higher education. Staff have been redeployed and severe new disciplinary measures have been imposed. Many Turkish academics have been sacked; many more have resigned and there is grave concern in the country among academics about falling standards in Turkish higher education.

The aim of this chapter is to explain why these problems have developed and have taken their particular form. In what follows the development of Turkish higher education will be examined first and some of the values which have inspired it. These developments are then set alongside patterns of social change to explain the social, religious and political differentiation among Turkish students. Since the quality of higher education is critical to a country's ability to profit from modern science and technology, the role of Turkish higher education will be discussed in relation to the economy and in particular to the formation of technically qualified personnel. Finally, the development of Turkish higher education since the military coup of 1980 will be discussed.

The theme which underlies the discussion is that within the unique developments of Turkish higher education there is an underlying logic at which work sets the constraints and opportunities on what can be achieved in Turkey given its particular economic structure, development strategies and state form.

DEVELOPMENT OF TURKISH HIGHER EDUCATION IN REPUBLICAN TURKEY

The development of higher education during the republican period has to be seen in the light of the social structure of Turkey in the years immediately following the First World War and the War of Turkish Independence. Three closely connected aspects of the society need to be stressed, the Ottoman state legacy of a failure to carry through reforms, the background and ideology of the republican leadership and, finally, the lack of a framework of modern higher education for the training of personnel other than highly placed military and state officials.

The Ottoman state had from the end of the eighteenth century acknowledged the need, particularly in the military field, to learn from developments in Europe. In 1795 an artillery school staffed by French officers was set up and was followed by schools for military engineering, medicine and a college of war. Later in the nineteenth century and the development of a secular educational system outside the traditional *madrasas* had led to the Civil Service School (*Mülkiye*) in 1859 and a law school in 1888. The *Mülkiye* developed throughout the second half of the century into an elite institution whose graduates came to occupy most of the important administrative positions in the empire (Frey, 1965; Roos and Roos, 1971). The graduates of this school along with those from the military academies, particularly the *Harbiye* (War College) were the training grounds for a new political elite which was secular in outlook and Western in orientation.

Frey (1965, p. 33) has shown that the development of this secular and modern system of higher education (supported as it was by a growth in prestigious secondary schools such as the Galatasaray *lise*) 'split the Ottoman ruling elite beyond repair'. Divisions emerged between modernisers and *madrasa*-trained scholars orientated more to Islam and the Ottoman state, an educational dualism which Frey (1965, p. 38) suggests 'resulted in the production of two conflicting mentalities'.

The Young Turk revolution of 1908 did little to resolve this and it was Atatürk who took up the challenge successfully to Westernise the Turkish educated elites. What Atatürk failed to do, however, was to modernise the mass of uneducated Turks who constituted the vast majority of his republic. In a very prescient comment, Frey (1965, p. 43) noted that 'This is an incredibly complex and delicate, even dangerous, assignment.' In post-Second World War Turkey, particularly in the most recent two decades the historic failure to Westernise the mass of Turks, particularly in rural areas, has had explosive political consequences which have brought the society close to civil war.

Şerif Mardin (1980, p. 40) has noted a feature of Ottoman reforms to education which explains a great deal of the subsequent difficulties faced by the Turkish republic under Atatürk in developing the country's economy; the fact that education expanded to fill official roles in the Ottoman bureaucracy. 'Educational institutions', he writes, 'were not created in Turkey to meet the needs of the sons of a solid bourgeousie whose parents were preparing them to join the family business by giving them the opportunity to learn bookkeeping and letter writing.' The contrast with Europe is clear and the consequences for social differentiation in Turkish society were to legitimate differences of status based on closeness to the bureaucratic and military leadership of the state. Since business, throughout the Ottoman period had been in the hands of ethnic and religious minorities – Christians, Armenians, Greeks and Jews – it had a lower status. The sons of the provincial notables who were educated in the professional schools sought their own futures not in trade but in public administration or the military. This explains a great deal of the political outlook and ideological stance of many of the Young Turks whose campaigning finally deposed Sultan Abdulhamid and of those after the debacle of the First World War who rallied to Mustafa Kemal (Atatürk) to fight for an independent Turkish Republic.

Atatürk himself told a congress of teachers before the battle of Sakarya that 'I am of the opinion that the principles of education and training which have been followed up to now are the most important factor in the decline of our nation's history' (Frey, 1965, p. 32). The social background on men like Mustafa Kemal encouraged them to identify strongly with the interests of the nation and the people rather than those of the central Ottoman elite and their religious supporters.

The ideological current which had influenced the Young Turks in their struggles against Abdülhamid were drawn from French positivism, the writings of Comte and later Durkheim which had been such a key influence on the philosopher and sociologist, Ziya Gökalp, the ideologist of the Young Turks. Şerif Mardin (1969, p. 277) has described them in this way:

> Educated in state schools established to modernise the bureaucracy, but brought up also with the idea of preserving the state, these young men found in the social engineering aspects of Comte the legitimation of their elitist outlook. Science was the rock on which they leaned.

And it was through education and nationalism strongly oriented to the West that they believed the future of Turkey lay. This starting point shaped their perception of what development had to mean for Turkey.

Gökalp, for example, saw the problems of the new Turkey as stemming from the fact the country contained three layers of people each different in education and civilisation from the other. These were the common people, the men educated in modern schools and those educated in *madrasas*. Each represented, respectively, the civilisations of the Far East, the West and the East. 'That means', he wrote, 'one portion of our nation is living in an ancient another in a medieval and a third in a modern age' (quoted in Frey, 1965, p. 39). The solution was the development of an education system which, secular in form would unite people in the one moral community which mattered, the nation.

Gökalp's ideas and his concept of *Türkcülük* - Turkism - stressing the unity of Turkish society and nation with patriotism replacing religion as the central core of the *conscience collective*, had a great influence on the subsequent course of the Turkish revolution and in particular on the development of education (Spencer, 1958). Such ideas coupled well with those of Mustafa Kemal that Turkey was a society in which there were clear divisions of occupation but none of social class and that the role of the state was to serve the people.

Any state requires educational institutions appropriate to its goals yet Atatürk had inherited a system which was poorly developed and in which, in its higher reaches, many were opposed to him. In 1933 he commissioned a report on the darülfünûn - the university - which showed it to offer low standard teaching and to lack any capacity for research.

The Law of Reorganisation of 1933 abolished the Ottoman institution and replaced it with the Univeristy of Instanbul. Staff were recruited carefully. They had to know a foreign language and several came from abroad, some as refugees from Nazi Germany. As late as 1949 there were still seventy-two foreign professors in Turkey's three universities and one writer felt able to report that 'Turkey is still reaping the benefits from having opened her academic doors to this oppressed intelligentsia' (Fotos, 1955, p. 251). New research institutes were created as well as courses on the history of the Turkish revolution. In 1937 the merged faculties of law, agriculture, language, history and geography formed the basis of the new University of Ankara.

The period of the 1930s was a difficult one for Turkey and the economy was badly affected by the world depression. It was the period of *étatism* during which the state pursued policies to develop industry through state economic enterprises and build up an infrastructure of economic organisation. These policies encouraged a much wider marketisation of the agricultural sector. They promoted the growth of provincial merchant interests and of a middle peasant group engaged in commercial agriculture (see Keyder, 1979).

The state introduced very strict labour laws modelled on Italian fascist legislation prohibiting unions and making strikes illegal.

During the later 1930s and throughout the Second World War the state managed to maintain the industrial sector of the economy but agricultural prices declined affecting the position of poorer peasants rather badly. This was a group which in any case was alienated from the regime on account of its militant secularisation policies.

The relevance of this for higher education is that a new pattern of social differentiation was developing in Turkey in which higher education played a key role in elite recruitment but one which inevitably brought it close to the centre of the political divisions in the society. In the post-war years, as will be seen, higher education became one of main sites of violent political conflict in Turkish society.

Higher education expanded rapidly from the early 1930s onwards. There were in total 6890 students in 1934–35; this figure doubled by 1940 and quadrupled to 25 000 in 1950 and in the ten years which followed it doubled to 53 000 in 1960 (OECD, 1965, p. 152). Given the values of the society, however, particularly the importance attached to employment in the state bureaucracy itself, it is hardly surprising that throughout this period the highest enrolments were in social science courses which throughout the period accounted for almost 50 per cent of all enrolments. This compares to a figure of about 20 per cent for science and technology courses.

During much of this period students were, as Fotos (1958, p. 254) described them, 'the very epitome of Turkish nationalism'. Their principal organisation was the National Students' Federation, a very loyal body which offered welfare support and social activities, especially on important national days. Fotos noted that 'There is a marked absence of radical leftist tendencies among Turkish university students.'

Turkish universities took no responsibility for student accommodation; their dormitories were privately sponsored often being supported by leading merchants, farmers or professionals from the provinces and charging nominal rents. The relevance of this is that links among students from the same province (i.e. among *hemşeri*) are strong in Turkey and this has important consequences later for how the student body divided along religious and political lines.

THE STRUCTURE OF HIGHER EDUCATION IN TURKEY

By 1971 Turkey had nine universities. Controlled and financed from the Ministry of Education the universities themselves, at least until the 1980 military coup, were from 1946 onwards autonomous institutions. The structure of their academic work was heavily influenced by the model of German universities with a great deal of status and power being attached to the senior academics who held personal chairs. Promotion was strictly regulated and slow and academic standards uneven. Low academic salaries were, in addition a strong cause for complaint among Turkish academics. Turkish criticism of the system during the 1960s focused on issues like overcrowding the inadequacy of *lise* graduates to the demands of university work, the lack of teacher-student contact and a reliance on formal teaching methods and limited text books, a method of teaching promoting memorisation and rote learning. Professor Okyar (1968, p. 224), then the professor of Economics at Hacettepe University and former Rector of the Atatürk university, criticised the universities in 1967 for poor standards of analysis, research and research training and low levels of exertion. 'Strong feelings', he wrote, 'and the stifling straightjacket of dogmatic thinking continue to influence attitudes and behaviour and the role of thinking in various ways'. The defence of autonomy, he felt, often prevented creative self-criticism and the system as a whole failed the economy in various ways.

Alongside the universities there were, until recently, a number of high institutes providing specialist training for the professions and for commerce as well as teacher training colleges. Many of these institutions have been incorporated into the university system as new universities have been established. There are now twenty-seven universities in Turkey each one suffering from the problems of rapid expansion, poor resources and inadequate teaching and research. The system as a whole does not dovetail at all well with the needs of the country for scientific and technical personnel. As has already been stressed, universities have been at the centre of the political strife which has taken place in Turkish society. These questions, to be understood, have to be set against the social and economic developments of the post-war period which generated new strains in Turkish society and against the pattern of student recruitments to higher education.

After the Second World War Turkey became part of a new structure of international relations which was itself bound up with power bloc rivalry between East and West. In response to Russian pressure on it in 1946 Turkey became part of the Western alliance. The country received Marshall Aid from 1946 onwards from the United States. In 1949 Turkey joined the Council of Europe; a year previously it had joined the OECD and in 1952 became a full member of NATO. From this period on (and following Turkish military involvement in the Korean War) the political, economic, military and educational links with the West have increased as has the volume of Western aid to the country.

Within this international framework Turkish higher education received a great deal of significant help from both in bilateral and multilateral aid (Stirling, 1976). Examples of such aid include the help given by France to the University of Ankara to complete a hydraulic laboratory. The British Council offers help with language training for Turkish students. The Germans have financed management education projects in Ankara university. The Atatürk University at Erzurum was helped considerably by a USAID programme involving staff from the University of Nebraska between 1955 and 1968 and the Middle East Technical University received considerable aid from diverse organisations, including USAID, CENTO, the Ford Foundation and OECD.

Paul Stirling (1976, p. 308) had analysed the pattern of aid from the West under five headings: the training of students and staff in foreign universities; the bringing of foreign staff to Turkey; contact between Turkish universities and universities abroad; the provision of capital and buildings; and, finally, 'the provision of models of university life, academic values, assumptions, standards, organisations'. What emerges is a complex pattern of exchanges which defy complete description. It is a pattern with considerable benefit to Turkish universities but Stirling has cautioned about some of the disadvantages and dangers. They concern research priorities and, as one might expect, given the logic of science and technology transfer between countries grossly unequal in terms of material resources, the cultural integration of Turkish society itself.

On the research question Stirling simply notes that almost all able Turkish staff in universities receive their research training abroad and return with research priorities defined in the West:

> Either by capturing domestic or foreign aid resources in Turkey, or by managing to finance regular visits abroad, they launch on research related not to the activities of other Turks, nor to their Turkish university, nor to the needs of Turkey. Many of Turkey's best university brains are, in horrific ways, clients of foreign universities, contributing yet further to the colossal advantage which the rich nations already enjoy in knowledge and research; the academic analogue of the Turkish emigrant workers. (Stirling, 1976, p. 308)

Stirling (1976, p. 323) asks: 'How far does the fact that so much of Turkish life is directly linked to foreign enterprises, models, institutions and sources of finance prevent Turkey from developing an indigenous natural culture of its own?'

In the absence of such a strong national frame of reference Turkish academics will face a dilemma of measuring their achievements against those of colleagues in the West and will always find their own achievement falls short on account of poorer resources, or, to deny the importance of such a comparison and risk not being part of an international order of science and scholarship.

This particular dilemma highlights another, that of how the educated Turk should relate to his or her less educated countrymen. Stirling has noted that Western influence on Turkish society has been to increase the gap between the majority of Turkish people and the educated elite. The differences between villagers and recent urban migrants and the Western-educated groups in terms of such things as taste in music, art and leisure, in 'political convictions and assumptions, in personal morality, in cosmology and religious belief are vast' (Stirling, 1976, p. 324). The basic expectations of the educated for a standard of life related to that of Europe are likely to increase their sense of difference from those whom they would claim to lead. These expectations, in any case, can only be met if the Turkish economy can be made to grow within an unequal distribution of incomes, for if the less well off increase their share of national income then it will be at the expense of groups whose expectations for a high standard of living are already high. It is these groups who value higher education and they are the ones, too, who have been severely worried in the past decade by high levels of inflation.

Özay Mehmet (1983) has noted that Turkey in the 1970s had a grossly unequal pattern of income distribution, one of the worst in the world among middle-income countries. He claims, too, that the structure of income distribution is dominated 'by a top-heavy, self-serving cluster of bureaucratic political elites on the centre allied, on the one hand, with landowning provincial polity and, on the other, with urban-centred monopolistic interests who often earn large profits and indirect state subsidies through their dealings with SEE [State Economic Enterprises]' (Mehmet, 1983, p. 57). During the period of rapid inflation during the 1970s the group, including the free professionals made gains in their incomes while farmers, industrial workers lost significantly. Civil Servants, Mehmet claims, maintained their income share but since these economic difficulties corresponded with growing levels of unemployment there was much in the failure of Turkey's development strategy and economic policies which fuelled political and revolutionary activity in the society.

For those in the higher status positions a claim to being well educated is a major plank of their self-respect and educational differences are powerfully acknowledged status criteria in Turkish society. The educated represent and echo to the great as opposed to folk traditions of Turkish culture. Closer inspection of the pattern of recruitment to higher education shows that it follows the same logic as that of secondary education. The system favours the better off, those from urban as opposed to rural areas, where most of the *lises* are and the children of officials as opposed to those of peasants or workers.

Andreas Kazamias (1966) noted in the 1960s that the pattern of opportunity in Turkey had the shape of a minaret, it was very narrow at the top. Those who succeed to higher education have first to be successful in the *lise*. In this way the inequalities visible at this level in the system are amplified. Regional inequalities in the distribution of secondary educational opportunities overlap with the inequalities of income and life style within the society and through this, influence considerably patterns of cultural transmissions, attitudes and opportunity in education.

Education is perceived in Turkey to be a central avenue of mobility but one which confers prestige rather than high income (see Aral, 1980). It seems also the case that opportunities for social mobility in Turkey since the Second World War have had a great deal to do with changes in the occupational structure of the society and migration to urban areas and less to do with real change in education.

The few studies which do exist on social mobility in Turkey are small scale and really do not sort these issues out. Something of the pattern of educational mobility is indicated in a study of university admission by researchers in Ankara. The survey, carried out in 1976 showed that one-third of applicants were from rural areas. One-third were women (although women constituted less than one-tenth of the applications from rural areas). One-third of all applicants and nearly one-half of those who passed the entrance examinations were from three large urban centres – Istanbul, Ankara and Izmir. Applicants from upper income families were much more likely than those from poor backgrounds to pass the examination (Özgediz, 1980). The composition of the student body and an indication of how this has changed over time is indicated in Table 11.1.

The patterns in this table are more important than the absolute

Table 11.1 Level of formal secondary and higher education by age and sex, Turkey 1980

Age group	Total	*Lise* % Male	*Lise* % Total age group	*Lise* % Female	Higher education % Male	Higher education % Total age group	Higher education % Female
11–14	4 194 081	–	–	–	–	–	–
15–19	4 877 556	58.8	6.3	41.1	73.9	0.1	26.0
20–24	4 144 144	67.6	9.9	32.3	65.8	3.6	34.1
25–34	6 090 104	67.8	4.0	32.1	77.7	4.7	22.2
35–44	4 422 557	66.8	1.8	33.1	81.0	3.0	19.0
45–54	3 831 626	66.9	1.3	33.0	84.8	1.5	15.2
55–64	1 961 499	68.6	1.6	31.3	86.5	1.8	13.5
65+	2 072 316	69.5	0.9	30.4	83.0	0.8	17.0
Unknown	94 106	64.8	3.8	35.3	89.1	4.7	10.9
Total	31 687 989	65.2	3.6	34.8	77.0	2.2	33.0

Source: Adapted from Census of Population. *Social and Economic Characteristics of Population 1% Sample Results* (Ankara: State Institute of Statistics 1980).

figures. What they show is that the younger age groups in the Turkish population have had a greater opportunity to attend *lises* than the older ones. On the other hand, there has not been such a great improvement in the proportion of the age group going on to university. Estimates about what the proportion is vary. In 1961 Kazamias (1966) estimated it at 1.0 per cent of the age group. In 1978 Hale (1978) estimated the figure to be between 6.4 and 7.8 per cent. These figures are lower than those reported in census returns.

What is perhaps clearer is the significant differences which exist between men and women in terms of their enrolment in the prestigious parts of the school system and in higher education. The participation of females has steadily increased over the years but the ratio is still about 65 : 36 in favour of men. It may well be the case, none the less, that in comparison to the Middle Eastern societies Turkey has done much more for the educational emancipation of women.

It should be noted, too, that the prestige attached to higher education varies according to the institution and even the faculty. The

Faculty of Political Science at Ankara is a very prestigious one. Its graduates have traditionally staffed the most important ministries in the state. Roos and Roos (1971, p. 22) have noted that the alumni of this institution make class histories read like a 'Who's Who in Turkey' for the republican period up to the end of the Second World War. Surveys of the social class background of graduates graduating between 1946 and 1955 and between 1958 and 1961 and a further survey in 1965 showed that about half came from official backgrounds, about a fifth from business backgrounds (Roos and Roos, 1971, p. 235).

There is little reason to be surprised by these patterns; they are the predictable outcome of a system of social stratification in a society which has always had a well-developed state and administrative apparatus and an undeveloped economy. The challenge to education planners in Turkey is to secure changes of a kind which are consistent with longer-term needs in the economy for trained personnel but which, in the short term, are politically feasible. The strong demand from *lise* graduates for places and political pressures, particularly from the provinces, that this demand should be met is difficult to square with national economic needs for better trained technicians and for a higher output of scientists and engineers.

The root issue here is the possibility of scientific and technological development in Turkey in a way which limits the country's dependency on outside aid. Critical to whether the country can mobilise its own scientific resources to develop its rich natural resources are the broad policies for science and education and research being followed. What these policies themselves can be is something constrained not just by available resources but by attitudes, expectations, and strategies of economic development.

SCIENCE, TECHNICAL TRAINING AND HIGHER EDUCATION

Since weaknesses in scientific and technical and vocational education are a common theme in all discussions of the Turkish secondary school system, it is no surprise that there are weaknesses, too, in the organisation of further technical education and in Turkish science as a whole. The roots of the problem go back, of course, to Ottoman times but they extend through the republican period to the present.

Ottoman modernisation plans in the nineteenth century acknowledged the importance of science and scholarship. In 1851 a Society of Knowledge (*Encümeni Daniş*) was formed modelled on the Academie Francaise but it collapsed in 1862 (Lewis, 1961, p. 437). The Ottoman Scientific Society was formed in 1861 and published scientific journals in which Western developments in science were reported. It was closed down in 1882 by Sultan Abdülhamid.

In the twentieth century science has found a place in Turkish universities but the output of scientists was described by Bernard Lewis (1961, p. 438) as late as 1961 as 'pitifully inadequate to the needs of a modern state and the volume of research well below the western level'. Successive five-year plans during the 1960s and 1970s have drawn attention to national shortages of technically trained personnel, particularly engineers (see Okyar, 1968). The need to develop technical education of all kinds and to move more resources in higher education into the applied sciences was the key theme which ran through the 1965 report of the Organisation of Economic Co-operation and Development (OECD) report on Turkey. This remains a persistent theme. A recent World Bank Report (1983, p. 5) on Turkey identified low labour productivity as one of the key constraints on economic development and set out the data in Table 11.2 on current shortages of scientific and technical workers.

These shortages are a reflection of long-standing preferences among school leavers for careers in social science, particularly law, poor facilities for scientific education and, perhaps, a feeling among students that Turkish industry cannot employ scientists at levels or with salaries appropriate to their education (World Bank, 1975). They are a reflection, too, of inadequate provision of science education in Turkish schools. It was reported in 1972, for instance, that teacher : pupil ratios in arts and humanities in schools were around 1 : 34. In physics, the figure was 1 : 75 and in chemistry 1 : 84 (State Planning Office, quoted in Weiker, 1981, p. 161).

The pattern of enrolments in universities and other institutes of higher education is further suggestive of these explanations. Science and engineering together still only make up barely one third of all higher education enrolments, a share of the total which has remained fairly stable over the past decade.

Lacking a strong national foundation of independent scientific research the education of those studying in higher education is not linked to developments in or the activities of scientific research. Although there are now twenty-seven universities in Turkey, university

Table 11.2 Demand and supply for professional scientists and engineers, technicians, skilled and semi-skilled workers in industry, 1985–95

Occupational category	Additional demand †	Supply	Supply as % of additional demand	Deficit as % of total labour demand in 1995
Professional scientists and engineers	175 000	120 000	69	17
Technicians	117 000	54 400*	46	31
Skilled and semi-skilled manual workers	2 447 000	1 430 000**	58	21

Notes: † Excluding upgrading requirement.
* Assumes † rapid growth of technician training institutes.
** Not including on-the-job training.

Source: World Bank (1983, p. 5).

research is concentrated both in volume and quality in just a few of these institutions in the large cities of Ankara, Istanbul and Izmir. Universities outside these cities do very little research (Sardar, 1982).

Turkey does have, however, an extensive framework of scientific policy-making and research organisation. The main scientific institution is Tübitak, the Scientific and Technical Research Council of Turkey. Tübitak sponsors many research groups in the basic sciences, in engineering, medicine, veterinary sciences and agriculture. It sponsors research and seeks overall to improve the quality of Turkish science and technology and in particular the training of Turkish research personnel. Through Turdoc, the Turkish Scientific and Technical Documentation Centre, which was established in 1966, efforts are made to facilitate the use of scientific and technical information from Turkey and from abroad. Sardar (1982) has summarised its activities this way: Turkish science policy emphasises technology much more than science. There is great emphasis on the transfer of technology, and 'techno-logical' progress and 'socioeconomic objectives of national economy' are seen purely in terms of transferring and securing Western technology.

It could hardly be otherwise given the world imbalance in scientific research and development and the dependence of modern science and technology on huge capital investments of a sort that poor countries simply cannot afford. Mehmet (1981, p. 58) has suggested that this strategy of high technology industrialisation based on imported technology was a major cause of Turkey's poor employment record and therefore something which contributed to the political instability of the society.

HIGHER EDUCATION AND POLITICAL VIOLENCE

During the period of the late 1960s and throughout the 1970s Turkish higher education was tragically caught up in the political conflicts of the society. It both reflected those conflicts and generated them and student political factionalism has been a factor prompting the Turkish military on three occasions to take over political power.

The vulnerability of institutions of higher education to political manipulations is not, of course, a phenomenon unique to Turkey or the Middle East in general. Higher education institutions in any modern society are necessarily sensitive to the political and economic changes going on around them for they are nearly always in the forefront of those changes. Their students are typically drawn from the elite social groups of the society and responsive to changes in society which affect their material interests in future employment. Teachers in these institutions are typically closely connected with political interest groups and state institutions and the most well known of them become important for their views across the whole range of legal, economic and sociopolitical issues throughout the society.

Turkey is no exception to this generalisation but the unique patterns of Turkish development have left distinctive marks on Turkish higher education undermining the Kemalist vision of what such institutions should be and what role their students should play in the society. Far from reinforcing the ideal of strengthening a *conscience collective* based on secularism, republicanism, and nationalism within which the educated would feel a special obligation to think scientifically and contribute to national development selflessly,

Turkish higher education, particularly from the late 1950s onwards, has been at the centre of political and ideological conflict.

There is no simple explanation for this. Some writers have explained the broad political malaise of Turkey during this period in terms of failure of leadership (see, e.g. Karpat, 1981). Şerif Mardin (1978) has discussed the political factionalism which brought Turkey to the point of civil war during the late 1970s in terms of a cultural dislocation of Turkish society consequential on the 'peasantisation' of urban areas and the break up of traditional social control. Yet others, particularly those on the left, see the political crises of Turkish society as a facet of Turkey's mode of capitalist industrialisation (see, e.g. Keyder, 1979).

These explanations are not necessarily mutually exclusive and the truth of the matter is that the political fractures of Turkish society have to be understood at several different levels and as being a consequence of problems connected with, on the one hand, the general phenomena of underdevelopment and rapid modernisation and, on the other, with the unique institutional and historical characteristics of Turkish society itself. Higher education is a sensitive barometer of both sets of issues.

The opening up of Turkey to democratic politics in 1950 and to economic policies which favoured private enterprise created a new set of opportunities in Turkey which favoured the interests of businessmen and richer peasant as against those of the traditional republican elites and the urban middle classes dependent of state employment. Increasing opportunities for exports following the Korean war facilitated a rapid development of the Turkish economy together with an acceleration of urbanisation. These developments had profound consequences for the shape of social inequality in Turkish society for the social structure of urban areas and for political life in general. New social and economic inequalities emerged. The Democrat Party, which ousted the Republican People's Party in the 1950 election, found its support among urban businessmen and richer peasants who benefited greatly from market liberalisation and from improvements in a transport infrastructure which itself had been made possible with Marshall Aid from the United States. Agricultural mechanisation increased as did rural migration to the cities and for the first time in Turkish history the peasantry acquired, through the Democrat Party considerable political clout and could raise questions about, for example, religious issues, which had for so long been off the political agenda in Turkey.

By the end of the decade, this particular structure of modernisation had run into serious economic and political difficulties. Economically there developed a serious problem of inflation as the government coped with a growing problem of import financing. This was a period when trades unions developed rapidly in Turkey under the overall guidance of the moderate Turkish Confederation of Trades Unions (*Türk-Is*). Opposition to Democrat Party rule came from younger members of the Republican People's Party and from the official class itself worried about a loss of prestige and the erosion of its income through inflation. This was also true of the military. Students were active in opposition to the government and the military coup of 1961 toppled the Menderes government in the name of democracy and justice.

It seems clear there was widespread concern about Democrat policies. A demonstration organised by school and university students in Istanbul in September 1955 against, ostensibly, Greek policies of *enosis* in Cyprus, degenerated into a riot, a rebellion as one historian put it, of the Istanbul *lumpen proletariat* against luxury and wealth (Ahmad, 1977). There was concern, too, that the Democrats were undermining the secular basis of the state by encouraging religious activity in the countryside and opposition to Kemalism. Students, however, were an important catalyst of the opposition to Menderes and as Şerif Mardin (1978) has said, they gained some reputation at the time as 'giant killers'.

The decade which followed the coup was for the universities one of great expansion. In 1960–61 65 000 students enrolled in universities. By 1970 the figure had increased to 159 000. During this same period there was considerable growth in teacher training and in religious colleges and it was the teacher training colleges where fascist groups among students were to find considerable support. It was a period of continuing rapid social change and one in which political factionalism among students, particularly among those on the left, increased and was coloured by the ideological currents of student protest in Europe, the United States and Japan.

The events of 1968 (the French student movement, the Russian invasion of Czechoslovakia, the Tet Offensive in Vietnam) had a great impact in Turkey among students. Left-wing students occupied the university of Istanbul and there were demonstrations against a visit of the United States Sixth Fleet to the city. It was a period of considerable factional in-fighting among different left-wing groups campaigning in and around the Turkish Labour Party and in the trades unions. Some of these groups took up guerrilla tactics against the state and imperialism (see Samin, 1981).

On the university campuses student politics erupted into intimidation of political opponents and to protests against university authorities. The affairs of the formerly apolitical National Students Federation were thoroughly politicised and a revolutionary youth movement (*Dev Genç*) emerged. Terrorist violence increased in the cities and when university campuses were eventually searched by security authorities they met with armed resistance Karpat, 1981).

In March 1971 the military intervened again to counter terrorism. Martial law was imposed and many arrests followed, particularly on the left. By 1973 the country was returned to democratic government and the Republican People's Party gained power. During the following few years student political violence increased, particularly violence between Right wing and left-wing groups. The right was by this time well organised and had its own terrorist factions. Şerif Mardin (1978, p. 234) summed it up this way: 'If the stronghold of the left was certain faculties of the universities, the stronghold of national socialism was the Ministry of Education and the system of state Teacher Training Schools.'

University professors were intimidated and some were shot. The leaders of the National Action Party were able to influence appointments and student admissions to the training colleges and while a military presence on campus controlled the violence in lecture rooms, it served merely to displace it to dormitories and to the streets (see Renda, 1980).

Beyond the left–right political divide this was a period during which religious groups in Turkey began to assert themselves. Right-wing political parties were able to make successful appeals to religious people on the theme of anti-communism and religious organisations among students sought to organise clandestinely in the universities. Such groups were and are still able to offer their members considerable support in such things as accommodation, companionship, help with textbooks and, during the troubles, personal protection.

During the period from 1975 onwards violence continued to escalate. Inflation increased, foreign indebtedness increased and organised government seemed impossible. In September 1980 the military intervened for the third time, this time under General Kenan Evren. The trigger for the coup, against a parliamentary background of the major parties being unable to agree on the election of a President of the Republic, was a demonstration in Konya of the ultra right and Islamic National Salvation Party of Erbakan. Konya is an important religious city, a centre of long-standing religious opposition to the republic. Some of the banners at the demonstration demanded a return to the law of the Sharia. Erbaken himself marched under a banner in arabic script on which was written the name of Allah.

The explanation for the coup lies deeper than this, of course, and relates to the role of the military in the Turkish state formation and to the structural problems of the society and the economy and the political system itself. Only this is clear; by the end of the decade Turkish society had become sufficiently polarised for the ideologies of both right and left to find ready support and that the fractures in the society were most obvious in its system of education. The competing ideological claims of the left and the right struck responsive chords among a student body which has grown rapidly and which experienced severe difficulties over accommodation, teaching and library resources. It was a body which was divided within itself along the very same lines which divided Turkish society as a whole.

MILITARY POLICIES IN HIGHER EDUCATION

Since students had played a major role in the political disturbances which prompted the military to intervene it was inevitable that the universities would be brought under stricter control. One Turkish academic in the Middle East Technical University told me that dealing firmly with disloyal groups among students was something close to the heart of General Evren. He had been incensed once at METU when students had not stood to attention while the national anthem had been played and affirmed that he would 'crush these elements'.

The new regime acted quickly on the universities and enacted a law on higher education (Law Number 2547) on 4 November 1981, a little under two months after the takeover of power. Article 4 of the new law set out the aims of higher education. These were:

a. To educate students so that they:
   (1) will be loyal to ATATÜRK nationalism and to ATATÜRK'S reforms and principles,

(2) will be in accord with the national, ethical, human, spiritual and cultural values of the Turkish nation and conscious of the dignity of being a Turk,
(3) will put the common good above their own personal interests and have full devotion for family, country and nation,
(4) will be fully conscious of their duties and responsibilities towards their country and will act accordingly,
(5) will have free though a liberal vision of world affairs and respect for human rights,
(6) will develop in a balanced way, physically, mentally, spiritually and emotionally,
(7) will prove to be good citizens contributing to the country's welfare and at the same time acquire the necessary skills for their future vocations.
(Higher Education Law, 1981)

The aims were elaborated further to charge higher education institutions to carry out research and to become 'recognised members within the world of science'. The basic principles behind these general aims are set out in the law as Atatürk nationalism, respect for Turkish mores and traditions, equality of opportunity in higher education and for science and technology to be in accordance with national needs.

Compulsory courses were introduced on Atatürk's principles 'and the history of the Turkish Reforms' as well as in the Turkish language and physical education and a foreign language. The whole of higher education was brought under the authority of a central body, the Higher Education Council, with members appointed by the Head of State, the Council of Ministers, the Chief of the General Staff, the Ministry of Education and from the universities themselves. In the latter case appointed members had to have at least twenty-five year's of service in academic fields. The overall aim of the Higher Education Committee was to plan the system of higher education.

The law changed fundamentally the structure of university government in Turkey and removed from universities the right they had to elect their own rectors. Under the new law rectors would be centrally appointed and the appointment of Dean of Faculty would have to be confirmed by the Higher Education Council. Changes were made in the system of appointing staff and in structures of promotion. The essence of these changes, which caused considerable consternation among academic staff, was that they could not be promoted within their own university, that they would have to be moved elsewhere first. The logic behind this was to enable new universities to be staffed properly and to spread senior academic staff more evenly across the country as a whole to assist university development in the rural areas. If staff refused redeployment they are considered under Article 41 of the new law to have, in effect, resigned. Regulations on student discipline were tightened as were the rules governing students rights to resit examinations. Article 59 of the new law stated quite specifically that politics and education were to be separated:

> Teaching staff members, and students of all levels, in institutions of higher education cannot be affiliated with political parties and their attached organisations; nor can they be involved in any political activity on behalf of a party. Membership of any society, excluding Voluntary Societies, is subject to the Rector's permission in writing.

The law amounts to a severe re-affirmation of Kemalist philosophy and its purpose is to bring the universities directly under central control to prevent the development of opposition politics within them. Built into the new regulations is the assumption that university autonomy was a concept that had been abused in Turkey and that the freedom universities had had to elect their own rectors and deans and to determine appointments to teaching posts had been corrupted by political factionalism on campus.

Turkish academics were clearly divided by all this. All felt the uncertainty of their new situation. The author was told by one senior academic that 'Turkish universities are in a state of shock under the new regulations. No one is certain of a job. Student numbers are to increase. Staff are to be reallocated. Research is to be centrally decided upon from proposals submitted by academics. Salaries are too low – about £70.00 per month – and morale has dropped.'

Another university teacher said that 'Nobody knows if they have a job next year. No planning is possible any longer.' Yet another added that university teachers had to be very careful what they said in lectures lest someone should inform on them to the military authorities accusing them of bias. The result was, of course, a severe self-censorship and a general feeling that the future would be bleak. Talk among university teachers was of resignation and impending resignations, of sackings and of their options for future employment. For under the new rules anyone who was sacked from the university would lose any entitlement to pension rights or to further employment by the state. All new appointments or redeployments would be vetted by the Higher Education Council and the security services to make sure that there were no political objections to particular members of staff.

The implementation of the new law since 1981 has raised some critical questions for Turkish higher education but the central ones revolve around three issues, those of the lack of autonomy of universities, the quality of higher education and the level of resources, both human and financial, which are available to the system.

The effective removal of university autonomy has caused considerable alarm in Turkish universities. The Higher Education Council has replaced nearly all rectors and deans with its own appointees and has been involved in a detailed way in planning national curricula for the universities and in reorganising their staffing structure. Bernard Kennedy, the *Times* correspondent in Ankara commented on these developments: 'In doing so it has spread a mixture of fear and indifference among a wide range of teaching staff, and confusion among all those connected with higher education' (THES, 11 February 1983, p. 8).

The Higher Education Council insists on strict adherence to rules which cover such detailed matters as academic dress and which to many academics and to anyone outside Turkey, seem absurdly trivial. Neither teachers or students are allowed, for example, to wear beards. Professor S. Erez, Professor of Obstetrics at Instanbul and chairman of the Turco-British Association, was, in fact, suspended from his post for refusing to shave off his beard and required to attend the Court of Decency to explain himself. The problem here is that the authorities see the beard as a symbol of left-wing sympathies. Turkey is a society where the symbolism of dress has considerable political importance. It was, after all, Atatürk himself who made the wearing of the Fez illegal thereby bringing his cultural revolution directly into the personal world of every Turk. Or, to put it differently, such dress regulations fuse the personal and the political in a way which obliges everyone to whom they apply to make a personal political statement on a daily basis.

More importantly, of course, the freedom of staff to write what they see as the truth has been curtailed absolutely. Those thought to be politically opposed to the regime are sacked. The Dean of Political Science at Instabul University was sacked for his political views and Yalçin Küçük was sentenced to eight years in prison for his book, *A New Republic*, which was considered a Marxist document (*THES*, 25

February 1983, p. 7). Notions of academic freedom which are central to how universities legitimate themselves in Western Europe are indeed foreign to the present system in Turkey.

There is, however, a growing discussion of this issue and particularly of the Higher Education Council itself under the leadership of Professor Doğramacı. It was reported recently, for example, in *Cumhuriyet* that the leader of the Social Democrat Party, Inönü, had criticised the university system. He is quoted as saying:

> There is no spirit in our universities. The desire to work, research and to think independently – these characteristics are lost. Independent thought has disappeared from the universities. If a university does not have academic autonomy it is like a bird with a broken wing. Whatever effort it makes it cannot fly. (*Cumhuriyet*, 2 October 1984)

Inönü followed this with the view that those members of staff who had been sacked from the system should be reinstated immediately.

The Higher Education Council has come under a great deal of criticism for what some see as its autocratic methods of making decisions and the sheer recklessness of some of those decisions, particularly the way it has expanded the university system while simultaneously getting rid of a large number of university staff on political grounds.

A recent article in *Cumhuriyet* by Dr Rauf Nasuhoğlu (1 March 1984) noted, for instance, that hundreds of senior staff had left the universities and had been replaced by less qualified people. According to his calculations the Ankara Faculty of Science has losts 101 members of staff and the Faculty of Medicine had lost sixty-eight. Three hundred and fourteen staff had left the Middle East Technical University. 'Our universities', he wrote, 'cannot survive this haemorrhage. We have fallen into a swamp of a system which is based on a personal autocracy.'

Nasuhoğlu went on to point out that the Higher Education Council interefered too closely with the work of universities and undermined the autonomy which, he felt, was a prerequisite for professional teaching and research. Even authoritarian states, he pointed out, had some degree of autonomy in their universities. Universities, he insists, require a basic respect for human rights, freedom of science and research and tolerance and that the only institution with any autonomy in the Turkish higher education system was the elite group within the Higher Education itself.

Criticism must be expressed within certain strict limits, however, and the Higher Education Council has recently allowed a more open discussion on autonomy. The reason can only be guessed at but one interpretation might be that the council values the opportunity such open discussion allows to affirm its own concept of autonomy. Professor Doğramacı, for example, is quoted by *Cumhuriyet* of 22 September 1984 as saying: 'In the universities there is no political interference.' His theme was that university rectors should be appointed and not elected; that student opinions should be consulted but that they should have no role in university government. The Higher Education Council, he said, was prepared to listen to complaints from students and that Turkey could be favourably compared to many West European countries in the degree of autonomy it allowed its universities.

Within these subtle rules of propagandising and criticising the strongest platform from which to comment is an Atatürkist one. Professor Necip Bilge criticised the Higher Education Council in *Cumhuriyet* of 22 February 1984 for not following strictly enough the methods of Atatürk in the field of university planning. Conceding the necessity of the Higher Education Council, he criticised the speed at which it opened up new universities and the insecurity this meant for university staff. Atatürk, on the other hand, had taken his time in bringing about reforms in universities and had accorded them more autonomy than the Higher Education Law did.

The autonomy issue is critical to all debates about the universities and to discussions of what kind of state exists in contemporary Turkey and it is clearly an issue which concerns the Turkish government since it bears directly on the image Turkey has in Europe and in the United States. The conditions of academic freedom, however, are not confined to the legal status of universities. They concern, too, the resources available for higher education and the quality of the teaching, learning and research which goes on within them. The issue of resources is urgent and serious since an already under-resourced system has expanded rapidly after the military coup and the consequences have been dire.

Since the coup, eight new universities have been opened in Turkey accommodating almost 90 000 students. The universities were formed by regrouping former higher education institutes and teacher training establishments and reflect that long-standing pressure of aspirations for university education which all post-war Turkish governments have had to cope with. In the academic year 1978–9 there were 319 715 students in universities. This figure dropped in the year following the coup to 240 364 but recovered to 268 000 by 1984 (*Newspot*, October 1984). The academic year 1984–5 began with 322 000 students (*Cumhuriyet*, 2 October 1984). The Higher Education Council is planning for 550 000 students by 1990 (*Cumhuriyet* 27 September 1984). In the academic year 1984–5 150 000 students were accepted into the system. This growth in numbers is fuelled by the academic amnesty which the Higher Education Council allowed to enable grade-repeating students to return to the universities in the hope of finishing their course. It is the case in Turkey that all young men must do national service. But only those with a diploma from the university can become reserve officers in the army. The indignity of an educated but unqualified Turk having to enter the army as an ordinary soldier is too unbearable so there has been a big response to the amnesty which allowed those formerly dismissed students to return to their colleges. It is not clear why the government should have conceded such an amnesty but one Turkish academic told the author he thought it was a political move. It is simply better to have members of the embattled generation of students in the system rather than outside it when they might become involved in terrorist politics again. This, of course, is only speculation.

There is no speculation necessary, however, about the outcome of this massive explosion of numbers, especially when it has been coupled by a massive reduction in teaching staff. Precise and reliable figures on staff reductions are difficult to find. Bernard Kennedy, the *Times* correspondent in Ankara, quoted recently a Turkish magazine which published the full list of 794 professors and lecturers who had actually been sacked or who had taken retirement since the Higher Education Council came into being (*THES*, 10 February 1984, p. 9). In May, however, Professor Doğramacı claimed that there had been no reduction in staffing, that those joining had replaced those who had left. Refuting suggestions in the press that 1188 staff had left, he claimed the figure was nearer 400. The larger figure being quoted was, he said, the result of staff redeployments and included people who were no longer counted as teachers and who would not necessarily return to higher education (*Cumuriyet*, 5 May 1984).

What the long-term consequences of such staffing changes means to the system as a whole cannot at this stage be assessed. What is clear, though, is that many universities are in considerable difficulty over teaching, accommodation and laboratory facilities and from a shortage of funds. Professor Tarakcıoğlu, the Rector of Gazi University in Ankara told the newspaper, *Milliyet* that:

> This year, 8,500 students were recruited through ÖSYM [i.e. the student recruitment office] 10,000 students through the academic amnesty. The number of students therefore rose to 48,000. This has stretched our capacity. In Ankara the most important problem is accommodation. In the technical faculties we have shortages of laboratories and material. Financial problems are common to all universities. (*Milliyet*, 29 September 1984)

The rector of Çukurova university is quoted by *Milliyet* as saying, 'In Adana we have accommodation for 700 persons. In fact, we have 8,500 students. We are under very grave pressure.' The Rector of Ankara University, Professor Somer, told the newspaper: 'The students in technical higher education are graduating from classrooms rather than workshops. But because we don't have finance we cannot establish workshops for them.'

Everywhere there are overcrowded lecture halls, problems of accommodation and lack of resources, particularly in some of the new universities and in those in rural areas. The Rector of Atatürk University, for example, noted a serious contradiction in Higher Education Council policies on staff redeployment:

> During the last three years, as a result of this rotation system, 27 teaching staff have come on a temporary basis. During the same period 11 professors, 25 docents, 15 assistant docents and 156 doctor assistants have left the university. Besides this quite a number of staff have asked permission to leave the university and they are preparing to leave. In order to keep our staff in our university the laws which govern established positions must be reconsidered to allow the universities in eastern Anatolia to have more posts. (*Cumhuriyet*, 3 October 1984)

The policy of recruiting staff to the undeveloped regions in the East might be well intended since it was the case, after all, that Turkish university teachers, seeing themselves as being essentially different from rural dwellers on account of their secular outlook, social status and general life style, were unwilling to work outside the big cities and in particular, outside Ankara and Istanbul. But the policy has clearly had unintended consequences and is, in fact, contradictory since it achieves the opposite of what is intended.

These difficult questions of staffing and resources affect students directly, bearing on the quality of the education they are offered and the circumstances in which they experience it. Accommodation is a serious issue and it may even be now influencing the level of demand for university places. The most recent figures on the level of applications for higher education indicate a drop in numbers despite the fact that the size of the 17–19 age group in the population is increasing. In 1981, 467 000 students applied for places and the intake was 100 000. In 1982 the figure had dropped to 408 000 with an intake of 120 000. And in 1983 it had fallen again to 360 000 with an intake of 150 000 (*THES* 4 February 1983). Competition is still intense, of course, and for those who are admitted there is a new regime of regular examinations to face for the Higher Education Council changed the regulations governing how many times a student can retake examinations and how frequently examinations should be set.

This pressure may be slightly less intolerable, however, than that of poor accommodation. *Cumhuriyet* carried an article on 3 October 1984 suggesting that many students were giving up their studies on account of the accommodation shortage. One female student is quoted as saying: 'I am the child of a worker. I could not get a place in a dormitory, The cheapest rent is 60 thousand lira. If we rent a flat with six friends each must pay 10,000 lira. Then what am I going to eat and how am I going to clothe myself? Perhaps I will go back home.' Dormitory allocation procedures are encouraged which favour young people from poorer families and the authorities are trying to encourage families in the bigger cities to take in students as lodgers, but there is no solution to the overall problem yet in sight.

The irony is that it was the difficult conditions which students faced which, during the 1970s and the times of the troubles, gave such an opportunity to religious groups to attract a student membership for they were able to supply help and friendship and welfare of a kind the universities themselves could not match. It is clear that the expansion of the system has done nothing to solve these problems; many of the structural features of university life which facilitated political and religious polarisation among students still remain, therefore, unchanged.

Student attitudes are influenced, too, by the quality of the education offered them and the pressure exerted on them to study. To avoid the problem of grade-repeating students, the Higher Education Council placed limitations on the number of times students could resit examinations and increased the number of examinations they must take. What this does is to make students even more reliant on rote learning from a limited range of texts. This, of course, is a problem in itself, the shortage of books, and it is made worse by the declining international value of the Turkish lira so that fewer books and journals from abroad can be bought. Students, therefore, have limited access to the literature of their subjects. One Turkish academic told me that 'memorisation and success at any cost were the cultural features of this society and a major feature of how students learn'.

The military coup has changed much in the organisation and in the functioning of Turkish universities although much, being deeply rooted in the character of Turkish society itself, has not changed. The long-term consequences of these changes cannot be anticipated. A sense of order reigns on Turkish university campuses but it must be doubted whether the changes which have taken place make any real contribution to the long-term problems of either higher education itself or Turkish society as a whole.

The expansion of university places does not itself do anything for the critical shortages of scientific and technical human resources the society faces. The movement of senior academic staff from one university to another may have an obvious political rationale but it does not facilitate good research. It breaks up research teams and removes from academics the ability to plan their work. Those Turkish scientists and scholars with an international reputation who have not already left the country to work elsewhere must be sorely tempted to do so on account of what are clearly deteriorating conditions of employment. Turkish universities have paid a high price for the political disorder which developed during the 1970s among their students. Their best hope for the future is that political stability will provide them with a little space within which to carry out their work all the while knowing that the criteria which matter most to their masters are political rather than academic and that the resources they need will not, in fact, be available. Turkey remains a poor society with a fragile economy, rising inflation and for the great majority of its people, a country with a low standard of living.

Conclusion

Conclusions are difficult and often too strained to give the appearance of a definitive end-point which has been reached. I shall not attempt such a conclusion since I cannot bring myself to believe that the kind of work I have been engaged in leads to precise conclusions or to finely elaborated theoretical propositions. Rather it leads to new questions.

Some of those questions are about theory and the manner in which changes in society and in education can be explained. Some are about method, about how to research and report change in the structure and functioning of education in different societies. Some are straightforwardly about history; about how decisions were taken, who took them and why. Since no sharp divide can be drawn between the past and the present, there are many questions to be asked about what is going on now in Egypt and Turkey. What are the educational realities to which current policies are addressed and which groups benefit most from them? These are,questions for further empirical research and there are many more like them. Perhaps the most important questions of all, however, are about practice, about how change can be implemented and directed and about what the priorities of educational planning should be and about who should determine those priorities.

There is a sense in which this whole book has been concerned with questions of this type. The policies which at various points in time governed educational development in the two societies and, of course, in the Western societies their leaders sought to emulate, have been described through the *actions* of different groups (and often of particular individuals) seeking to realise what they took to be their best educational interests. It is not surprising that from the end of the eighteenth century onwards the actions that mattered were those of military elites who sought the training of specialists rather than the promotion of general elementary education.

The *logic of the situation* which those elites were in was one of the military and technical superiority of the West and of the long term decline of the Ottoman state. Their *perception* and *understanding* of that situation reflected their own education and position within the state. What they could do to halt decline and strengthen themselves was constrained by their *resources*, their *power* and by *traditional modes of thinking* throughout the society. In short, their *opportunities* to achieve the changes they desired were severely limited.

These limitations were not all features of the Ottoman state itself, however; they were set, too, by the logic of capitalist development in the West as this influenced the economic, political, military and intellectual life of the empire. That logic dictated that Ottoman modernisation would be of a defensive kind.

The legacy of the eighteenth- and nineteenth-century modernisation was felt in the twentieth century in the situations confronting Egyptian and Turkish nationalists. Both Atatürk and Nasser were military men, heirs to the modernising traditions of their countries and both were limited in what they could achieve by the poverty and the class systems of their societies and in particular by the absence of efficient mechanisms through which they could communicate to the mass of the people they sought to lead. Nor was the international situation in which they lived supportive of their ambitions.

Atatürk and Nasser were not the ciphers of class interests or of historical forces beyond their control; they were men of imagination and power who knew what they wanted for their countries and who were able, for a while, with military support to define their own political space. They were men of action whose priorities were clear. Their failure to impose those priorities on others and to build institutions which reflected them lends support to a most important conclusion: the priorities of policy must always adjust to the practicalities of politics. The two, in fact, are inseparable and both have to be understood historically.

What is politically practical, however, is not something which is settled by the character of political life in the dependent society itself; it is something circumscribed by the actions of the powerful groups of those societies which dominate the world economy. This has been one of the central tenets holding the argument of this book together; underdevelopment is a *relationship* but one which changes through time, through political and economic *action* and *conflict*.

It follows that solutions to the problems of underdevelopment – of poverty, disease, squalor and ignorance – have to be sought *simultaneously* in both the developed and the underdeveloped societies. The problem is not simply one of increasing the flow of aid from the rich to the poor. Such a view has gained in respectability since the publication of the Brandt report of 1980. But aid, as it is now widely understood, can increase dependency and fails to challenge the structure of an international order which functions to reward those already rich at the expense of those who are poor.

Nor is it a problem of improving the quality of aid and of putting greater emphasis on such aims as rural development, basic education and improvements in the lives of women. All of these are important and improvements here have been recognised in current discussions of development. Since Brandt and the discussions which have followed its publication, such goals have become part of an orthodoxy of development planning (Brandt, 1980; Garrett, 1984)

There is much that is valuable in these discussions especially the recognition that the rationale for aid giving in Western societies should be drastically improved. It is important, therefore, to understand the political dynamics of the developed societies as part of the problem of underdevelopment. Changes in the pattern and volume of aid, of trade and investment and in the character of scientific and technical co-operation presuppose substantial alterations of outlook, understanding and political direction in the developed societies themselves.

How such changes could be brought about in societies which are increasingly nationalistic and 'cold-warpolitan' in their world outlook and increasingly materialistic in their collective sense of the good life, is one of the most urgent questions their peoples face. This observation applies with almost equal force to the societies of the communist world which are, of course, major aid donors in the Middle East and elsewhere in the underdeveloped world.

It is no part of this analysis to suggest that underdevelopment is entirely an externally inflicted phenomenon. Such a view is both from a practical and theoretical point of view unhelpful. Dependency, as several writers have pointed out is not a one-way relationship (see, e.g. Ball, 1981). Others have underlined that, especially with respect to education, there are many barriers to improvements which are specific to many Third World societies themselves and to the educational institutions within them (see Watson, 1984). These barriers are concerned with state policies and educational practice, with the resources applied to education and with how such resources are monitored and controlled.

The state in Egypt and Turkey is not merely, *pace* Marx, the executive office of a ruling class. The experience of the two societies under Atatürk and Nasser is that the state itself can nurture new social classes. In both countries a state bourgeoisie has developed dependent on state employment and one which, through its own actions has nurtured the growth of both capitalists and proletarians. State policies must be seen as having their own dynamic apart from the framework of international relations within which they developed. It was not under the weight of an externally imposed necessity that Nasser guaranteed state employment to university graduates, that President Sadat allowed the Egyptian migration stream to develop. Both policies have had profound consequences for the demand for education in Egypt, consequences which were not intended and which have led to large numbers of people being educated far in excess of the capacity of the Egyptian economy to absorb them.

This is not to deny, of course, the importance of external influences. Egypt was, after all, invaded by Britain on two occasions and both countries in the period since the mid-1950s have been in receipt of massive aid finance and technical assistance designed, as I have shown, to keep them both within a Western sphere of political influence.

There comes a point, however, when the distinction between what is external and what is internal to a society becomes unhelpful. The long-standing influences in the realm of ideas and in the way in which Western values have, over a period of almost two centuries penetrated into modes of thinking in the Middle East, is a case in point. The modernising elites of the Ottoman Empire and the nationalists of the twentieth century arrived at their notions of what development should mean through their reading of Western economic, scientific, military and political achievements. But their notions were their own, part of their whole understanding of their societies and of their place within them.

What was not so clear to them was that the ideas they admired – science, constitutional government, a free press, 'modern education' and, above all, national self determination – were not just ideas; they were simultaneously political and cultural forms which, in the European case, expressed the interests and aspirations of a new class, the industrial and commercial bourgeoisie seeking to establish its own legitimacy against older aristocratic elites and to justify its own domination of a growing industrial working class. The values which the reformers admired were those of a class-divided society.

This was particularly true in the case of education. It is something of an irony, therefore, that what was conceived of as a liberating and modernising demand for education came to be focused on institutional forms which, in the West, were designed for the purposes of social control and social selection. For in the West educational institutions functioned and unintentionally continue to do so in ways which *exclude* people from access to high status occupations. Max Weber noted this long ago in his famous essay on bureaucracy (Gerth and

Wright Mills, 1970). Bureaucracy, he noted, brought with it a system of specialised examinations and the requirement in modern capitalism for expertly trained technicians and clerks carries such examinations all over the world.

'The development of the diploma from universities. and business and engineering colleges', wrote Weber, 'and the universal clamour for the creation of educational certificates in all fields make for the formation of a privileged stratum in bureaus and offices' (Weber, 1970, p. 241). He pointed clearly to the significance of such developments:

> When hear from all sides the demand for an introduction of regular curricula and special examinations, the reason behind it is, of course, not a suddenly awakened 'thirst for education' but the desire for restricting the supply of these positions and their monopolization by owners of educational certificates. (Weber, 1970, p. 242)

Weber wrote this before the First World War and clearly had capitalist societies in mind. Already by that time the organised labour movements of the West had established their claims for a share of educational certificates and the gradual extension of opportunities to acquire them in the twentieth century is arguably one of mechanisms through which working-class consent to the status quo has been secured. The extension of educational opportunity to working-class people lends credence to the view that prestigious careers are open to the talented and not merely the high born. It is a view which, to be widely believed, must ignore the routine ways in which educational selection reflects social inequalities and inhibits the development of talents of a more diverse, often practical kind and can contribute to turning people away from an interest in further education.

Education on models such as this has played a major role in the Middle East in generating new forms of social inequality. Those who have derived most benefit and advantage from it have secured their advantage at the expense of the educational life chances of the poor both in urban and rural areas. The poor have themselves experienced gains from the expansion of formal education and their aspirations are now focused on gaining even greater access to it. But they are in a race which they cannot win and the allocation of state resources to formal education of a hierarchical, selective kind is simultaneously to prevent resources being allocated to non-formal education programmes tuned to a wider range of needs and interests and targetted specifically to the most disadvantaged groups. It is one of the mechanisms reinforcing the cultural disjunctions which separate the educated from the mass of the people. This cultural disjunction finds further expression in demands from the educated for yet more education, often abroad to gain prestigious doctorates and among the poor, especially in rural areas, to a mistrust of innovative educational strategies geared to local needs. Only that education which leads to a certificate carries any value.

This situation is not one which remain unchallenged. Among government planners in both societies and the aid agencies with which they work these problems are recognised and the overt policy goals in both Egypt and Turkey are to attach more weight to practical scientific and technical training and basic education. The main challenge has come, however, through Islam. The faith itself has become a vehicle for political opposition which can unite people from diverse class backgrounds. Islam has always been a potent framework of values, aspirations and identity which could be set against the encroachments of the West and the new forms of social inequality and national divisions which modernisation inspired.

Fears among secular military elites that Islamic values were being powerfully reasserted in Turkey was one of the factors prompting the *coup d'etat* of 1980. And there is growing evidence in Turkey today of an effort to give Islam a higher profile in the nation's education now that the army's political control is secure. The reason, no doubt, is related to Turkey's economic drive to trade more with the Arab states. To do so successfully, Turkey has to give the appearance at least of being a good Islamic country. In Egypt the Islamic associations among students remain a potent political force cultivating quiet opposition to President Mubarak, the Camp David agreements and to many facets of economic and political life in Egypt.

It is not possible in a study such as this to derive practical conclusions about educational policies in Egypt and Turkey. It is not, in any case, a task which an uninvited outsider should undertake. There are clues in the analysis, however, which prompt new questions for policy makers and those their work affects. They fall, I think, into three main groups, those concerned with history, those with comparisons with the developed world and those focused on present policies and programmes.

The point about history is straightforward. Solutions to the problems of the two societies must be worked out in relation to their own cultural traditions and historical experience. That experience needs to be under constant review. It offers examples of educational practice of a challenging and innovative kind. Examples of these would include the village institute programmes in Turkey and the literacy drives of the Arab Socialist Union in Egypt in the early 1960s. Both achieved notable success in literacy development and, in the Turkish example, of rural development. The failures, too, must be faced.

Comparison of their problems with those faced by the developed societies is an urgent task for modernity, too, has its problems. The educational institutions of the West are too deeply implicated in reproducing social inequalities to provide an acceptable model for the future in Egypt and Turkey and the cultural and political and scientific forms encoded in Western educational practice need to be critically assessed to judge which needs in the society or, more accurately, which interests, they best reflect. There is a wide critical debate going on in the West about the structure and purpose of education and about alternatives to current practice. It covers such themes as adult and continuing education, of how best to relate educational provision to the needs of the economy, of how to build up structures of life-long education and how to broaden the access of working class people, women and ethnic minority groups to further and higher education. It is a debate carried on with increasing ideological acrimony as Western governments, faced with deepening economic difficulties seek to reduce public expenditure and improve the cost effectiveness of the services they still provide.

This is not the place to enter into such debates or assess the longer-term viability of current patterns of educational provision. It is a debate which should be joined, however, by educators in the Third World and particularly in the Middle East. For some of the problems with which it is concerned are of common interest. They include how best to meet the needs of migrant workers and their children. Western Europe and Germany in particular has a large population of Turkish migrant workers. Egypt is a labour exporting country and throughout the whole Gulf area there are major problems in coping with the social and educational consequences of labour migration. The transfer of technologies and technical personnel raises questions about technical training, the needs of overseas post-graduate students and the best forms of aid and technical assistance to achieve self-sustaining patterns of development. The critical discourse about these matters should be broadened out and the international agencies which could facilitate such dialogue should be strengthened. How that should be done is yet another question.

Whether such discussions can be opened up in ways that are mutually beneficial to the developed and the underdeveloped societies is clearly a matter which will be decided politically. Educators have a role to play here; so, too, does social research into educational practice and change. If this book contributes in a small way to opening up that area of critical discourse for those who study Egypt and Turkey then it will have made a useful practical contribution to policy.

Bibliography

ABADAN-UNAT, N. (ed.) *Women in Turkish Society* (London: E. J. Brill, 1981).

ABDEL-FADIL, M. 'Educational Expansion and Income Distribution in Egypt', in G. Abdel-Khalek and R. Tignor (eds), *The Political Economy of Income Distribution in Egypt* (London: Holmes & Meier Publishers, 1982).

ABDEL-KHALEK, G. 'Looking Outside or Turning North West? On the Meaning and External Dimension of Egypt's Infitah 1971–1980', *Social Problems*, vol. 28, no. 4 (April 1981).

ABDEL-KHALEK, G. 'Foreign Economic Aid and Income Distribution in Egypt', in G. Abdel-Khalek and R. Tignor (eds), *The Political Economy of Income Distribution in Egypt* (London: Holmes & Meier Publishers 1982).

ABDEL-KHALEK, G. and TIGNOR R. *The Political Economy of Income Distribution in Egypt* (London: Holmes & Meier Publishers, 1982).

ABRAMS, P. 'Towns and Economic Growth', in P. Abrams and E. A. Wrigley (eds), *Towns in Societies* (Cambridge and London: Cambridge University Press, 1978).

ABRAMS, P. *Historical Sociology* (Cambridge and London: Cambridge University Press, 1982).

AHMAD, F. *The Turkish Experiment in Democracy 1950–1975* (London: Hurst for the Royal Institute of International Affairs, 1977).

AHMAD, F. 'The Political Economy of Kemalism', in A. Kazancīgil and E. Özbudun (eds), *Atatürk. Founder of a Modern State* (London: C. Hurst, 1981).

ALTBACH, P. G. 'The University as Centre and Periphery', in I. J. Spitzberg, Jr. (ed.), *Universities and the International Distribution of Knowledge* (New York: Praeger, 1980).

AMBROSE, S. E. *Rise to Globalism. American Foreign Policy 1938–1970* (Harmondsworth: Penguin Books, 1971).

AMIN, S. *The Arab Nation: Nationalism and the Class Struggle* (London: Zed Press, 1978).

AMMAR, H. *Growing up in an Egyptian Village* (London: Routledge & Kegan Paul, 1954).

ANDERSON, P. *Lineages of the Absolutist State* (London: New Left Books, 1974).

ARAL, S. 'Social Mobility in Turkey', in E. Özbudun and A. Ulusan (eds), *The Political Economy of Income Distribution* in Turkey (New York: Holmes & Meier Publishers, 1980).

ASFEC (The Regional Centre for Functional Literacy in Rural Areas), *Silver Jubilee* (Cairo: Sirs-el-Layyan, 1978).

ASFEC *Basic Education in Egypt. Theory and Practice* (Cairo: Sirs-el-Layyan, 1981).

ASHBY, E. *Universities: British, Indian, African. A Study in the Ecology of Higher Education* (London: Weidenfeld & Nicolson, 1966).

ATIYAH, E. *An Arab Tells His Story. A Study in Loyalties* (London: John Murray, 1946).

AYUBI, N. 'The Egyptian "Brain Drain": A Multidimensional Problem', *International Journal of Middle East Studies*, 15, (1983).

BAER, G. *Studies in the Social History of Modern Egypt* (London: University of Chicago Press, 1969).

BALEMIR, W. Socio-Economic and Demographic Determinants of Rural Education. A Report Presented to the Middle East Research Program in Population and Development, Ankara (1981).

BALL, S. 'The Sociology of Education in Developing Countries', *British Journal of Sociology of Education*, vol. 2, no. 3, (1981).

BAŞGÖZ, I. L. and WILSON, H.E. *Educational Problems in Turkey 1920–1940* (The Hague: Indiana University Publications, 1968).

BECK, L. and KEDDIE, N. (eds) *Women in the Muslim World* (Cambridge and London: Harvard University Press, 1978).

BERQUE, J. *Egypt. Imperialism and Revolution* (London: Faber & Faber, 1972).

BIRKS, J. S. and SINCLAIR, C.A. *International Migration Project. Country Case Study: Arab republic of Egypt* (Durham: University of Durham, 1978).

BOWEN, J. *A History of Western Education. Vol. 3. The Modern West* (London: Methuen, 1981).

BRANDT, W. *North–South: A Programme for Survival* (London: Pan Books, 1980).

BRAUDEL, F. *Civilization and Capitalism 15th–18th Century. Vol. 1. The Structures of Everyday Life* (London: Collins, 1981).

BRAUDEL, F. *Civilization and Capitalism 15th–18th Century. Vol. 2. The Wheels of Commerce.* (London: Collins, 1982).

BRONOWSKI, J. and MAZLISH, B. *The Western Intellectual Tradition* (Harmondsworth: Penguin Books, 1963).

BROWN, D. (Director, US Aid, Cairo) *Economic Development in Egypt – An American's Perspective* (Cairo: American Embassy, 1982).

CACHIA, P. *Taha Husayn His Place in the Egyptian Literary Renaissance* (London: Luzac, 1956).

COLLINS, R. 'Some Comparative Principles of Educational Stratification', *Harvard Educational Review*, vol. 47, no. 1, (1977).

COWEN, J. *Joseph Cowen's Speeches on the Near Eastern Question: Foreign and Imperial Affairs: and on the British Empire* (Newcastle-upon-Tyne: Andrew Reid, 1909).

CROMER, Earl of, *Report by Her Majesty's Agent and Consul General on the Finances, Administration and Condition of Egypt and the Sudan*. Cmnd 1012 (London: HMSO, 1902).

CROMER, Earl of, *Reports by Her Majesty's Agent and the Consul-General on the Finances, Administration and Condition of Egypt and the Sudan*. Cmnd 1951 (London: HMSO, 1904).

CROMER, Earl of, *Modern Egypt. Vol 2* (London: Macmillan, 1908).

DERVIS, K. and ROBINSON, S. 'The Structure of Income Inequality in Turkey 1950–1975' in E. Özbudun and A. Ulusan (eds) *The Political Economy of Income Distribution in Turkey* (New York: Holmes & Meier, 1980).

DESSOUKI, A. E. H. 'The Politics of Income Distribution in Egypt', in G. Abdel-Khalek and R. Tignor (eds), *The Political Economy of Income Distribution in Egypt* (London: Holmes & Meier Publishers, 1982).

EL-DIN EL-SHAYYAL, GAMAL 'Some Aspects of Intellectual and Social Life in Eighteenth-Century Egypt', in P. M. Holt (ed.) *Political and Social Change in Modern Egypt* (London: Oxford University Press, 1968).

DPT (Devlet Planlama Teskilat) *Yili Programi* (Ankara, 1982).

FAKSH, M. 'Education and Elite Recruitment: An Analysis of Egypt's Post-1952 Political Elite', *Comparative Education Review* vol. 20, no. 2 (June 1976).

FAKSH, M. 'The Consequences of the Introduction and Spread of Modern Education: Education and National Integration in Egypt', *Middle Eastern Studies*, vol. 16, no. 2 (May 1980).

FISCHER, M. J. 'Islam and the Revolt of the Petite Bourgeoisie', *Daedalus* (Winter 1982).

FISCHER, W. and LUNDGREEN, P. 'The Recruitment and Training of Administrative and Technical Personnel', in C. Tilly (ed.), *The Formation of National States in Western Europe* (Princeton, New Jersey: Princeton University Press, 1975).

FISEK, S. 'Changes Upset Progressives', in *The Times*, (4 April 1977).

FLINN, M. W. 'Social Theory and the Industrial Revolution', in T. Burns and S. B. Saul (eds), *Social Theory and Economic Change* (London: Tavistock Publications, 1967).

FOSTER, P. *Education and Social Change in Ghana* (London: Routledge & Kegan Paul, 1965).

FOTOS, E. 'An Appreciation of Turkish University Life', *Middle Eastern Affairs*, vol. 6, (August–September 1955).

FREY, F. W. *The Turkish Political Elite* (Cambridge, Mass.: MIT Press, 1965).

FRIERE, P. *The Pedagogy of the Oppressed* (Harmondsworth: Penguin Books, 1970).

FRIERE, P. *Education: The Practice of Freedom* (London: Writers and Readers Publishing, 1972).

GALTUNG, J. 'Towards a New International Technological Order', in W. Morehouse (ed.), *Science, Technology and the Social Order* (New Brunswick, New Jersey: Transaction Books, 1979).

GALTUNG, J. 'Literacy, Education and Schooling – for What?', in H. J. Graff (ed.), *Literacy and Social Development in the West* (London: Cambridge University Press, 1981).

GARRETT, R. M., (ed.), *Education and Development* (London: Croom Helm, 1984).

GELLNER, E. 'Doctor and Saint', in Nikki R. Keddie (ed.), *Scholars, Saints, and Sufis* (London: University of California Press 1972).

GELLNER, E. *Muslim Society* (London: Cambridge University Press, 1981).

GERSCHENKRON, A. *Economic Backwardness in Historical Perspective: A Book of Essays* (Cambridge, Mass.: Belknap Press, 1962).
GERTH, H. and WRIGHT MILLS, C. *From Max Weber: Essays in Sociology* (London: Routledge & Kegan Paul, 1970).
GIBB, H. A. R. and BOWEN H. *Islamic Society and the West* (London: Oxford University Press, 1969).
GIBB, H. A. R. *Islam* (Oxford: Oxford University Press, 1978).
GILSENAN, M. *Recognising Islam. An Anthropologist's Introduction* (London: Croom Helm, 1982).
HALE, W. M. *The Republic of Turkey* (International Migration Project, University of Durham, 1978).
HALL, B. L. 'Knowledge as a Commodity: the Inequalities of Knowledge Creation', in I. J. Spitzberg, Jr. (ed.), *Universities and the International Distribution of Knowledge* (New York: Praeger, 1980).
HAMPSON, N. *The Enlightenment. The Pelican History of European Thought, Vol. 4* (Harmondsworth: Penguin Books, 1968).
HANSEN, B. and RADWAN S. *Employment Opportunities and Equity in Egypt* (Geneva: International Labour Office, 1982).
HAY, D. *Europe in the Fourteenth and Fifteenth Centuries* (London: Longmans, 1966).
HERMAN, R. 'Britain Slips Down the Science League', *New Scientist*, (9 August 1984).
HEYWORTH-DUNNE, J. *An Introduction to the History of Education in Modern Egypt* (London: Frank Cass & Co., 1968).
HILL, C. *Intellectual Origins of the English Revolution* (Oxford: Clarendon Press, 1965).
HILL, C. *The World Turned Upside Down. Radical Ideas During the English Revolution* (Harmondsworth: Penguin Books, 1975).
HOBSBAWM, E. J. *The Age of Revolution 1789–1848* (New York: Mentor Books, 1962).
HOBSBAWM, E. J. *Industry and Empire* (London: Penguin Books, 1971).
HOLMES, G. *Europe: Hierarchy and Revolt 1320–1450* (Fontana, 1975).
HOLT, P. M. (ed.) *Political and Social Change in Modern Egypt* (London: Oxford University Press, 1968).
HOOKER, A. H. Report of the Council of Cairo Non-Official British Community to the Mission of Enquiry (Milner Commission), (Durham University: Sudan Archive 162/6/8, 1920).
HOPKINS, N. 'Tunisia: An Open and Shut Case', *Social Problems*, vol. 28, no. 4 (1981).
HOPWOOD, D. *Egypt: Politics and Society 1945–1981* (London: George Allen & Unwin Publishers, 1982).
HOWARD-MERRIAM, K. 'Women Education and the Professions in Egypt', *Comparative Education Review*, vol. 23, no. 2 (June 1979).
HUIZINGA, J. *The Waning of the Middle Ages* (London: Penguin Books, 1979).
HUSSEIN, M. 'Nasserism in Perspective', *Monthly Review*, vol. 23, no. 6, (November 1971).
HUSSEIN, M. *Class Conflict in Egypt* (New York: Monthly Review Press, 1973).
HUSSEIN, T. *The Future of Culture in Egypt* (Washington, DC: American Council of Learned Societies, 1954).

HYDE, G. D. M. *Education in Modern Egypt. Ideals and Realities* (London: Routledge & Kegan Paul, 1978).

IBRAHIM, Saad Eddin 'Social Mobility and Income Distribution in Egypt 1952–1977', in G. Abdel-Khalek and R. Tignor (eds), *The Political Economy of Income Distribution in Egypt* (London: Holmes & Meier Publishers, 1982).

IBRAHIM, Saad Eddin 'Anatomy of Egypt's Militant Islamic Groups', mimeo (American University of Cairo, 1980).

INALCIK, H. *The Ottoman Empire. The Classical Age 1300–1600* (London: Weidenfeld & Nicolson, 1973).

JANSEN, G. H., *Militant Islam* (London: Pan Books, 1979).

Joint Egyptian–American Team, *Basic Education in Egypt* (Washington: Human Resources Management, 1979).

JOHNSON, R. 'Notes on the Schooling of the English Working Class 1780–1850' in R. Dale *et al.* (eds) *Schooling and Capitalism: A Sociological Reader* (Milton Keynes: The Open University Press, 1976).

KANDIYOTI, D. 'Social Change and Social Stratification in a Turkish Village', *The Journal of Peasant Studies*, vol. 2, no. 2 (1975).

KARPAT, K. H. 'The Transformation of the Ottoman State 1789–1908', *International Journal of Middle Eastern Studies*, 3, 1972.

KARPAT, K. H. 'The People's House in Turkey 1931–1951', *Die Welt Des Islams*, vol. 15 (1974).

KARPAT, K. H. *The Gecekondu: Rural Migration and Urbanization* (Cambridge: Cambridge University Press, 1976).

KARPART, K. H. 'Turkish Democracy at Impasse: Ideology, Party Politics and the Third Military Interval', *International Journal of Turkish Studies*, vol. 2, no. 1 (1981).

KAZAMIAS, A. M. *Education and the Quest for Modernity in Turkey* (London: C. Tinling, 1966).

KAZANCIGIL, A. and ÖZBUDUN, E. (eds) *Atatürk. Founder of a Modern State* (London: C. Hurst, 1981).

KAZANCIGIL, A. 'The Ottoman-Turkish State and Kemalism', in A. Kazancigil and E. Özbudun (eds) *Atatürk. Founder of a Modern State* (London: C. Hurst, 1981).

KEDDIE, N. R. (ed.) *Scholars, Saints and Sufis* (Berkeley: University of California Press, 1972).

KERR, M. H. 'Egypt', in J. S. Coleman (ed.), *Education and Political Development* (New Jersey: Princeton University Press, 1965).

KEYDER, C. 'The Political Economy of Turkish Democracy', *New Left Review* 115, (May–June 1979).

KEYDER, C. *The Definition of a Peripheral Economy: Turkey 1923–1929* (Cambridge and London: Cambridge University Press, 1981).

KINGSFORD, W. E. Report of the Council of Cairo Non-Official British Community to the Mission of Enquiry (Milner Commission), (Durham University: Sudan Archive 162/6/8, 1920).

KORAYEM, K. *The Government Policies and the Labour Market in Egypt* (Cairo: Institute of National Planning, February 1984).

KUMAR, K. *Prophecy and Progess. The Sociology of Industrial and Post-Industrial Society* (Harmondsworth: Penguin Books, 1978).

LANE, E. W. *The Manners and Customs of Modern Egyptians* (London and Toronto: J. M. Dent & Sons, 1917).

LAPIDUS, I. *Muslim Cities in the Later Middle Ages* (Harvard: Harvard University Press, 1967).
LEVY, R. *The Social Structure of Islam* (Cambridge: University Press, 1957, reprinted 1969).
LEWIS, B. *The Emergence of Modern Turkey* (London: Oxford University Press, 1961).
LIAS, C. R. *Education in Egypt*, Memorandum to Information Committee for the British Mission of Enquiry (Milner Commission), (Durham University: Sudan Archive, 695/1/1, 1920).
LICHTHEIM, G. *Imperialism* (London: Allen Lane, The Penguin Press, 1971).
LUTFI AL-SAYYID, A. *Egypt and Cromer. A Study of Anglo-Egyptian Relations.* (London: John Murray, 1968).
LUTFI AL-SAYYID MARSOT, A. *Egypt's Liberal Experiment: 1922–1936* (London: University of California Press, 1977).
LUTFI AL-SAYYID MARSOT, A. *Egypt in the Reign of Muhammad Ali* (Cambridge: Cambridge University Press, 1984).
MAGNARELLA, P. J. *Tradition and Change in a Turkish Town* (London: John Wiley & Sons, 1974).
MAKAL, M. *A Village in Anatolia* (London: Vallentine Press, 1954).
MARDIN, Ş. *The Genesis of Young Ottoman Thought. A Study in the Modernization of Turkish Political Ideas* (New Jersey: Princeton University Press, 1962).
MARDIN, Ş. 'Power, Civil Society and Culture in the Ottoman Empire', *Comparative Studies in Society and History*, vol. II, no. 3 (June 1969).
MARDIN, Ş. 'Ideology and Religion in the Turkish Revolution', *International Journal of Middle East Studies*, 2 (1971).
MARDIN, Ş. 'Youth and Violence in Turkey', *Arch. Europ. Sociol.* XIX (1978).
MARDIN, Ş. 'Turkey: The Transformation of an Economic Code', in E. Özbudun and A. Ulusan (eds), *The Political Economy of Income Distribution in Turkey* (New York: Holmes & Meier Publishers, 1980).
MARLOWE, J. *Cromer in Egypt* (London: Elek Books, 1970).
MEHMET, O. 'An Assessment of Manpower and Educational Planning in Turkey: Shifting from Long-Term Forecasting to Employment Policy', *International Journal of Manpower*, vol. 2, no. 2 (1981).
MEHMET, O. 'Turkey in Crisis: Some Contradictions in the Kemalist Development Strategy', *International Journal of Middle East Studies*, vol. 15 (1983).
MERTON, R. K. 'Puritanism, Pietism, and Science' in *Social Theory and Social Structure* (Glencoe, Ill.: The Free Press, 1957).
MESSIHA, S. A. *Export of Egyptian School Teachers. Cairo Papers in Social Science* (Cairo: American University of Cairo, 1980).
MILNER, Lord *Report of the Special Mission to Egypt, 1921*. Cmnd 1131 (London: HMSO, 1921).
MINISTRY OF EDUCATION *Perspectives in Education in Modern Egypt* (Cairo, 1979).
MINISTRY OF EDUCATION *Education in Egypt* (Cairo, 1976).
MINISTRY OF EDUCATION *Education in Egypt* (Cairo, 1981).

MOORE, B. Jr. *Social Origins of Dictatorship and Democracy: Lord and Peasant in the Making of the Modern World* (London: Allen Lane/Penguin Books 1967).
MOORE, C. H. *Images of Development. Egyptian Engineers in Search of Industry* (Cambridge, Mass.: MIT Press, 1980).
MORRIS, J. *Pax Britannica. The Climax of an Empire* (Harmondsworth: Penguin Books, 1979).
NCFER (National Council for Educational Research) *Developing and Innovating Education in Egypt. Policy and Plans* (Cairo, 1980).
NEF, J. U. *Cultural Foundations of Industrial Civilization* (Cambridge: Cambridge University Press, 1958).
OḠUZKAN, T. *Educational Systems. An Introduction to Structures and Functions with Special Reference to Turkey* (Istanbul: Bogazici University Publications, 1981).
OECDE (Organization for Economic Cooperation and Development,) *The Mediterranean Regional Project* (Paris, 1965).
OKYAR, O. 'Universities in Turkey', *Minerva*, vol. 6 (Winter 1968).
OWEN, R. *The Middle East in the World Economy 1800–1914* (London: Methuen, 1981).
OZANKAYA, Ö. 'Social Life in Four Anatolian Villages' in *Bulletin of the Social Science Faculty Ankara University*, vol. 27, no. 3, 1973.
ÖSGEDIZ, S. 'Education and Income Distribution in Turkey' in E. Özbudun and A. Uluson (eds), *The Political Economy of Income Distribution in Turkey* (New York: Holmes & Meier, Inc, 1980).
ÖZBAY, F. 'Education and Labor Force Participation of Turkish Women as a Function of the Rural Property System', A paper given at the 9th World Congress of Sociology, Uppsala, Sweden 1978.
ÖZBAY, F. and BALEMIR, W. 'School Attendance and its Problems in Turkish Villages 1975', Unpublished report presented to IDRC Hacettepe Institute of Population Studies, 1978.
ÖZBUDUN, E. and ULUSAN, A. (eds) *The Political Economy of Income Distribution in Turkey* (New York: Holmes & Meier, Inc, 1980).
PELLETIERE, S. C. *Press and the Politicization of Young Egypt: The Process of a Revolt* (London, England and Michigan, USA: University Microfilms International, 1979).
PIERCE, J. E. *Life in a Turkish Village* (New York: Holt, 1964).
REID, D. M. 'Educational and Career Choices of Egyptian Students, 188–2 1922', *International Journal of Middle East Studies*, 8 (1977).
RENDA, I. 'Existing, not Educating', *The Times Educational Supplement* (8 February 1980).
REPP, R. 'Some Observations on the Development of the Ottoman Learned Hierarchy', in N. R. Keddie (ed.), *Scholars, Saints and Sufis* (Berkley: University of California Press, 1972).
RICHMOND, J. C. B. *Egypt 1798–1952 Her Advance Towards a Modern Identity* (London: Methuen, 1977).
ROBERTSON, J. M. *Letters from an Egyptian to an English Politician upon the Affairs of Egypt* (London: George Routledge & Sons, 1908).
ROBINSON, R. D. *The First Turkish Republic. A Case Study in National Development* (Cambridge, Mass.: Harvard University Press, 1963).

RODINSON, M. *Islam and Capitalism* (Harmondsworth: Penguin Books, 1980).
ROOS, L. L. and ROOS, N. P. *Managers of Modernization: Organizations and Elites in Turkey 1950–1969* (Cambridge Mass.: Harvard University Press, 1971).
ROPER, J. *The Women of Nar* (London: Faber & Faber, 1974).
ROSE, H. and ROSE, S. *Science and Society* (Harmondsworth: Penguin Books, 1969).
ROTHSTEIN, T. *Egypt's Ruin. A Financial and Administrative Record* (London: A. C. Fifield, 1910).
RUGH, A. *Coping with Poverty in a Cairo Community* Cairo Papers in Social Science, vol. 2. (Cairo: American University of Cairo, 1981).
SAAD, S. L. *Dropout from Primary Education During the Years 1956/7–1978/9: A Statistical Study* (Cairo: National Centre for Educational Research, 1980).
SAADAWI EL, N. *The Hidden Face of Eve* (London: Zed Press, 1980).
SAFTY M EL, 'Youth, Religion and Violence: The Case of an Egyptian Militant Islamic Group, A Sociological Perspective', Mimeo (Cairo: American University of Cairo, 1982).
SAGASTI, F. R. 'The Two Civilizations and the Process of Development', *Prospects*, vol. X, no. 2 (1980).
ST JOHN, B. *Village Life in Egypt* (New York: Arno Press, 1973).
SAMIN, A. 'The Tragedy of the Turkish Left', *New Left Review*, no. 126 (March–April 1981).
SARDAR, Z. *Science and Technology in the Middle East* (Harlow, Essex: F. H. Books, 1982).
SCOTT, R. B. 'Qur'an Courses in Turkey', *The Muslim World*, vol. LXI, no. 4 (October 1971).
SEMMEL, B. *Imperialism and Social Reform. English Social-Imperial Thought 1895–1914*, (London: George Allen & Unwin, 1960).
SHAPIN, S. and BARNES, B. 'Science, nature and control: interpretating Mechanics' Institutes', in R. Dale, G. Esland and M. MacDonald (eds), *Schooling and Capitalism* (London: Routledge & Kegan Paul, 1976).
SHAW, S. *History of the Ottoman Empire and Modern Turkey Vol. 1* (London: Cambridge University Press, 1976).
SHAW, P. 'Manpower and Educational Shortages in the Arab World: An Interim Strategy', *World Development*, vol. 9, no. 7 (1981).
SHEPARD, W. 'The Dilemma of a Liberal: Some Political Implications in the Writings of the Egyptian Scholar, Ahmad Amin (1886–1954)', in E. Kedourie and S. G. Haim (eds), *Modern Egypt. Studies in Politics and Society* (London: Frank Cass, 1980).
SILVERA, A. 'The First Egyptian Student Mission to France under Muhammad Ali', in E. Kedourie and S. G. Haim (eds), *Modern Egypt: Studies in Politics and Society* (London: Frank Cass, 1980).
SMITH, C. D. 'The Intellectual and Modernization: Definitions and Reconsiderations: The Egyptian Experience', *Comparative Studies in Society and History*, (1980).
SPENCER, R. F. 'Culture Process and Intellectual Current: Durkheim and Atatürk', *American Anthropologist*, 60, (1958).

STEPHENS, R. *Nasser. A Political Biography* (Harmondsworth: Penguin Books, 1971).
STIRLING, P. *Turkish Village* (New York: John Wiley & Sons, 1965).
STIRLING, P. 'Turkey', in N. Parkinson (ed.), *Educational Aid and National Development. An International Comparison of the Past and Recommendations for the Future* (London: Macmillan Press, 1976).
STONE, F. 'A Pioneer in Turkish Village Revitalization', *Hacettepe Bulletin of Social Sciences and Humanities*, vol. 2, no. 2 (1970).
SWANSON, E. V. et. al. 'The Retention of Literacy/Numeracy Skills: An Overview for Basic Education in Egypt', in ASFEC (The Regional Centre for Functional Literacy in Rural Areas), *Basic Education in Egypt. Theory and Practice* (Egypt: Sirs-el-Layyan, 1981).
SZYLIOWICZ, J. S. *Education and Modernization in the Middle East* (Ithaca: Cornell University Press, 1973).
TAWNEY, R. H. *Religion and the Rise of Capitalism* (Harmondsworth: Penguin Books, 1972).
TAYLOR, A. J. P. *The Trouble Makers. Dissent Over Foreign Policy 1792–1939* (London: Hamish Hamilton, 1957).
TIBAWI, A. L. *Islamic 'Education'* (London: Lusac, 1972).
TIGNOR, R. L. *Modernization and British Colonial Rule in Egypt, 1882–1914* (New Jersey: Princeton University Press, 1966).
TIGNOR, R. 'Equity in Egypt's Recent Past: 1945–1952', in G. Abdel-Khalek and R. Tignor (eds), *The Political Economy of Income Distribution in Egypt* (London: Holmes & Meier Publishers, 1982).
TILLY, C. (ed.) *The Formation of National States in Western Europe* (Princeton, New Jersey: Princeton University Press, 1975).
TRIMBERGER, K. *Revolution from Above. Military Bureaucrats and Development in Japan, Turkey, Egypt and Peru* (New Jersey: Transaction Books, 1978).
UNDP (United Nations Development Programme), *Background Information on the Activities of the United Nations Development Programme and Associated Programmes in Egypt*, (1981).
UNESCO (United Nations Educational, Scientific and Cultural Organization), *International Yearbook of Education*, vol. XXXIII (Paris, 1981).
UNITED NATIONS *Conference on Science and Technology for Development 78–2065*, Second Draft, National Paper of Egypt (New York, 1978).
VATIKIOTIS, P. J. *The Modern History of Egypt* (New York: Frederick A. Praeger, 1969).
VEXLIARD, A. and AYTAC, K. 'The "Village Institutes" in Turkey', *Comparative Education Review*, 8 (1964).
WAARDENBURG, J. 'Some Institutional Aspects of Muslim Higher Education and Their Relation to Islam', *Numen*, vols 11–12, (1964–65).
WALLERSTEIN, I. *The Capitalist World-Economy. Essays by Immanuel Wallerstein* (Cambridge and London: Cambridge University Press, 1980).
WARD, N. *Technical Education in Egypt*, Mimeo (Cairo: British Council, 1979).
WATERBURY, J. *The Egypt of Nasser and Sadat. The Political Economy of Two Regimes* (Princeton, New Jersey: Princeton University Press, 1983).

WATSON, K. (ed.), *Dependence and Interdependence in Education. International Perspectives* (London: Croom Helm, 1984).
WEBER, M. 'The Social Psychology of World Religions', in H. Gerth and C. Wright Mills, *From Max Weber* (London: Routledge & Kegan Paul, 1970).
WEBER, M. *Economy and Society* (Berkeley: University of California Press, 1978).
WEIKER, W. F. *The Modernization of Turkey: From Atatürk to the Present Day* (New York: Holmes & Meier, 1981).
WIKAN, U. *Life Among the Poor in Cairo* (London: Tavistock Publications, 1976).
WILLIAMS, J. *Education in Egypt before British Control* (Birmingham: Frank Juckes Ltd, 1939).
WILLIAMSON, B. *Education, Social Structure and Development* (London: Macmillan, 1979).
WORKING PARTY ON CHRISTIAN MINORITIES OF TURKEY *The Situation of the Christian Minorities of Turkey since the Coup D'Etat of September 1980* (report published by the Churches Committee on Migrant Workers in Europe, 1982).
WORLD BANK *Education. Sector Working Paper* (Paris, 1974).
WORLD BANK Staff Appraisal Report: Third Education Project. *Arab Republic of Egypt*, Report no. 3096-EGT, (1980).
WORLD BANK *Turkey: Prospects and Problems of an Expanding Economy* (Washington, 1975).
WORLD BANK *Turkey: Sector Memorandum. Industrial and Vocational Training* (Washington, 1983).
YUSSEF GAMAL AL-DIN, N. *Selection for University Education in Egypt: Practice, Philosophy and Perspective.* PhD Thesis (Durham: University of Durham, 1979).
ZAHLAN, A. B. (ed.) *Technology Transfer and Change in the Arab World* (Oxford: Pergamon Press, 1978).
ZAHLAN, A. B. *Science and Science Policy in the Arab World* (London: Croom Helm, 1980).
ZAHLAN, A. B. (ed.) *The Arab Brain Drain* (London: Ithaca Press for the United Nations, 1981).

Index